Holy Terror

The Inside Story of Islamic Terrorism

Amir Taheri

Hutchinson
London Melbourne Auckland Johannesburg

This edition first published in 1987 by Hutchinson Ltd, an imprint of Century Hutchinson Ltd,
Brookmount House, 62–65 Chandos Place, London WC2N 4NW

Century Hutchinson Australia Pty Ltd
PO Box 496, 16–22 Church Street, Hawthorn, Victoria 3122, Australia

Century Hutchinson New Zealand Limited
PO Box 40–086, Glenfield, Auckland 10, New Zealand

Century Hutchinson South Africa (Pty) Ltd
PO Box 337, Bergvlei, 2012 South Africa

Filmset by Deltatype, Ellesmere Port
Printed and bound in Great Britain by Anchor Brendon Limited, Tiptree, Essex

British Library Cataloguing in Publication Data

Taheri, Amir
Holy terror.
1. Shīah — Near East 2. Islam and politics — Near East 3. Near East — Politics and government.
I. Title
322′.1′0956 D562.8

ISBN 0 09 165970 1

Holy Terror

The Inside Story of Islamic Terrorism

By the same author

The Spirit of Allah: Khomeini and the Islamic Revolution

Contents

It is in the nature of Islam to dominate, not to be dominated, to impose its law on all nations and to extend its power to the entire planet.

Shaikh Hassan al-Banna, founder and Supreme Guide of the Muslim Brotherhood

Introduction

Is there such a thing as Islamic terrorism? Is Islam a religion of terror? These questions have been asked at various levels ever since a group of militant 'students' seized the American Embassy compound in Tehran on 4 November 1979 at the start of one of the longest hostage-holding crises since World War II. The answers have differed widely, according to their source. Some Muslim intellectuals and political leaders have reacted with outrage to the very idea of discussing the possible existence of an Islamic version of terrorism.[1] Certain Western and Israeli writers and politicians, on the other hand, have gone out of their way to 'prove' that Islam and terrorism are synonymous and that Islamic politics inevitably lead to violence and terror. A number of not very talented social caricaturists in the West, notably in Hollywood, have even created a new version of the quintessential 'baddy' – the Islamic terrorist who devotes his life to hijacking passenger aircraft and planting bombs in kindergartens. Cinema audiences in the United States and western Europe cheer when the forces of good, symbolized by the US Delta Force,[2] smash their way into the hideout of Islamic terrorists to put them to death and liberate their hostages.

Such a crude and blatantly racist approach to the problem does no one any good; it prevents an objective understanding of a phenomenon which, having asserted its bloody presence on a global scale, seems likely to remain a feature of international life for some time to come. Whipping up hatred against Muslims in the West will no doubt harm Islam's image as a religion with a universal vocation, but I believe that the attitude of those Muslim intellectuals and political leaders who seek to avoid such uncomfortable questions altogether will prove more damaging to Islam in the long run.

It is almost unnecessary to ask why the term 'Catholic' or 'Christian' terrorism is not used in the West to refer to the Irish Republican Army or the dozen or so terrorist organizations active in South America. The answer is obvious. The IRA or the Peruvian Shining Path do not kill in the name of religion, but describe themselves respectively as 'nationalist' and 'Maoist'; in other words, they are political organizations using terror to further their objectives. The aim of the IRA is the reunification of Ireland within a single republic; the Shining Path dreams of establishing a Marxist state based on Mao Tse-tung's reading of Leninism.

The Islamic Jihad Organization, on the other hand, the Party of Allah and the scores of other, much smaller groups using violence and terror to promote their causes, would be insulted if described as political organizations seeking political goals. They recruit their members in the name of Islam and are led by religious officials. Their long-term objective is the conversion – 'by force if necessary'[3] – of all mankind to the faith of Muhammad. In this they differ from the 'traditional' Palestinian organizations which since 1967 have used a range of violent methods in their struggle against Israel. No one would describe al-Fatah, for example, as an Islamic organization, although its leader, Yasser Arafat, alias Abu-Ammar, and more than 95 per cent of its members are Muslims. Even the notorious Sabri al-Banna, alias Abu-Nidal, can hardly be described as an 'Islamic' terrorist, despite his recent rediscovery of Allah and even more recent rejection of his socialist beliefs in favour of the teachings of the Qur'an. Arafat's aim is purely secular: he wants to create a Palestinian state on at least part of the territory currently occupied by Israel. Abu-Nidal must also be described as a 'secular' leader: he works for whoever pays best, and in this capacity served Saddam Hussein of Iraq as well as Moammar al-Gaddafi of Libya before returning to his original paymaster, Syria's Hafez al-Assad.[4]

The distinction is important, for if we are to understand the political tremors that have sent shock waves through the Muslim world, we must resist the temptation to accept Israeli contentions that the Palestine Liberation Organization, the

Abu-Nidal gang and the Khomeinist terror organizations in the Middle East are all parts of a single entity. Whether well-meaning Muslim intellectuals admit it or not, there exists today a phenomenon justifiably described as 'Islamic' terrorism. It is a movement quite distinct from other groups using political violence in the Middle East and beyond in the name of nationalism or of one of the many different brands of communism. But why the inverted commas? Because whilst the doctrine as well as the practice of the fundamentalist movement is directly traceable to Islam, both as revealed in the Qur'an and as described in the Hadiths,[5] Islam is not limited to what the Partisans of Allah believe or do. In other words, Khomeini's teachings are Islamic, but Islam is not limited to what Khomeini teaches. A comparison could be made with the Inquisition, which, although rooted in a strict reading of Christianity, did not encompass the much wider universe of Christ's message. The vast majority of Muslims would probably not see their beliefs, hopes and aspirations reflected in the action of suicide bombers in Beirut or the throwing into the sea of a crippled American passenger on the *Achille Lauro*.[6] But some, especially among the politically active minority, would heartily approve the use of violence against the 'infidel' in almost any circumstances.

A universally acceptable definition of terrorism is impossible, for one man's terrorist will always be another's freedom fighter, but it can be said with certainty that terrorism is what terrorism does. Everyone recognizes it, regardless of ideological differences, even though they may not be prepared to admit it in public. Soviet leaders, for example, have on a number of occasions advised Libya to modify its policy of support for terrorist groups, but they would never admit that Colonel Gaddafi's Jamahiriyah had anything to do with terrorism.[7] One could say that any deliberate use of violence outside the internationally recognized norms of war, and for the purpose of provoking fear in the service of a political cause, constitutes an act of terrorism. The fact remains, however, that what the world is facing today is not a continuation of the old-style, 'classical' terrorism traditionally employed by political movements basing themselves on armed struggle. Many liberation movements, ranging from the Algerian Front de la Libération Nationale (FLN) to the Cypriot EOKA and the two guerrilla movements in Rhodesia,[8] used terror tactics as part of their overall military strategy; they resorted to acts of terrorism without becoming terrorist organizations. The same could be said of the Zionist movement which, through groups such as Irgun and Stern, made effective use of terror against the British in the 1940s in mandate Palestine.

An analysis of present-day forms of terrorism is long overdue. It is surprising that, although the West in general[9] and the United States in particular are prime targets of most forms of contemporary terrorism, these countries have done so little to define and understand the danger. Four types of terrorist movements can be identified today. The first can be described as 'national' in that they are basically active within given nation-state boundaries – any overspill of terrorist activity beyond their borders is incidental. These movements, which tend to be centrifugal and secessionist in nature, base themselves on the principles of nineteenth-century-style nationalism. The IRA, the Basque ETA, and the various Kurdish autonomist organizations in Turkey, Iran and Iraq fall into this category, as do such outwardly religious movements as the Khalistan[10] in the Punjab and the Moro Liberation Front (MLF) in the Philippines.[11] Most of these movements espouse radical, often proto-Marxist, politics and are generally believed to enjoy direct or indirect support from Soviet bloc countries. Most, however, remain outside the East–West ideological rivalry that dominates much of international politics. Jonas Savimbi's UNITA movement in Angola[12] began with vaguely Marxist sentiments and ended up an ally of South Africa. The three Eritrean liberation organizations have changed their ideological colours a number of times to suit the needs of the moment.

In the second category are a whole series of urban guerrilla groups which, unable to appeal to any important section of society, are drawn into a form of political gang warfare with the police before being isolated and defeated. The Red Brigades in Italy, the Baader-Meinhof group and its successor, the Red Army Faction, in West Germany, the Weathermen in the United States and the CCC[13] in Belgium provide some examples. Inspired by different interpretations of Marxism-

Leninism, these groups are generally hostile to the Soviet Union on ideological grounds while considering the United States their number one enemy.[14]

The third type of terrorism is practised by the remnants of the old-style guerrillas, principally in Latin America. The Sandinistas became a household name after overthrowing Anastasio Somoza's dictatorship in Nicaragua in 1979, and have emerged as the new shining example of liberation movements in Central America. Influenced by Marxism-Leninism, but deeply nationalistic and drawing much of their support from middle-class intellectuals, these guerrilla movements now practise terrorism of a kind and on a scale that would have been totally unacceptable to the Che Guevara generation. The advent of democracy in Latin America has deprived most of these groups of their basic *raison d'être* and in the next few years they may well be replaced by smaller, more tightly knit urban terrorist groups. The prospect of a guerrilla army marching on the capital, having conquered the countryside after the pattern of Cuba or even Nicaragua, is daily becoming more remote.

The fourth type of terrorism that the world has witnessed since the 1960s is publicity-seeking,[15] and is basically aimed at focusing attention on particular grievances or causes. The early hijackers from the People's Front for the Liberation of Palestine (PFLP) went out of their way to make sure that no harm came to their hostages. Their aim was to force public opinion, throughout the world but more specifically in Israel and the United States, to listen to the grievances of the Palestinians. Such tactics have been used by a wide range of organizations seeking radical change in society: the African National Congress (ANC), for instance, uses similar methods in its campaign against the white South African government in Pretoria.

Publicity-seeking terrorism is at times practised by mercenary terrorists who sell their services to various radical states. These mercenaries do not represent any real cause and, despite the political trappings they like to give themselves, are no different from the hired killers of the underworld. One well-known example is the notorious, Venezuelan-born Illych Ramirez Sanchez, alias Carlos, who until his unexplained disappearance in 1982 worked on behalf of Libya, Syria, and for a limited time Soviet bloc Intelligence services.[16]

Political movements practising publicity-seeking terrorism, whether inside the target country or elsewhere, often do so because they are incapable of waging an effective war on the armed forces of the state they want to overthrow. By hijacking a passenger aircraft they not only state their cause but also unknowingly advertise their military impotence. School children blown to bits in a Palestinian 'guerrilla' attack on an Israeli bus serve as substitutes for the Israeli soldiers whom the 'guerrillas' cannot kill on the battlefield. Publicity-seeking terrorism, which starts out as no more than the means of achieving a broader politico-military strategy, eventually becomes an end in itself, rendering the organization practising it incapable of responding effectively to changing political conditions. In some cases it is the states which finance 'guerrilla' groups that insist on seeing some proof of the groups' ability before they unloose their purse strings; 'guerrilla' movements in the Middle East keep collections of videotapes and other documentation to demonstrate their prowess.[17] Publicity-seeking terrorism is at times specifically ordered by governments as a means of achieving clearly defined diplomatic goals. Syria and Libya, which, together with South Yemen and, until 1984, Algeria, formed the so-called Arab 'Steadfastness Front', reacted to the signing of the Camp David accords between Egypt and Israel by ordering a series of dramatic terrorist attacks, mostly on soft targets in western Europe.[18] Finally, a guerrilla organization sensing a decline in its prestige may also have recourse to acts of publicity-seeking terrorism. Yasser Arafat's al-Fatah (Victory) organization, the main group within the PLO, ordered the hijacking of the liner *Achille Lauro* as a means of reasserting its position as a fighting force in the wake of the Israeli raid on the Palestinian headquarters near Tunis in 1985.[19]

The fifth form of terrorism, described as 'Islamic' for reasons already stated, is a new phenomenon with very deep roots.[20] It is different from all other forms of terrorism in at least three important respects. First, it rejects all the contemporary ideologies in their various forms; it sees itself as the total outsider with no option but to take control or to fall, gun in hand.[21] It cannot even enter into talks with other terrorist movements which may, in some specific cases at least, share its tactical objectives. Considering itself as an expression of Islamic revival – which must, by definition, lead to the conquest of the entire globe by the True Faith – it bases all its actions on the dictum that the end justifies the means. Recourse to terrorism is, therefore, one means among many that the fundamentalist movement uses and will continue to use in its campaign to create a universal Islamic state and to spread the rule of Islam throughout the world. 'The world as it is today is how others [i.e. the infidels] shaped it,' wrote the late Ayatollah Muhammad Baqer al-Sadr. 'We have two choices: either to accept it with submission, which means letting Islam die, or to destroy it, so that we can construct the world as Islam requires.'[22] Another leading theoretician of fundamentalism, Mostafa Chamran, wrote: 'To us the East is like the West. Both are enemies. Communism is as much an enemy as are liberalism and socialism and democracy. We are not fighting within the rules of the world as it exists today. We reject all those rules.'[23]

Ignoring the special characteristics of Islamic terrorism, a number of governments and even church organizations have tried to open up an ecumenical dialogue with the fundamentalists, often with the aim of freeing hostages. President Jimmy Carter, whose administration showed symptoms of the Stockholm Syndrome in dealing with the Islamic Republic over the hostage issue, had his fingers burned when he tried to appeal to the 'spiritual' sentiments of the Tehran ayatollahs. Believing that Khomeini would appreciate the President's distinction as a born-again Christian, Carter made strenuous efforts to give his messages to the Ayatollah a strongly religious tone. But the attempt misfired, for Carter did not realize that Khomeini would never be wooed by such protestations of piety on the part of the 'chief of the infidels'. Andrew Young, Carter's Ambassador to the United Nations, did no better even though he was prepared to describe Khomeini as 'a twentieth-century saint'. The experience of Britain's Archbishop of Canterbury, Dr Runcie, was no happier. His special envoy Terry Waite, a man of great courage and immense patience, failed to secure the release of British and American hostages in Lebanon in 1985 partly because he ignored the fact that, from the point of view of the Partisans of Allah, Dr Runcie is not only in no position to speak in the name of God but deserves particular enmity as 'chief of the Cross-worshippers'.[24]

The second characteristic that distinguishes the Islamic version from other forms of terrorism is that it is clearly conceived and conducted as a form of Holy War which can only end when total victory has been achieved. The term 'low-intensity warfare' has often been used to describe terrorism,[25] but it applies more specifically to the Islamic kind, which does not seek negotiations, give-and-take, the securing of specific concessions or even the mere seizure of political power within a certain number of countries. The point was well made by Hussein Mussavi, one of the leaders of fundamentalism in Lebanon, on 14 November 1985: 'We are not fighting so that the enemy recognizes us and offers us something. We are fighting to wipe out the enemy. We will not take the path of shame. . . .'[26] What is demanded, in other words, is not even a negotiated surrender, but the enemy's total annihilation.[27] For the time being, at least, the prospects for drawing Islamic terrorist organizations into some process of diplomatic dialogue must be considered fairly remote. Even those states which patronize most of the Islamic terror groups have discovered that their influence has certain limits when it comes to urging negotiation. Syria, having failed to persuade an Islamic terror group that had kidnapped four Soviet diplomats in Beirut in 1984 to release their hostages, was eventually forced to enlist the services of other terror gangs in Lebanon in order to satisfy the demands of its Kremlin allies.[28]

The third specific characteristic of Islamic terrorism is that it forms the basis of a whole theory both of individual conduct and of state policy. To kill the enemies of Allah and to offer the infidels the choice between converting to Islam or being put to death is the duty of every individual believer, as well as the supreme – if not the sole – task of the Islamic state. One of the principal leaders of the international Islamic terror movement, Ayatollah Fazl-Allah Mahalati, wrote:

> A believer who sees Islam trampled underfoot and who does nothing to stop it will end up in the seventh layer of Hell. But he

> who takes up a gun, a dagger, a kitchen knife or even a pebble with which to harm and kill the enemies of the Faith has his place assured in Heaven. An Islamic state is the sum total of such individual believers. An Islamic state is a state of war until the whole world sees and accepts the light of the True Faith.[29]

This attitude of exclusivism prevents Islamic fundamentalists from forming even tactical alliances with other movements sharing many of their more important objectives. On a visit to Nicaragua in 1984 the Prime Minister of the Islamic Republic, Mir-Hussein Mussavi Khamaneh'i, promised the Sandinista government a comprehensive package of aid in the name of 'our common struggle against the American Great Satan'. On his return to Tehran, however, he was unable to fulfil his promises because clerical members of the Islamic Majlis (Parliament) refused to 'squander what belongs to believers on helping non-believers'. The fact that the Nicaraguan Foreign Minister was a Catholic priest, and thus a leading 'Cross-worshipper', was cited as a major reason for refusing to help that country.[30]

Islamic terrorism has played a constant key role in revivalist movements in the Muslim world during the past 150 years. And, despite vehement protests from Westernized Muslim intellectuals, the idea of 'murdering, maiming and menacing' the enemy for the purpose of hastening the final triumph of Islam has always held a very strong appeal among the Muslim masses.

But is Islam a religion of terror? No more, and probably no less, than other major religions. It is certainly based on the fear of Allah and makes liberal use of the threat of damnation in Hell. The terror that the world is witnessing today in the Middle East and beyond is directly traceable to the basic teachings of Islam. But a true understanding of Islam cannot be confined to the use of terror in its service. Inaugurated as a proposed code of individual and social ethics, Islam quickly developed into a religion because of the genius of the Prophet Muhammad. Nor did it stop there, but became a culture, a way of life, and eventually a complete and dynamic civilization. What the fundamentalists are now trying to do is to ignore Islam's experience during the fourteen centuries of its existence, and to reduce it once again to the embryonic form it had in Medina when Muhammad ruled. The fundamentalists, terrorized by their vision of the contemporary world, seek safety and protection in a past that did not exist as they imagine it today. Fear of life makes them worship death. They long to return to the womb of history, where they hope to feel warm once more in a cold world.

1

The City of Faith and the City of War

> The dagger, poison, the
> revolver. . . . These are the weapons
> of Islam against its enemies.
>
> Shaikh Hassan al-Banna[1]

Muna el-Saeed[2] is the eighteen-year-old daughter of a small shopkeeper in Baalbek, in Lebanon's Bekaa Valley. Old photographs show her to have been a typical Arab beauty with the dark, deep eyes of a desert gazelle. It was because she was so beautiful that she attracted numerous suitors from the age of nine – the age at which Islam permits 'women' to become wives or legal concubines.[3] But Muna had preferred to study, dreaming of one day attending the American University in Beirut. Now her beauty is gone and she may never become a bride. It was on the eve of 'Ashura in 1985 that her life changed.[4] Returning home from a visit to a friend, Muna was surrounded and attacked by a group of youths – all members of Hezb-Allah, the Party of Allah. They objected to the 'lax way' in which they thought she was dressed, and accused her of 'insulting the blood of the martyrs' by not having her hair fully covered. Then one of the youths threw 'a burning liquid' on her face while the others shouted: 'Allah is the greatest! Khomeini is the chief!'

'Next,' Muna remembers, 'I was in hospital with my family at my bedside.' The 'burning liquid' had been acid, and Muna, nicknamed 'the playful one' by her parents, was disfigured, her face turned into a horrifying mask. Months of treatment, including plastic surgery in France, all paid for by 'people of goodwill', have failed to undo the damage done by the Baalbek zealots. But it is not only her body that has been affected. 'I feel that my soul is burning too, and covering my vision with foglike smoke,' she relates. 'My attackers told me that I did not belong to the City of Faith and that I was an agent of the City of War.' The division of the world into two mutually exclusive camps – the City of War and the City of Faith – lies at the heart of Islam's traditional view of existence. Places where Islam rules supreme and its laws are strictly obeyed are known as Dar al-Iman[5] or the City of Faith. The rest of the world is signified under the title of Dar al-Harb[6] or the City of War.

Muna is not the only victim of the Party of Allah's hostility to those whom they call agents of the City of War. Since 1980 scores – some say hundreds – of women have suffered the same fate in Baalbek, in Beirut, in southern Lebanon and in many other Muslim cities from Tunis to Kuala Lumpur. Radical Islam has declared war on the infidels and considers its first and foremost task to be the full cleansing of the City of Faith. People found ignoring or even slightly transgressing divine rules on any matter, including the way the faithful should dress, lay themselves open to the wrath of teenage revolutionaries thirsting to kill in the name of an ideal they only half grasp. The primary victims of Islamic terrorism are the Muslims themselves, for the emerging fundamentalist movement throughout the Islamic world is still seeking to establish political control of its own society before it can mobilize the forces necessary for a global Holy War against the City of War. Domestic enemies of Islam must be destroyed or driven from power before the Partisans of Allah can think of conquering other lands.

At the head of the list of these domestic enemies are all the present-day governments of Muslim countries, with the sole exception of Ayatollah Khomeini's Islamic Republic. Next come the middle classes and more or less Westernized intellectuals who 'have sold their souls to Satan'.[7] Religious minorities, such as Baha'is in Iran, Chinese Buddhists in Malaysia and Maronite Christians in Lebanon are also enemies that ought to be eliminated or subdued. The list does not end there. As in the story of Muna el-Saeed, it also includes women who do not 'dress properly' and those who 'deviate from the norms in any way'.[8] 'Every single lock of hair that shows from beneath a *chador* carelessly worn is like a dagger aimed at the heart of our martyrs,' said Hojat al-Islam Ali-Akbar Hashemi Rafsanjani.[9] He added: 'America cannot defeat Islam with all the tanks, bombers and missiles Reagan commands. But Islam will be defeated if its womenfolk refuse to cover their hair and wear proper clothes.'[10]

In countries where the Partisans of Allah are still weak and not fully organized they act as missionaries of the Faith. In Malaysia, for example, they tell 'deviationist' Muslims: 'Obey the rules, or Allah will damn you!' In West Beirut, where they have been in control since December 1985, their message is slightly different: 'Obey the rules, or we will murder you!' These architects of the City of Faith have no time for the niceties of political language.

Since Islam cannot abdicate from its mission to bring the whole of humanity to its own path – the 'Right Path' – relations between the City of Faith and the City of War cannot but be hostile. As long as Islam is not strong enough to impose its will on the inhabitants of the City of War by force, it may observe a period of truce. But there can never be peace between the two. A state of truce could be tolerated as long as the two warring camps touched one another only at their physical frontiers. The real danger came when the City of War started to conquer the land of Islam from within. 'The infidels,' wrote Ayatollah Fazl-Allah Mahalati,

> had no need to attack us with their armies. Islam was defeated by its own rulers, who ignored Divine Law in the name of Western-style secularism. The West captured the imagination of large sections of our people. And that conquest was far more disastrous for Islam than any loss of territory. It is not for the loss of Andalusia [i.e. the Spanish *Reconquista*] that we ought to weep every evening – although that remains a bleeding wound. Far graver is the loss of large sections of our youth to Western ideology, dress, music and food.[11]

All this makes for a divided society, at war against itself. Another leading ideologist of the Party of Allah, Ayatollah Muhammad Baqer al-Sadr, wrote of 'the confusion, the tearing apart of oneself' that is experienced by Muslims living in states where the rules of Islam are imposed 'only in part'.

> A Muslim who lives within a social order that is in contradiction to

> the Qur'an and Islam finds out that in many circumstances he is obliged to act in contradiction to [his beliefs]. What should he do? When in the mosque, should he reject what constitutes his life in the shop, the office or the institute? Or should he opt for his everyday life and reject what he worships? He cannot have it both ways. He must either turn his back on the mosque, in which case he enters a destructive spiritual vacuum, or he must withdraw from active life and be deprived of participation in society. By renouncing the active life of the community, he would become a force of negation. Society thus loses, little by little, the capacities of its purest children.[12]

The belief that Islam cannot allow a secular power structure is no longer limited to the clergy and their followers among the literate elements in Muslim societies. Even Western-educated intellectuals who had, until the Islamic Revolution of Ayatollah Khomeini in Iran, argued that a 'soft and gradual separation of the mosque and state would not be impossible',[13] have now changed their minds. 'The very concept of a secular Muslim society is impossible by definition,' said Habib Boulares, a leading Arab scholar with impeccable Western credentials, and a member of the Tunisian National Assembly. 'Islam does not admit the notion of religion as the private affair of individuals.'[14] Under Islam it is not religion that is a part of life, but life a part of religion. Khomeini never tires of reminding us that the Prophet Muhammad was also a politician, a sovereign, a head of state and a chief executive. 'If we accept secularism and allow our rulers to be chosen by the ordinary people from among ordinary politicians, we will not have to wait long before we see the end of Islam,' says the Ayatollah.

This rejection of secularism and the sustained hatred of Western ways have led many European and American commentators to conclude that what we are witnessing today is the violent rejection by the Muslim masses of all that the West has to offer. The fact is, however, that the masses in question have been led to reject a certain version of the West presented to them by often corrupt and incompetent rulers on the one hand and power-seeking clergy on the other. Khomeini's Islamic Revolution in Iran and the rise of fundamentalist movements throughout the Muslim world are described in the West as a backlash to what is seen as a programme of hasty modernization. This analysis, attractive at first sight, leads to the inevitable conclusion that the world's estimated 1000 million Muslims[15] should be allowed to exclude themselves from the mainstream experience of humanity in the name of a return to the source and traditional values. The Islamic backlash and the violence it has provoked are thus regarded by some observers of the Third World as not only inevitable but also desirable. However, a closer examination of Muslim history in the past 150 years shows that true Westernization was never made available to the masses. A number of distinct attempts were made to give the traditional Oriental system of rule certain Western trappings. Western theories of administration, Western weapons systems and military doctrines and, in one or two cases, certain aspects of Western education were adopted by the modernizers. But it was all aimed at strengthening the position of the state, which in practice meant the absolute power of one man. In Egypt, Turkey and Iran Khedive Mehmet Ali Pasha, Nassereddin Shah, Kemal Atatürk and Reza Shah all tried to Westernize their respective societies, but their principal aim in so doing was to strengthen their own rule at the expense of all the other institutions of society. Westernization in the form of human rights, the rule of law, a pluralistic system of government, freedom of expression and enterprise, and equal rights for women and religious and ethnic minorities has never been offered to, and as a consequence never been rejected by, the Muslim masses. In fact, whenever such aspects of Westernization were offered, they were enthusiastically accepted. The Turks have had little difficulty in appreciating the liberties that a Western-style multi-party parliamentary system could offer, and in Iran the leading ayatollah of the day was hanged in public in 1911 because of his opposition to the creation of a Western-style Parliament.

The problem is that most advocates of modernization in Islamic countries have not been prepared to go the whole way and accept that they, and the institutions they represent, must relinquish some of their privileges in order to attract mass support for their project. Reza Shah presided over Iran's first attempts at industrialization, but he could not resist the temptation to increase his personal wealth in the process. In Turkey Atatürk created a one-and-a-half-party system[16] but he himself remained above it all, a demi-god known as the Father of the Turks and certainly enjoying far greater absolute power than had any Ottoman sultan. Muhammad Reza Shah gave Iranian women the right to vote, but did not complete this reform by making sure that women's votes, as well as men's votes, meant anything in deciding the nation's policies. The Tunisian leader, Habib Bourguiba, is often cited as a leading modernizer in the Islamic world. True, he virtually abolished the fasting month of Ramadan and imposed a number of legal reforms in favour of women; the other side of the coin, however, is that he gave himself the title of the Great Combatant[17] and decided to stay at the helm for life. His personal powers go far beyond those wielded by any medieval bey.

Apart from their greed for personal power and profit – a greed shared by the intellectuals[18] – Westernizers in the Muslim world have also suffered, and continue to suffer, from another important handicap. They are assumed to represent the interests of the big, formerly colonial, powers. This handicap is all the more debilitating in the case of countries which never came under direct colonial rule: there the foreign colonial power hid behind the local ruling elites which, while trying to pose as independent, had no means of defying the wishes of their distant masters. They could not throw off the colonial yoke without mobilizing the support of their own masses, but this was impossible because they lacked all legitimacy in the eyes of the public. In countries which experienced direct colonial rule, however, the elites were able to secure the necessary degree of legitimacy by leading the independence movement.[19]

The question of legitimacy is of crucial importance to the stability of any form of rule. Until the abolition of the Caliphate in 1924 the problem was hardly ever posed in the Islamic world. The Ottoman Sultan was the Caliph of all Sunni Muslims, whether or not under his direct rule. For the Shi'ites legitimacy was shared between the grand ayatollahs on the one hand and the Shah on the other.[20] The Constitutional Revolution in Iran[21] and the break-up of the Ottoman Empire reopened the question of legitimacy. In Iran, the constitutionalists tried to solve the problem through an ingenious formula according to which all power belonged to the Hidden Imam,[22] who represented the divine will, while the exercise of that same power was the exclusive prerogative of the sovereign nation. This complicated theory of legitimacy might have worked had it not been ignored by all those concerned in its implementation. The people, however, accepted it, thus providing an important example of how a Western style of government can be welcome in a Muslim land provided it is not presented as a violent break with tradition. In some other Muslim countries the army, itself a product of colonial rule in most cases, has played the role of arbiter of power either by directly involving itself in government[23] or by using various political parties as instruments for imposing its will. In either case, however, the ruling military have failed to solve the problem of legitimacy.

A number of so-called traditional regimes have tried to secure for themselves a measure of legitimacy through reference to tribal or religious credentials. The King of Morocco, who traces his roots back to the Prophet Muhammad himself, describes himself as the Emir al-Momeneen, or the Commander of the Faithful, and claims to rule on behalf of his holy ancestor. In Jordan the King is first and foremost a hereditary tribal chief who also traces his ancestry to the Prophet. The Saudi royal family presents itself as the custodian of Mecca and Medina, Islam's holiest places, as well as the protector of the Wahabbi faith. In Oman, Kuwait, Qatar, Bahrain and the seven emirates of the Persian Gulf the rulers are chiefs of powerful clans which owe much of their influence to their wealth and the role they play in the oil-based economy. Among them only Kuwait has succeeded in giving its government a broader base by creating a parliamentary system, which – surprisingly – seems to have won a measure of credibility among the people. The dissolution of the parliament and the suspension of parts of the constitution in the spring of 1986, however, underlined the fragility of the Kuwaiti experience. The one Muslim country where a more or less parliamentary system was functioning in 1986 was Malaysia, but even there the legitimacy of state power was subject to growing doubts on the part of the country's Muslim majority. Malaysian fundamentalists have for years claimed that the government in Kuala Lumpur was secretly committed to full-scale secularization and that it had 'sold its soul to Hindus, Buddhists and foreign capital'.[24]

In the eyes of the fundamentalists, the official government of the country, being illegitimate if not downright hostile to Islam, belongs to the City of War and must therefore be fought or, if that is not possible at present, shunned and boycotted. Almost all Islamic states have conscription laws, because they have great difficulties in getting young men to join the army. Not a single Islamic state has succeeded in creating an efficient system for collecting direct taxation: the payment of taxes to an illegitimate authority is considered an act of sacrilege to Islam. Instead, the people pay the religious authorities substantial sums of money in the form either of *khums* or of *zakat*.[25] Had it not been for indirect taxation, foreign aid and the control of major revenue-earning exports, very few of the Islamic states would be in a position to finance even their day-to-day operations.

The present-day Muslim fundamentalist sees himself in the same position as Muhammad before he left Mecca for Medina. The government of Mecca was considered Satanic and illegitimate, and those who supported it mocked the Prophet and even threw stones at him.[26] Their aim was to force Muhammad to submit to a power that defied Allah, but he preferred to go into exile rather than bow to Satanic rule. His move from Mecca to Medina in AD 622 is known as the *hegira* or withdrawal. Leaving one's home town or village, which implies abandoning many friends and relatives as well as a certain rhythm of life, is always a painful decision for a Muslim. Thus the *hegira* from Mecca to Medina is seen as an act of courage and self-sacrifice on the part of the Prophet. And since every Muslim must model his life on that of the Prophet and imitate his doings,[27] it is incumbent on him to withdraw from a social and political system that is manifestly un-Islamic. Muslims should train themselves to spot the hand of Satan wherever it happens to be at work. The identification of *kufr* or infidelity, which is the same thing as obedience to Satan, is a prime duty for every good Muslim.[28] Once *kufr* has been identified one must fight to eradicate it or, if one is unable to do so for any reason, flee from it, perform a *hegira*. 'Fleeing from what is unbearable [i.e. on religious grounds] is an attribute of the prophets,' runs an Arab proverb. The concept of identifying *kufr* in order to withdraw from it has been developed by scores of fundamentalist thinkers from Mawlana Abol-Ala Mawdoodi[29] to the youthful militants of the Takfir wal-Hegira movement in Egypt. This is how the latter group understands the concept:

> Allow ourselves to sink into corruption, which already covers us up to the neck, or to save our body and our soul, withdraw? This is the choice that we followers of Muhammad have in Egypt today. Should we stay in these cities, these Sodoms and Gomorrahs of the present time – cities where every particle of air is burdened with the rot of corrupt life? Should we have dealings with the government of the Pharaoh – a government which is totally committed to Satan? Or should we leave all behind and go – go into the desert and live among the beasts in order to protect the purity of our Faith?[30]

All those who fall outside the realm of true Islam are described as *aghyar*, literally 'the others', and are in turn divided into several categories. First, there are those Muslims who have taken the path of *dhalal* (perdition) – without, however, being fully aware of the calamity they court. These wayward lambs must be brought back to the flock through advice, cajolement and 'a little force, if necessary'.[31] The people of *dhalal* must be 'reconverted to true Islam' one by one. 'We must argue with them, remind them of what Allah expects us to do in this world, and pray on their behalf,' wrote Ayatollah Hossein-Ali Montazeri.[32] 'But we must at all times remember that our task of guidance has a limit in time. Once that limit is reached, the people of *dhalal* must be shunned and boycotted and left to their fate. From then on their account is with Allah only.'[33]

Next among the *aghyar* are the *munafeqeen* or hypocrites who, while professing to be good Muslims, think 'other thoughts in secret and miss no opportunity of enjoying themselves'.[34] They must be given adequate warning to change their ways and to return to Islam, but they will in the end have to be dealt with severely. 'Killing a hypocrite who refuses to reform is more worthy than a thousand prayers,' said Ayatollah Muhammad Muhammedi Guilani, the Islamic judge in Tehran's sinister Evin Prison.[35]

Then comes the category of *ahl al-dhimma* or the people of the head tax, in other words Christians, Jews and Zoroastrians who, although recognized as legitimate religious minorities, must pay head tax to the Islamic authorities. The fact that Egypt's 10 million Coptic Christians, representing more than a fifth of the country's population, have not paid the *dhimma* tax for nearly two centuries is advanced as one of the main grievances of Islam in Egypt by those who claim to represent the True Faith.[36] The *dhimmis* and other infidels who may harbour hostile intentions towards Islam must be considered enemies making war on Allah. Their punishment is death.

The concept of *aghyar* is not limited to persons and communities; it also covers the realm of thought. All thoughts, ideas, doctrines and philosophies that are not squarely based on Islam belong to the realm of 'others', and he who 'thinks other thoughts' is as 'dangerous to Islam as he who points his dagger in the direction of Islam', in the words of a leader of the Lebanese Sunnis.[37] These 'other thoughts' include almost the whole of Western political experience, and it is in this sense that fundamentalist Islam rejects the West. But this rejection at a theoretical level concerns the clergy and their militant supporters, and not the masses, who have seldom had an opportunity to share the experience in question. The fundamentalists recognize democracy as 'an enemy of Islam', for it gives men – who are nothing but *abids* (slaves) of Allah – the right to legislate their own affairs. Khomeini says that democracy 'leads to prostitution'. Other fundamentalist thinkers see it as an obstacle to their dream of conquering the whole world for Islam. Shaikh Saeed Shaaban, leader of the Sunni majority in Tripoli, Lebanon's second largest city in terms of population, developed the theme in these words:

> We must reject democracy in favour of Islam, which is the unique [political] perfect system worked out by the Almighty. . . . Our march has just begun and Islam will end up conquering Europe and America. . . . For Islam is the only [path to] salvation left for this world in despair. . . . It is our mission to bring salvation to the entire world. And let no one think that we are Utopian dreamers.[38]

Despite their many doctrinal differences on a number of essential points, all Muslim fundamentalist movements share the belief that the elimination of the *aghyar*, whether on an individual and spiritual basis or through the conversion or expulsion of non-Muslim communities, is an important form of Jihad or Holy War. 'Muslims cannot remain indifferent to the fact that non-Islamic thoughts may cross their minds,' wrote the fundamentalist theoretician Abdul-Karim Biazar-Shirazi. 'The danger of our minds being invaded by so much that is alien to Islam becomes daily greater. Thus our vigilance must also increase in proportion [to the danger].'[39] So how does a true Muslim wage his Holy War against the *aghyar*? How does he fight the City of War wherever and in whatever form it may reveal itself? The same writer suggests an answer:

> Several steps must be taken. The first is that of *tazkiah*, which means bringing under control the rebellious self which exists in every being. Without this, even the most steadfast of believers will be in danger. Voices murmur in their ears, inviting them to enjoy the delights of this world, asking them to be merry and to forget Allah. . . . The second step is that of *takfir*, which means pointing the finger at things or persons who do not comply with [the laws of] Islam. . . . How scared of *takfir* are the enemies of Islam! True believers should shout from the rooftops the names of those who are not true to Islam; should expose their identity to [the community]. Our blessed Prophet said that traitors are cowardly! How cowardly are traitors to Islam when we hit them upon the head with the mace of *takfir*. . . . He who points the finger of *takfir* at an idea condemns it for ever in the eyes of Muslims. He who points the finger of *takfir* at a person or group of persons who refuse to see the light of Islam and embrace it signs the death sentence of that individual or community. For the step that must follow *takfir* is known as *tathir*, which means purification. Could a responsible doctor [of medicine] see microbes in a body through a microscope and do nothing about what he sees? The answer is clearly no. The same can be said of true believers, who cannot see agents of corruption acting within the body of the community without seeking to destroy them. . . .[40]

Since the victory of Khomeini's Islamic Revolution in Iran and the emergence of well-structured fundamentalist organizations in other Muslim countries, this three-stage process of self- and community-cleansing has developed into a collective crusade against any person or any non-Muslim community which might in any way threaten the unanimity of true believers. Members of the Party of Allah and its many offshoots throughout the Muslim world are put through a rigorous programme of self-purification before being authorized to act as social purifiers. The young Partisans of Allah who threw acid at Muna al-Saeed were merely doing their natural duty in accordance with the most deeply felt convictions of fundamentalism. They could not remain indifferent to microbes in the body of society. And what 'microbe' is more dangerous than the sight of a beautiful young woman who refuses to cover herself with the *hejab*?[41]

In 1976 Iran was shocked by the news of the murder of a young university student who had joined one of the many anti-Shah Islamic groups. The student, Majid Sharif-Vaqefi, had subsequently quarrelled with his fellow-believers on a point of ideology. He had been promptly pronounced 'unclean' and murdered, his body incinerated in a coal-fired heater. His assassins, later arrested and tried, expressed 'pride and joy' at their deed: Sharif-Vaqefi, they said, had 'polluted his mind with filthy alien thoughts' and had thus sealed his own death warrant; his body had to be incinerated because 'a contaminated corpse would pollute the earth'.[42]

One theme common to all fundamentalist thinkers is that Islam aims at *towheed*, or one-ness; this means one-ness not only of ideas but also of behaviour. Uniformity and unanimity are supreme values for the fundamentalist. 'We must make sure that the same word is on every lip,' wrote Khomeini. 'Even if the word spoken has no place in the hearts of some of the people who pronounce it, it is still better that everyone says the same thing.'[43] Another authority, Fath-Allah Bidar, writes about 'one-ness' as a supreme Islamic goal:

> The people of Jesus[44] have four different versions of what their Prophet wanted them to learn. . . . Hence the door is open to confusion, to debate and dissent, to someone saying this and someone else saying that. In Islam, however, there is only one Qur'an and not four. It means that Allah wants true believers to think exactly the same and behave in harmony and live in tranquillity with one another. This is why those who suggest other [thoughts] or try to to be different are divisive elements,

schismatics who ought to be brought back into the fold or eliminated. . . .[45]

When the fundamentalists act from a position of weakness, the process of cleansing society from dissent and individual idiosyncrasies rests on a fourth 'pillar' – that of *tabligh*, which means propagation of the Faith. *Tabligh* is necessary until such time as the machinery of state has been taken over by true believers, and can be undertaken in a variety of ways ranging from the setting up of Qur'anic schools to the assassination of 'especially notorious enemies of Islam'.[46]

Adding to the number of believers and reducing that of the infidels is one of the most important duties of the militant fundamentalist. The number of believers can be increased by producing many children, and by converting the infidels – which at the same time, of course, reduces the numbers of infidels. But what about those 'enemies of Islam who shall in no circumstance return to the Right Path'?[47] They should be either disfigured so that 'they are recognized by the ugliness of their faces that reflects the ugliness of their souls', or 'eliminated'.[48] The authority to kill such 'forsaken souls' is drawn from a saying attributed to the Prophet: 'Kill the troublemaker before he can harm you!'[49]

The dictum that the end justifies the means is adopted by all fundamentalist organizations in their strategies for achieving political power and imposing on society their own view of Islam. What is important in every action is its *niy'yah*, its motive. No means need be spared in the service of Islam as long as one takes action with a pure *niy'yah*. Nakir and Munkar, the two angels in Islam who interrogate the dead shortly after burial, never waste time putting questions about means; instead, they emphasize the importance of aims. Those who have served Allah, and worked and fought to spread the True Faith across the globe, will be directed towards Paradise; Hell awaits the rest. The means all come from Allah, and must be seen as signs pointing to the kind of action He desires. Khomeini explained how Allah gave Abraham an axe with which to smash the idols in Mecca, while Moses received a staff which he turned into 'a deadly weapon against the Pharaoh'.[50] Another theoretician of the fundamentalist movement, Muhammad-Taqi Partovi, put the point slightly differently: 'It is Allah who puts the gun in our hand. But we cannot expect him to pull the trigger as well simply because we are faint-hearted.'[51] One of the heroes of fundamentalism, Muhammad Navab-Safavi, developed the argument even further:

> We know of no absolute values besides total submission to the will of the Almighty. People say: 'Don't lie!' But the principle is different when we serve the will of Allah. He taught Man to lie so that we can save ourselves at moments of difficulty and confuse our enemies. Should we remain truthful at the cost of defeat and danger to the Faith? We say not. People say: 'Don't kill!' But the Almighty Himself taught us how to kill. Without such a skill Man would have been wiped out long ago by the beasts. So shall we not kill when it is necessary for the triumph of the Faith? We say that killing is tantamount to saying a prayer when those who are harmful [to the Faith] need to be put out of the way. Deceit, trickery, conspiracy, cheating, stealing and killing are nothing but means. On their own they are neither good nor bad. For no act is either good or bad on its own, isolated from the intentions that motivated it. Look at a kitchen knife. Is it either good or bad? With it a housewife can cut the meat she needs for her daily stew. A miscreant could use it to end the life of a true believer. And a soldier of Islam could use it for piercing the black heart of a harmful one.[52]

A true believer cannot remain indifferent to the political fate of the society in which he lives. Islam is a thoroughly political religion, and cannot be put in a position of weakness simply because some means and tactics may be considered immoral. Khomeini wrote: 'Consider the case of our blessed Prophet. He made [war] plans for thirteen years and spent another ten years fighting his wars. He did not say: "What have we got to do with politics?" '[53]

Means used in the service of the cause can be blessed, and in so doing rendered noble, in a number of ways. One means of blessing a gun intended as an assassination weapon against a harmful one is to take it to a holy shrine and move with it around the tomb of the Imam. Another way is to have inscribed on its barrel the names of the Five People of the Shawl[54] or a verse from the Qur'an. A simpler method is to whisper a suitable verse into the barrel of the gun before firing it. The gun with which a Partisan of Allah shot and killed the

Egyptian President Muhammad Anwar Sadat on 6 October 1981 was inscribed with the words 'In the Name of Allah the Avenger!'[55] And the acid that disfigured Muna al-Saeed? It was, perhaps, blessed in its container by a shaikh[56] of the Party of Allah.

2

The Weed in the Garden of Allah

The Unbelievers follow
falsehood while the Believers
follow the Truth. When you meet
the Unbelievers strike off their
heads, and when you have laid
them low bind them firmly.

Qur'an, *sura* XLVII, verses 3 and 4

'The world is a beautiful garden created for Man by Allah,' wrote Sayyed Muhammad Qutb, one of the saints of Islamic fundamentalism.

> The creator of the garden has sent us His directions for its use in the form of revealed religion. What is the central message of these divine directions? It is, simply, to root out the weed that grows wild in this garden and that, if allowed to spring up and to spread, will smother it to death. Now who is to stop the weed, to eliminate it [altogether]? The answer is every one of us. For every one of the believers must fight this war.[1]

According to fundamentalist Islam, the inhabitants of Allah's garden are divided into three categories: the *mustanbat*, those who have full knowledge of their religious duties; the *mustakbar*, those who oppress and exploit humanity or simply mock the Faith; and, finally, the *mustazaf*, the oppressed and the weak who are not aware of the teachings of Islam or, for whatever reason, are not capable of implementing them. Everyone should aim to achieve the status of *mustanbat*, and every *mustanbat* is a warrior of Allah provided that he meets four conditions.[2] A warrior of Allah is personally responsible to his creator and must, 'when he has no friends', perform his duties single-handed. One of his most important tasks is to protect the *mustazaf*, the vulnerable section of the community, and to guide them in all matters. Equally vital, however, is that he should 'strike off the head of Unbelievers'. Every *mustanbat* can act as a judge of others provided he bases himself firmly on the rules of the Faith. He can pass sentence of death on anyone even without referring to a recognized judge or *qadhi*. It is, of course, highly recommended that he should secure the consent of a *qadhi* before proceeding to eliminate one of the weeds, but the absence of a *qadhi* or any difficulty in obtaining the desired death sentence need not prevent a warrior of Allah from carrying out what he considers to be a divine judgement. Once a weed is clearly recognized as an enemy of the Faith he becomes *mahdur ad-damm* – one whose blood must be shed.

The assassination of President Sadat by a group of Islamic fundamentalists must therefore be seen as the continuation of a tradition which began with the dawn of the Faith. Three out of the four Caliphs who succeeded the Prophet were assassinated by those who considered them to have become weeds.[3] Omar Ibn Khattab, the second Caliph and the architect of Islam's greatest conquests after the Prophet, was struck down by a poisoned dagger wielded by Firuz, alias Abu-Lowlow, on 3 November 644.[4] The third Caliph, Othman Ibn Affan, was murdered at his home by a group of soldiers on 17 June 656.[5] Ali Ibn Abi-Taleb, the fourth Caliph and the first Imam of the Shi'ites, suffered the same fate when one Abdul-Rahman Ibn Muljam struck him down with a long sword in February 661 at the mosque of Kufa in Mesopotamia.[6]

The tradition thus established was to continue throughout the history of Islam. Muawwyyah, who succeeded in ousting the House of Ali from power in order to found the Umayyid Dynasty, was himself subjected to several unsuccessful assassination attempts. Hassan, Ali's elder son and a pretender to the title of Caliph until he abdicated this right in favour of the Umayyid ruler, also suffered an attempt on his life. But it was not for another four hundred years that assassination as a means of implementing divine will was developed into an integral part of all radical readings of Islam.

The man responsible for this development was Hassan

Sabbah, born in Qom, 150 kilometres south of Tehran, in the mid-eleventh century. Brought up as a Shi'ite,[7] he had every reason to be unhappy in an Iran dominated by the Sunni faith and ruled by the Turkish Seljuk Dynasty. Hassan, who was considered clever enough to study theology, was sent to Neyshabur, 1100 kilometres east of present-day Tehran, to attend the *maktab*[8] of Imam Muwaffiq.[9] But Hassan was not to become a mere *faqih* or doctor of divinity, content with adjudicating theological disputes. He believed that Islam, or at least the Shi'ite-Ismaili version of it to which his family subscribed, was a religion both of action and of reflection. Almost a modern revolutionary, Hassan understood the four phases of a successful politico-religious movement: study, propagate, organize and attack. He also knew that a genuine revolutionary movement needs at least one 'liberated zone' from which to launch its bid for the conquest of the world.

This liberated zone Hassan was to seek all over the Seljuk Empire, which at the time extended from Mesopotamia to Central Asia. At the end of a long journey that took him to the four corners of that empire, Hassan found the region of Dailam, a section of the Elburz mountain range that seals off the Iranian plateau from the Caspian Sea, most suitable. Here, both slopes of the Elburz are covered by dense pine forests. The valleys, however, grow a number of crops ranging from wheat and barley to hashish. Fruit and olive orchards as well as rich vineyards make the region more attractive than most other parts of the vast country. Hassan arrived in the village of Rudbar in about July 1090, in the company of a group of disciples, for a period of repose and reflection. He was by then convinced that his movement would not long survive the pressures of clandestine life. Any serious politico-religious movement would sooner or later need to create its ideal society, even on a miniature scale if necessary, in order to convince the mass of the *mustazaf* of its ability to 're-create the world as Allah wished it'. Islam's kingdom, unlike that of Christ, does not belong to the hereafter and must be created here and now.

According to Hassan's followers it was the Almighty Himself who led their guide to Rudbar, for it was near this peaceful village of no particular distinction that Hassan found the fortress of Alamut, which he was to turn into his liberated zone and base of operations. All that remains today of the fortress, some 140 kilometres west of Tehran, is a mass of ruins often covered by snow. But it is not difficult to see and to feel that there is indeed something special about Alamut. Here, the deep violet and ochre rocks seem to be much darker than anywhere else in the mountains, and the view of sheer rocks nibbling at the heavens inspires feelings of awe even in the most unemotional visitor. The fortress was built on the crest of the mountain but with its foundations hidden, so as to create the impression that the huge edifice was somehow suspended in the air above a deep, dark precipice. Constructed of light grey rock, presumably brought from other parts of the mountain, the tall watch-towers of the fortress had a dominating view of the plain that runs all the way to Qazvin.[10] Local folklore dated the fortress to the mythological Aryan kings of ancient Iran, but it may have been constructed during the rule of the Buyid kings a couple of centuries before Hassan reached it. The fortress, which bore the apt name of Ashianeh Oqab (Eagle's Nest), was occupied at the time of Hassan's arrival by a descendant of Imam Ali, who acted as the governor of the region on behalf of the Seljuk Sultan. Hassan kept his intention to take over the fortress a secret until the end of that fateful summer. No soldier of Allah should give out unnecessary information even to his closest friends; the Prophet said: 'He who keeps secrets shall soon attain his objectives.'

Hassan made use of his presence in the village to convert some of the local peasants. His austere lifestyle, his erudition and his charisma won over most of them, while the local governor, occupied by the joys of the flesh, knew nothing of the danger growing all round him. Hassan, acknowledged as *murshid* or guide within a few days, was soon to be given the title of Deh-Khoda, literally the God of the Village, but taken to mean 'ruler'. In September 1090 he was already inside the Eagle's Nest, preparing to seize it. He did not have long to wait, and the 'divine signal' to take over the fortress came before the month was out. The governor was allowed to leave with a few of his possessions and a message of 'contempt and defiance' for the Turkish Sultan.[11]

Within less than two years Hassan had organized his liberated zone into the headquarters of a revolutionary movement that sent tremors into the heart of the Seljuk court. He divided his fraternity into three categories. First were the *murshids* or guides, who devoted themselves to study and to the preparation of propaganda material. Then there were the *da'is* or propagators, who were sent on proselytizing missions throughout the Muslim world. These *da'is* were often men of great learning who, instead of enclosing themselves in *maktabs* where they would be instructing only a few pupils, toured the countryside to take the message to everyone, including the humble and the poor. As master polemicists the *da'is* would go to any *maktab*, *madrassah*[12] or mosque to measure the strength of their faith as well as their own powers of persuasion against that of traditional teachers. Nasser Khosrow Qobadiani, one of the greatest of all Persian poets, was among the *da'is* propagating the reformed doctrine of Ismailite Shi'ism.[13] Finally came the *fedayeen* – those prepared to sacrifice their lives, as well as to kill, for Allah. It did not take long for the reputation of the *fedayeen* and their poisoned daggers to reach all parts of the empire, and the term *fedai* and its plural *fedayeen* were to achieve a permanent place in Islamic political vocabulary. Thousands of members of the Palestine Liberation Organization, for example, describe themselves as *fedayeen*, as do Marxist-Leninist urban guerrillas in Iran.[14]

In 1092 the Seljuk Sultan Malek-Shah, no doubt taking the advice of his Grand Vizir Nizam al-Mulk, sent a spy to Dailam to find out at first hand about the activities of this strange and increasingly dangerous sect. The spy, Emir Arsalan Tash, organized a network of informers in and around Alamut and spent several months compiling a chilling report. As a result of his information the Seljuk state made a sustained effort to reduce the fortress and to put Hassan and his immediate companions to death.

Arsalan Tash's report describes Hassan's hideout in the following words:

> Alamut is one of the most important forts in the Rudbar region. Built at an inaccessible height, it is known as the Eagle's Nest, a name fully justified by its impregnable situation. [The fort]

resembles the shape of a kneeling lion with its head resting on the earth. The walls are carved out of the rock. There are no accessible paths and the defence [of the fort] is therefore easy. To reach it one has to climb tiny stairs or, rather, holes carved out of the mountainside. Inside the wall there is a village whose population works day and night to construct new walls and to dig huge basins for conserving honey, oil and wheat in sufficient quantities to maintain a sizeable garrison. The fort itself is built on top of a gorge. And since fortifications are unnecessary on this side the walls are much lower. They can see that [these walls] cover fields and orchards. As far as the inhabitants of the village are concerned, they are the subject of strange rumours in the region. [According to these rumours] the man who calls himself the Lord of the Mountain began by throwing out of Alamut, together with their entire families, all deformed, old or sick men – making exceptions only in the case of those who were masters of a rare science or craft. He also expelled [from the village] all musicians and story-tellers. But the number of inhabitants has continued to grow. Hardly a day passes without the arrival of new Ismailis from the four corners of the globe or the appearance at the gate of those desirous to learn about the new doctrine of the religious-military order created by Hassan Sabbah. Even without taking into account the village, the fort has over a hundred guards, divided into several companies on the basis of a mysterious hierarchy. They are all blindly devoted to their master.[15]

This account, although only partially accurate when checked against other documents, including Hassan's autobiography, nevertheless contains most of the themes of a ferocious propaganda campaign launched against the sect. The secret nature of some aspects of the organization within the citadel of Alamut was almost certainly the result of habits formed by Hassan and his partisans during years of clandestine struggle against the state. But Seljuk propaganda presented this as a sure sign that Hassan was head of a *batini* group, that is, Zoroastrians who hid their true faith behind an Islamic façade. The Ismailis were identified also with Qarmatis, who were accused of being worshippers of ancient Aryan deities. Nizam al-Mulk, who was himself at times accused of harbouring a secret desire to return Iran to its pre-Islamic past, knew that Hassan's image could be demolished in the eyes of the Muslims only if he could be portrayed as a corrupt, pleasure-seeking and ostentatious ruler. Nizam understood Muslim psychology well, and his remarks ring perfectly true even today:

> The example of austerity is far more effective than that of corruption. The heretic [i.e. Hassan Sabbah] knows full well where he is heading. His long experience, his deep knowledge of men and his profound study of politics and history have taught him that impiety and corruption might, at times, bring about the fall of a dynasty but could never serve as a basis for founding a new one. He knows that he must make himself respected and that the mass [of the people] cannot be controlled without order. He also knows that religion and ethics are the only [effective means] of guaranteeing the obedience of the people.[16]

It was Nizam al-Mulk's undoubted talent for political propaganda which enabled the Seljuk state to contain the danger of Alamut, and to portray Hassan and his followers as a community of loose souls totally devoted to immoral pleasure. Reports that Alamut had been turned into an earthly version of Paradise, where houris – both male and female[17] – were present to satisfy every desire of the *da'is* and the *fedayeen*, were spread throughout the empire by Nizam's agents and repeated by orthodox mullahs from the pulpit of every mosque in the empire. Hassan had sentenced all the top dignitaries of the Seljuk state to death, and was answered in kind when mullahs in the pay of the Grand Vizir declared him to be an enemy of Allah whose blood ought to be shed. It was war. But Hassan's disciples managed to last longer than the Seljuk state. Despite occasional military defeats, some quite severe, the *fedayeen* kept their efficient war machine in good order. And before the eleventh century was out, they had created a string of other strongholds – almost all patterned on the model of Alamut – in the remote mountain regions of Iran. Hassan's followers became a state within the state: the City of Faith existing alongside the City of War. There could be no peace between the two, and every truce dictated by circumstances was used to prepare for the next battle.

During the Crusades, Hassan's followers turned their deadly attention to the warriors coming from Europe to fight Islam. The *fedayeen* would introduce themselves into the Christian camp by stealth, or disguised as merchants and journeymen, in order to put their poisoned daggers to use. This was the West's first-ever encounter with Islam's Holy Terror, but Hassan's followers had already spread terror throughout the vast realm of Islam itself. Among their more illustrious victims were Malik-Shah himself, who was put to death by poison, and Nizam al-Mulk, who was 'ripped apart'.[18] Scores of orthodox Islamic leaders, judges, teachers and prayer leaders also perished, together with countless state functionaries. Many of the *fedayeen* died in the performance of their sacred duty, but the prospect of death did not seem to discourage the followers of the Old Man of the Mountain. To despise death was one of the highest values promoted in the tightly knit community; the poet Nasser Khosrow wrote:

> Man's fear of death is an illness
> Whose only medicine is the science of the Faith.

But was 'the science of the Faith' enough to make the *fedayeen* kill and die without hesitation? Almost certainly not. The *fedayeen* were subject to long periods of intense propaganda in which they took part in a series of initiation ceremonies. Contemporary reports speak of the 'glimpse of Paradise' which the *fedayeen* were allowed to catch as part of their 'progress towards the Truth'. The Paradise in question may have been a beautiful Persian garden, but it certainly was not the fairytale land of milk and honey and incense described by anti-Ismaili historians. The *fedayeen* must also have been initiated in the use of narcotics. Hashish was grown in that part of Iran since long before the advent of Islam and may have been used, together with another plant with narcotic properties, known as *shahdaneh* (royal seed), in religious ceremonies in pre-Islamic Iran. Most historians affirm that the Alamut community knew of both hashish and *shahdaneh* and made regular use of it. Some accounts speak of hashish being smoked at initiation ceremonies, while others say it was mixed with yoghurt and drunk by the faithful. In either case, the effect was to alter the level of consciousness and create 'the illusion that the user was about to enter Paradise'.[19]

A recent historian, Silvestre de Sacy, wrote about the use of hashish by the *fedayeen* of Alamut:

> At the time of the power of the Ismailites, the hallucinogenic preparations [they knew] were not generally known to the

> Muslims. It was not until much later that this knowledge was brought from the eastern provinces, probably from India itself, into Persia. . . . No doubt the Ismailites, whose religion has a number of points in common with Indian dogmas, had learned of the use of [hashish] much earlier and kept their knowledge a precious secret and one of the most powerful instruments at their disposal.[20]

It is also possible that Hassan had discovered a magic potion by mixing wine with opium. The Rudbar region produces excellent grapes, which until the Islamic Revolution in 1979 were made into both wine and arak.[21] Opium poppies grow in the Qazvin Plain not far from Rudbar, and opium must have been known to Hassan and his disciples. The term *hashasheen*, or smokers of hashish, began to be applied to Hassan's followers soon after Nizam al-Mulk's murder; it stuck, and later entered Western languages as 'assassin'.

The attitude of contemporary Islamic fundamentalism towards the movement of the Assassins says something about their ideological confusion. Hassan Sabbah and his Assassins are described as 'heroes of Islam', while there is talk of the effective role they played in spreading terror among the European Crusaders. Muslim writers have penned countless novels, short stories and plays in which Hassan is depicted as an Avenger of Allah putting the infidel to flight. But when it comes to Hassan's revolutionary struggle against the established Islamic order of his time, widely differing views are expressed. The revolutionary fundamentalists such as Khomeini avoid the subject altogether. Militants of the Islamic Left, however, consider Hassan to have been an early exponent of 'Marxism in an Islamic context'.[22] The conservative and traditionalist writers and thinkers see in Hassan exactly what Nizam al-Mulk saw in him: a power-hungry politician devoted to returning Iran to its pre-Islamic beliefs through the use of pseudo-Islamic concepts. Some of Khomeini's opponents in the Arab world, notably in Iraq, which has been at war with the Islamic Republic since 1980, describe Khomeini as a latter-day version of Hassan Sabbah – a 'magus dreaming of reviving the Persian Empire and restoring the worship of the Holy Fire'.[23]

The *fedayeen* may or may not have drawn their inspiration

from hashish, although there is nothing in their own literature to hint even remotely that this was the case,[24] but they certainly used political assassination as a weapon against their enemies. They did not invent political murder; as we have already seen, this method of eliminating the enemies of Allah was already known to the Kharejites,[25] who included among their victims Imam Ali. But it was Hassan Sabbah who developed political murder as an important element in a coherent theory of political power. The lessons he taught were never forgotten in the Islamic world, and today attract more disciples than ever.

3

The Blood of Brothers

> Those who are against killing
> have no place in Islam. Our Prophet
> killed with his own blessed hands.
> Our Imam Ali killed more than
> seven hundred on a single day. If
> the survival of the Faith requires
> the shedding of blood, we are there
> to perform our duty.
>
> Ayatollah Sadeq Khalkhali, Islamic judge

One evening in March 1928 Hassan al-Banna, a primary schoolteacher in the Egyptian city of Ismailia, had just completed his sunset prayers. Humid heat enveloped the featureless city named after Khedive Ismail, but now controlled by the Suez Canal Company, a Franco-British concern. Just as al-Banna, known to everyone in the neighbourhood as Shaikh Hassan because of his reputation as a master of Islamic science, was preparing to settle down for the night he heard a knock on his door. When he opened it he found himself face to face with six men, all wearing an expression of grim determination.[1] Shaikh Hassan was only twenty-two and, as an underpaid teacher, could not afford servants; having led his visitors into the tiny reception room he had to leave them for a few moments in order to make some tea. On his return he found them all still standing. They bowed their heads in a gesture of respect as the young teacher entered the room. 'Thou art our master and our guide,' they said in unison. Shaikh Hassan motioned them to sit on the floor in a semi-circle, and served them the tea he had made. It was an assembly of the *owlia* or friends, the ideal company in which every Muslim would wish to find himself. They were all only in their twenties, and yet in every word and movement they displayed a gravity associated with much older men in the Islamic East.

One of the guests began to speak, explaining the purpose of their visit:

> 'We despise this life, which is one of dishonour and enslavement. Arabs and Muslims no longer have a place here in this country, nor do they enjoy any dignity. And they do nothing about their state of bondage as wage-earners working for foreigners. As for us, we have nothing to offer but our blood, which circulates in our veins with boiling rage. We have nothing but our souls, which sparkle with faith and dignity. We have nothing but our lives and these few coins that we have saved on our children's food. We do not see how we ought to act. But thou hast the answer. We do not know how to serve the fatherland, the faith and the Muslim *Ummah*.[2] Thou hast the answer. Here is what we demand of thee today: we offer thee all that we possess in order to be liberated from this ignoble dependence; we put ourselves in the hands of Allah. And thou shalt be responsible to Him [on our behalf]. Thou shalt be responsible for us and our actions, responsible for an entire community of devoted [fighters] which takes an oath in front of Allah to live only according to His religion and to die for Him – to seek none but Him. In short, we shall be a community that deserves to be victorious despite its small numbers and the limited means of struggle at its disposal.'[3]

With tears in his eyes Shaikh Hassan accepted the offer, and then suggested that all present take an oath of fidelity to the cause and the organization.[4] The meeting continued through the night as Shaikh Hassan and his guests discussed the 'tragic state' in which Islam found itself as a result of the treachery of its rulers and the lethargy of its masses. They also discussed possible names for their new organization. Several traditional ones were suggested: they could, for example, call themselves a *tariqa* or 'path', of which scores already existed in Egypt and other Muslim countries; or they could form a club, imitating the Westernized intellectuals, or an association, or even a union or political party. But Shaikh Hassan would have none of these. What was starting at his house in Ismailia on that fateful night would be something entirely different; it would mark 'the return of combative Islam' and should therefore be known by an original name. Shaikh Hassan closed the debate with these words: 'We shall avoid formalities and official ceremonies. Our gathering shall be, first and foremost, [the expression of] an idea. . . . We are all brothers in the service of Islam. We are, therefore, the Muslim Brotherhood.'[5]

At first glance, Ismailia appears an unlikely place for the birth of a militant Islamic movement which, given Egypt's situation in those days as a virtual colony of Britain, could not fail to be xenophobic. Ismailia was, in a sense, a child of the Suez Canal Company. It owed its *raison d'être* to the Canal which provided some 90 per cent of Egypt's foreign earnings. More than a third of the city's working population were employed by the company and their salaries, very high by Egyptian standards of the time, gave the local economy a degree of buoyancy unknown in most other parts of the country.

In Ismailia, the infidel and his way of life were omnipresent while Islam was pushed into the background and confined to a few semi-derelict mosques. The town boasted several bars, billiard halls and brothels as well as a night club where the infidels and their Egyptian 'lackeys' drank beer, listened to music and indulged in the pleasures of the flesh. Many Muslim women had cast off their veils and appeared in the streets, in offices and even in the bazaar with their hair uncovered and their legs showing from under short skirts. An increasing number of young men had shaved off their beards and wore European suits complete with ties, despite the suffocating heat of the city. To Shaikh Hassan, Ismailia must have appeared like Sodom and Gomorrah combined.

'The people of Ismailia had all but forgotten their Creator,' wrote one of Shaikh Hassan's admirers, Saleh Habibi.

> They pronounced the word 'Allah' every now and then. But that was done out of habit and signified nothing. Prayers were still performed by most people, but that too was little more than a ritualistic act. Islam was considered decadent and dying and the future was shaped in the West. People had been won over by the idea of having a good life in this world, regardless of the questions that would be asked in the next.[6]

Perhaps more serious from Shaikh Hassan's point of view was the fact that a large number of young men in Ismailia had rallied to the Wafd[7] party, which openly advocated the Westernization of Egypt. The message of the Wafd encompassed all the hatred that Shaikh Hassan felt against Egypt's foreign masters, who, despite formal recognition of the country's independence in 1922, intervened in every aspect of the nation's political and economic life. The Wafd wanted to throw foreigners out of Egypt and reassert national sovereignty, but its ultimate aim was the Westernization of Egypt and it considered the suppression of backward Islamic ideas a step along that path. As Shaikh Hassan saw it, the Wafd might one day succeed in expelling all Europeans from Egypt, but would at the same time establish a secular way of life; the Europeans would go, but their civilization would remain. It was, perhaps, because Ismailia was the archetypal City of War in Egypt at that time that Shaikh Hassan had chosen it as the starting point of his Jihad.

Born in Muhammadiah, some 150 kilometres northwest of Cairo, Hassan al-Banna came into contact with the idea of an Islamic revival at an early age. His own father, who was a theology teacher and part-time Islamic judge as well as running a watch repair shop to augment the family's income, was a graduate of the prestigious al-Azhar theological college in Cairo. Hassan, sent to a Qur'anic school at the age of eight, was soon characterized by his teachers as a precocious genius. By the time he was thirteen he had already attended a number of religious meetings organized by semi-secret Islamic societies. As he was active in school politics, it was only natural that he should be present, leading a dozen classmates, at the riots of 1919 which shook Egypt and eventually forced Britain to recognize the country's independence.

The almost inevitable contact with Sufism gave Hassan a taste for philosophical speculation and doubt while attending Cairo's Dar al-Ulum, or House of Sciences, which in fact was a graduate school of literature. But Hassan was no Sufi by temperament. He was not one to withdraw from the world and devote himself to meditation on abstract issues. He was a man of action, and was strongly attracted by political power. His membership of the Hassafiyah Society of Sufis, following his full initiation that gave him the right to wear the white turban and long coat of the order, was to prove no more than a brief respite in his turbulent life. His flirtations with poetry also proved transient, and before he had turned twenty he had decided that he would become a teacher, a propagator of the Faith. He explained his decision in these words: 'Our youth is submerged in perplexity and doubt, and apostasy is more present than Faith. I must serve as a counsellor and a teacher. I shall devote myself to the education of children during the day and the education of their parents in the evenings. The nights I shall devote to study and prayer. . . . This is a pact between Allah and myself.'[8]

At the time when Shaikh Hassan and his six companions were setting up the first *halqah* or 'link' of what was to become 'a steadfast chain binding Muslims together throughout the world', Egypt was the intellectual centre of Islam and the idea of an Islamic Renaissance was very much in the air. After a lapse of nearly half a century, the teachings of Sayyed Jamaleddin Assadabadi[9] had sunk in among the intellectual elite. Both a pan-Islamist and a freemason, Assadabadi had never quite decided what he wanted. He had been more of an agitator than an original thinker, vacillating between the prospect of a modernized Islam joining the progressive states of Europe on the one hand, and the temptation of returning to a golden past on the other. His revolutionary phraseology had conquered the Muslim imagination from his native Iran to Egypt, where he had been a frequent traveller and preacher.

Sayyed Jamaleddin's vitriolic attacks on 'corrupt rulers' had produced at least one dramatic result. One of his distant admirers, Mirza Reza Kermani, a student of theology, had decided to do his individual duty towards Allah by murdering Nassereddin Shah, the reformist Qajar monarch who sat on the Peacock Throne.[10] In 1922, however, Shaikh Hassan al-Banna's 'seething passion'[11] for radicalizing Islam stopped short of advocating assassination as a means of fulfilling divine wishes. Shaikh Hassan admired Sayyed Jamaleddin's role as a teacher and preacher, but not as a revolutionary leader. The young Ismailia schoolmaster also studied with great care the work accomplished by Shaikh Muhammad Abduh, Sayyed Jamaleddin's most illustrious disciple.

The founder of the Muslim Brotherhood followed the ongoing debate on the future of Egypt through the pages of *al-Manar* (*The Lighthouse*), an erudite periodical edited by one of Abduh's disciples, the Syrian-born Rashid Raza. In a sense the al-Manar group could be described as the founding fathers of Islamic fundamentalism in the twentieth century.[12] But they differed in one important aspect from the later fundamentalists, including, from the 1930s onwards, al-Banna himself – they believed that Islam's victory must be achieved on 'the battlefield of ideas'. Fighting them at the time on that battlefield in Egypt were a number of politicians and intellectuals who openly advocated the political Westernization of the Muslim world. Some of these Westernizers, like Taha Hussein who served for a while as Minister of Education, were to become bestselling authors, thus demonstrating that a genuine audience for Western ideas existed in Egypt.

Another contemporary group that influenced al-Banna's formative years in a number of ways was the band of tribal warriors who were conquering virtually the whole of the Arabian peninsula, with the the exception of Yemen, Oman and the Persian Gulf coasts, under the leadership of Abdul-Aziz Ibn Sa'ud. Fervent followers of the eighteenth-century Islamic teacher Abdul-Wahhab, these 'rising stars of the desert'[13] owed much of their success to their ability to whip up among their tribal supporters a degree of religious zeal unknown for centuries even in the birthplace of Islam. Their belief that nothing could resist a combination of the Holy Book and the sword produced handsome dividends when they founded the Kingdom of Saudi Arabia in 1929.[14]

Shaikh Hassan had by then been secretly converted to the cult of action. After years of teaching and preaching at schools and mosques he had concluded that what mattered was political power, and not winning a few debates in the pages of obscure journals which few people read and fewer understood. The emblem he chose for the Muslim Brotherhood showed that he shared Abdul-Aziz's belief: it consisted of a Qur'an protected by two crossed scimitars, below which was the motto: 'And Be Ready!'[15] Shaikh Hassan also made his own the dictum that the end justifies the means – which was, as explained above, to become virtually an article of faith for future fundamentalists. Needing money to get the new society moving, Shaikh Hassan did not hesitate to accept a gift of 500

Egyptian pounds, a considerable sum in those days, from the Suez Canal Company. Several Brothers were, however, so outraged at this that they left the new organization altogether.[16] Shaikh Hassan attached no importance to widespread rumours that he had been picked up by the British – who still dominated Egyptian politics – and by the royal court at Cairo, as a man who could stem the tide of popular support for Wafd's brand of nationalism. The fact was, however, that the king and his entourage, as well as the monarchist press, did whatever they could to promote the Muslim Brotherhood, while the Company persisted in its generosity by offering as 'modest gifts' to the Brothers a plot of land on which to build a school and a mosque, as well as a fully completed mosque.

Shaikh Hassan's apparent absence of scruple in accepting donations from the very infidels he had vowed to chase out of Egypt did not in the end mean any modification of his anti-British campaign. As soon as he was sure he could stand on his own feet he began to advertise his admiration for the Italian fascist dictator Benito Mussolini and, later, for Adolf Hitler. It is quite possible that the Brothers were the origin of rumours that Mussolini was an Egyptian Muslim, that his real name was Musa Nili (Moses of the Nile), and that Hitler too had secretly converted to Islam and bore the name of Hayder or 'the brave one'. Saying special prayers for an Axis victory became a frequent feature of the Brothers' gatherings during World War II.[17]

It was, no doubt, under the combined influence of King Abdul-Aziz of Saudi-Arabia on the one hand and the European fascist and Nazi movements on the other that Shaikh Hassan began thinking of creating a military arm for his movement. The decision was announced to a handful of disciples in 1938, shortly after Shaikh Hassan al-Banna had been formally chosen as the Supreme Guide of the organization. In his first speech as Supreme Guide, Shaikh Hassan announced that the rules of Islam must be imposed in Egypt 'by force if necessary'; 'the battle of ideas' was no longer sufficient. He also announced his intention of creating 'a solid, alternative administration' – a parallel government in fact – which would, when the time came, take over the government of the country. Finally, a relentless war would be waged against 'the heathen, the apostate, the deviant', who would, when judged too dangerous, be put to death in the name of Allah.

When Shaikh Hassan launched his Holy War the organization he had founded a decade earlier had become the strongest and best organized political force in Egypt. The Muslim Brotherhood, now with its headquarters in Cairo where the Supreme Guide had taken up residence after leaving Ismailia, boasted a membership of more than half a million, with a further 2 million described as 'sympathizers or aspiring members'.[18]

By the time Rommel's Afrika Korps landed in Libya, the Muslim Brotherhood was convinced that it would be able to take over the government of Egypt within a few months. This conviction was based on two assumptions: one was that the Allies would be defeated by the Axis,[19] and the other was that the Egyptian state, lacking popular support and always considered as something of an 'imposition from the outside',[20] would fall apart under the Brotherhood's political propaganda and the campaign of selective assassinations soon to be unleashed. Both assumptions were to prove wrong, with disastrous consequences for Shaikh Hassan and his friends.

The Muslim Brotherhood's military wing was originally intended to lead a popular uprising in favour of the Axis forces, but, as an Allied victory became increasingly inevitable, it was turned into a reserve of the movement with the vague idea of some day seizing power through a coup d'état. Scores of young officers were seduced by the movement's passionate militancy and opposition to foreign domination,[21] but none would take part in the series of terrorist attacks that the Brotherhood launched in Egypt and elsewhere shortly after the end of World War II. Shaikh Hassan's campaign of terror was to become a model for future fundamentalist movements, notably in Iran and Lebanon. Cinemas were dynamited and hotels and restaurants catering for 'the infidel and the heretics' were set on fire. Women wearing 'inadequate dress' were the victims of knife attacks, and homes said to belong to apostates were raided and ransacked by angry believers gathering for 'spontaneous demonstrations'. But it was the series of spectacular assassinations that followed, which in the end established the pan-Islamic reputation of Shaikh Hassan's movement. The Supreme Guide of Cairo was to find himself a worthy heir to his namesake, the Old Man of the Mountain, nearly a thousand years before him. A secret court, headed by Shaikh Hassan himself and including two or three other 'judges', organized the trial *in absentia*[22] of those in prominent places who were 'causing corruption on earth'.[23] The assassins of the Middle Ages were back with a vengeance.

Among those murdered were two Prime Ministers, Ahmad Maher and Noqrachi Pasha, while a third Premier, Mustafa Nahas Pasha, managed to survive three attempts on his life. Less fortunate were the Interior Minister, Amin Othman Pasha, the Police Chief, Selim Zaki Pasha, the Chief Justice, Ahmad al-Khazindar, and dozens of other officials as well as businessmen and intellectuals.

Frustrated by the tediously slow pace of the return to Islam in Egypt, and constantly tempted by the 'delights of the other side of the Mediterranean', by 1945 the Shaikh and his friends had completely succumbed to the temptation of pushing history ahead under 'the whip of our will'.[24] The whistling of every bullet fired by one of Shaikh Hassan's *fedayeen* sent an echo throughout the Muslim world and encouraged hundreds of young men from Turkey, India, Afghanistan, Iran and Iraq to travel to Egypt to join the Brothers and learn from them the 'art of eliminating the weed'.[25] Before the Muslim Brotherhood was formally banned, in December 1948, it was estimated to have trained more than a hundred terrorists from Muslim countries other than Egypt. And yet the venerable Shaikh missed no opportunity to deny having anything to do with terrorist activity. He had learned from the Shi'ites the art of *taqiyah*, or keeping one's convictions a secret, whenever and wherever it was profitable to do so.[26] The mass arrest of Brotherhood members and the ensuing lengthy interrogation of hundreds of militants, in January 1949, convinced the Egyptian police that Shaikh Hassan had been the mastermind of all the political murders that had rocked the country. Shaikh Hassan was to die, but not after a regular trial; he was simply to be eliminated, just as he had organized the elimination of so many of his real or imagined enemies. He was executed on 12

February 1949, but the Brothers were not to disappear with their Supreme Guide.

The question of what to do about the Brothers divided Egyptian government leaders for several months. In the end the advocates of a fresh attempt at collaboration won against those who wanted the campaign of repression launched at the end of 1948 to continue until the clandestine organization was totally destroyed. It is almost certain that King Farouk, whose father King Fuad had partly financed the movement in its very early days, played a key role in tipping the balance in favour of the collaborationists. He saw the Muslim Brotherhood as a powerful force with which to counter-balance both the nationalist and the proto-communist groups that were just beginning to make their influence felt in Egypt. Farouk was also instrumental in the choice of the relatively moderate Shaikh Hassan al-Hodeibi as al-Banna's successor and the new Supreme Guide. Hodeibi immediately designated al-Banna 'al-Murshid al-Shaheed' (The Martyred Guide), in the hope of persuading the more militant Brothers that the dead leader's radical policies would still be pursued. The militants, however, would have none of Hodeibi, and soon rallied around Salih al-Ashmawi, a firebrand and convinced advocate of perpetual Holy War, who led the Brothers until the end of 1951.[27]

The Muslim Brotherhood's failure to seize power through either spreading the word or gunning down the enemies of the Faith left the movement without an alternative strategy. The Brothers never recovered from their repeated errors in gauging the public mood. Their recipe for change through assassination focused the limelight on them, but secured them no share in real power. The failure of their strategy in Egypt was quickly repeated by similar failures suffered by the offshoots of the movement in Syria, Iraq, Yemen and Iran.[28] In Egypt the Brothers contributed to the destabilization of the constitutional monarchy, and thus paved the way for the seizure of power in 1952 by a secret society of young army officers calling themselves Zubat al-Ahrar (Free Officers). Many of the Free Officers had at one time or another been attracted by the ideas of Shaikh Hassan and his movement, but none was prepared to hand over to the leadership of the fundamentalist movement the prize they had won through their coup d'état.

Very quickly they started to show the distrust that all armies in the Muslim world have traditionally felt towards various brands of fundamentalism. Even when it proclaims itself to be an instrument of Islam, a Muslim army shows little inclination to share power with doctors of theology, regardless of their zeal in imposing the rules of the *shari'ah* or divine law.[29]

Within less than two years of the overthrow of the monarchy, all power was concentrated in a Revolutionary Command Council (RCC) headed by a young colonel of the infantry, Gamal Abdul-Nasser. General Muhammad Neguib, the titular head of the 'revolution', was already retired, while Major Abdul Ra'aouf, the Brothers' man inside the RCC, was imprisoned on a charge of conspiracy against the state. The honeymoon between the Brothers and the new republic proclaimed by the Free Officers was to end in a bitter divorce, followed by a ruthless campaign aimed at wiping out Shaikh Hassan's movement.

Nasser had at first presented himself as a soldier of Islam, dedicated to creating an Islamic society. The first version of the pamphlet entitled *Philosophy of Revolution* and published in his name was a virtual rewrite of the Brothers' propaganda sheets. But once the new ruler had decided to break with the Brothers he ordered a new version which, duly published in 1955 soon after the crackdown against the Muslim Brotherhood, presented Nasser as a socialist devoted to *uruba*[30] and progress in the Western sense of the word.[31]

One reason for Nasser's decision to destroy the Brotherhood may have been that, having seized power, he now had access to a secret report on the infiltration of the armed forces by the movement. Completed in 1952 shortly before the coup d'état, the report had arrived too late for the royal police to take any action. What Nasser saw in it now more than frightened him: the Brothers were almost everywhere within the armed forces, which Nasser had seen as his own powerbase.[32] The colonel[33] began preparing his plan for the dismantling of the Muslim Brotherhood in the summer of 1954, after the leadership of the Brothers had announced its resolute opposition to a new Suez Canal treaty negotiated with Great Britain. The treaty was signed on 19 October 1954, and three days later an attempt was made on Nasser's life in

Alexandria. The would-be assassin, Lieutenant Muhammad Abdul-Latif, missed his target despite the fact that he was less than twenty metres away. Was it, perhaps, because he had been an associate of Nasser's during the latter's flirtations with the Brotherhood? Was not the whole episode prearranged by Nasser himself in order to win popularity and to trump up a seemingly valid excuse for ordering a massacre of the Brothers? The movement's literature abounds in 'proof' that the Alexandria assassination attempt was totally stage-managed by Nasser and masterminded by two foreign propaganda experts: Josef Buenze, a German Nazi who had sought asylum in Egypt, and James Eichelberger, a United States diplomat who had been acting virtually as an adviser to Nasser for some time before the Alexandria episode.[34] In later years Nasser's successor, Sadat, seemed to exonerate the Brotherhood and blame the attempt on the *raïs*'s life on 'adventure-seeking counsellors'.[35]

Whatever the truth about the Alexandria conspiracy, Nasser was able to justify his earlier decision to outlaw the Brotherhood and his new plan for consigning them to 'the dustbin of history'.[36] More than a thousand members of the movement were arrested, together with their Supreme Guide, Shaikh Hassan al-Hodeibi. A revolutionary court, consisting of three army officers including Anwar Sadat, sat almost non-stop for weeks to decide the fate of the 'plotters'. Several leading members of the movement were sentenced to death and hanged, among them Abdul-Qader Auda, Muhammad Farghali and Yussef Tal'at. Scores of prisoners were tortured and many died for unexplained reasons while serving their sentences in concentration camps set up by Nasser. The government also carried out a vast purge of the army and the civilian administration. Thousands of people suspected of being members of or sympathizers with the Brotherhood were dismissed, often without the legal compensation customary even in Nasser's Egypt. The intended annihilation of the Brothers gave Nasser's secret police, the Mukhabarat,[37] then in its infancy, an opportunity for speedy growth. Within a few years the newly established republic was all but dominated by this organization, which by promoting a climate of fear and suspicion prevented the new institutions of the state from striking real roots in the country. Nasser's republic became a police state incapable of solving Egypt's political and economic problems and unable to realize the global ambitions of the *raïs*. The Brotherhood in Egypt was not to recover from the savage suppression ordered by Nasser, but the Nasserist state was in the long run to prove the real loser in the confrontation. By singling out the Brotherhood as its principal enemy, the state cut itself off from the vast Islamic population in Egypt. It had no choice but to turn to the Left, eventually ending up as an ally of the Soviet Union.

One unintended effect of Nasser's attempt to exterminate the Brotherhood was its speedy domination by radical elements. Hodeibi's soft line had failed and the pious Shaikh, now in prison, had no choice but to approve – albeit it with his silence – the emergence of Sayyed Qutb, a noted hard-liner, as the virtual leader of the movement. Qutb, imprisoned along with other Brothers at the start of the persecution, did not waste time in praying for an accommodation with Nasser. He put his pen to work and sent from prison little 'papers' which dealt with all the main political issues of the day as well as the subtleties of Qur'anic teaching. They were read and debated in hundreds of secret cells set up throughout Egypt, from which were to emerge the militant fundamentalists of the 1980s who, rejecting the Brotherhood as 'conservatives', would attempt a return to the tradition established by Hassan Sabbah and his medieval Assassins. Sayyed Qutb was their teacher before becoming their model and idol.

Nasser's secret police, however, did not immediately appreciate the potential threat that Qutb could pose to the stability of the regime, and allowed him to go free before serving his full sentence. Qutb immediately devoted himself to rethinking the movement's strategy and giving the secret cells a measure of rationalization. The central theme that Qutb developed was simple enough: Islam could not accept any compromise with other religions or political doctrines concerning the way of life in a Muslim community. Such a compromise would lead to *iltiqat* or hybridization.[38] Islam had to remain pure, and be applied as a total system of life and not in bits and pieces. To achieve the complete reorganization of society in accordance with the rules of the Qur'an it was vital that every Muslim, male and female, should undertake his personal Jihad against the usurper power. Under Hodeibi the Brotherhood had fostered the illusion that the movement's collective responsibility somehow diluted the individual Muslim's duty towards Allah. Qutb now reversed the formula by calling on all believers to assume their individual duties and to 'execute the will of Allah' as they saw fit, regardless of whether or not they had any possibility of harmonizing their activities through a single organization.

By the end of 1964 the Egyptian secret police had convinced Nasser that the Muslim Brotherhood was fully reorganized and planning a series of assassinations to be followed by a military coup d'état aimed at overthrowing the regime. How much of this was true it is difficult to state with certainty even today. In any event, a second wave of repression hit the Brotherhood in 1965. Thousands were arrested and thrown into military prisons and concentration camps. Hundreds died and many were hanged, including Sayyed Qutb himself. He was quickly honoured by his followers with the title of *shaheed* or 'martyr'.[39]

Between 1971 and 1986 both Sadat and his successor, General Muhammad Hosni-Mubarak, tried to bring the Brothers into the state system. They succeeded as far as the official leadership of the movement was concerned, but the real militants who were ready both to die and to kill remained committed to the destruction of the Egyptian republic and to its replacement by an Islamic government. In 1971 Shaikh Omar al-Talmassani, officially declaring himself to be the Supreme Guide, reorganized the remnants of the Brotherhood as a political party seeking a share in power. He even went as far as rejecting any use of violence for the achievements of Islamic goals within a Muslim country. From 1980, until his death in May 1986 in Geneva, Shaikh Omar used what was left of his prestige and that of the Brothers for the purpose of combating what he described as 'Egyptian Khomeinists'. He felt no sympathy for President Sadat's assassins, and stated that the movement was now part of the system created by Nasser.[40]

4

The Sayyed Who Saw the Light

> Throw away your worry beads and buy a gun. For worry beads keep you silent while guns silence the enemies of Islam.
>
> Muhammad Nawab-Safavi[1]

Najaf, an oasis city in the heart of the Iraqi desert, was not exactly the sort of place one would choose for a holiday in the summer of 1938. Constantly enveloped in a thin mist of hot dust and with temperatures rising to 45° Centigrade, this stop on a once busy caravan route was, on the eve of World War II, as far removed as possible from the events that made history. Dominated by the golden dome of the mausoleum of Ali, the fourth Caliph and the first Imam of Shi'ism, Najaf was said to earn its livelihood in two ways: exporting mullahs and importing corpses. Each year the city's two dozen theological colleges produced enough turbaned heads to supply the needs of the faithful throughout the Shi'ite realms in Iraq, Iran, Lebanon and faraway British India. Rich Shi'ites were prepared to pay hefty prices for tiny graves that would one day house their remains near the shrine of the Master of the Pure.[2] The city had a third source of income, however, in the shape of the several thousand pilgrims who came each year to pray for salvation, to demand a cure for various illnesses, or simply to spend a few weeks away from it all with a *seeghah* or temporary wife and in the company of learned mullahs, who for a modest sum offered entertaining and instructive exposés on topics such as the origin of Man and the way the djins organize their affairs.[3] The fact that Najaf was hemmed in on all sides by ever-expanding graveyards and that nearly half its eighty thousand population consisted of amateur or professional beggars, soothsayers, fortune-tellers and pickpockets did not seem to discourage the pilgrims.[4] For those who had the privilege of praying at the shrine of Ali and that of his son Hussein, the third Imam, in Karbala, also in Iraq, would have all their sins forgiven by Allah. In addition the city produced – even though in very small quantities – some of the best dates in the world, and boasted a bustling market where a variety of contraband goods could be obtained.

It was perhaps this last feature of life in the holy city more than anything else that brought a young mullah there that summer of 1938. For Sayyed Muhammad Nawab-Safavi, then in his thirties, had neither accompanied a corpse for burial nor did he share the belief that all Muslims needed to do was to pray at a holy shrine. Finally, he was not interested in temporary concubines, for a passion far stronger than any which could be inspired by carnal pleasure filled his entire existence. He was thinking of 'doing something about Islam',[5] and he was looking for inexpensive guns in Najaf's 'smugglers' bazaar'.

A native of the central Iranian village of Saveh, Sayyed Muhammad had witnessed and personally suffered from the campaign that Reza Shah, the founder in 1925 of the Pahlavi Dynasty, had launched against the Shi'ite clergy as part of his plans to Westernize the country. Reza Shah had ordered the unveiling of women, which had forced many pious families to perform *hegira* and go into voluntary exile. Sayyed Muhammad had taken his mother, two sisters and one younger brother to the holy city of Karbala which, as part of the newly created Iraqi state, escaped Reza Shah's enforced modernization plans. He had then travelled to Cairo, where in 1936 he had frequented several Muslim Brotherhood mosques and attended a number of their secret meetings. For a while he had thought of attending the al-Azhar theological college, which would have meant defying a Shi'ite rule that discouraged mullahs from studying at a Sunni centre of learning. In 1937 he had met Shaikh Hassan al-Banna, the Supreme Guide, at the Cairo home of the latter's father, Abdul-Rahman. The encounter had ended with the two men feeling an intense dislike for one another. Sayyed Muhammad had apparently tried to persuade the Supreme Guide that the only way to prove the sincerity of the Brotherhood was through a mass conversion of its members to Shi'ism; Shaikh Hassan, for his part, found his generally low view of Shi'ite mullahs confirmed by Sayyed Muhammad's arrogance, which was matched only by his ignorance of the issues.[6] The meeting did, nevertheless, persuade Sayyed Muhammad that Islam, which he described as 'a sword in the shape of a faith',[7] needed a dedicated group of fighters prepared to kill and to die for the glory of the Holy Book. It is not known whether Sayyed Muhammad was taught how to use a gun by any member of the Muslim Brotherhood, but certainly by the time he returned to Iraq and visited Najaf in search of weapons he was considered a fairly good shot.[8] How he would have loved to gun down that Pahlavi tyrant in Tehran.

While in Cairo Sayyed Muhammad had had another curious experience. One day as he was leaving the Hussein Mosque in the heart of the city a well-dressed stranger approached him and asked whether they could talk. He turned out to be a talent scout for a new Egyptian film company. 'Your future is in films,' the stranger told Sayyed Muhammad who, appalled at the very idea, shook 'with rage for a long time'.[9] The talent scout had not been altogether wrong, however. The Iranian mullah was tall, handsome and graceful: without his well-trimmed beard he might have been taken for a John Gilbert lookalike.

Sayyed Muhammad differed from Shaikh Hassan on one major issue: he did not believe that Islam could be constructed through a mass movement. A frequent theme in his few writings is the fact that the Prophet Muhammad began his conquest of the world single-handed and was for years head of a small group of believers. 'Why should we think that by becoming many we can solve the problems of Islam?' he was to tell his disciples years later. 'Let us be few, but a united and determined few. We must be the few who show the path to the rest who have not seen the light.'[10]

He also disapproved of Shaikh Hassan's tactic of dynamiting cinemas, restaurants and other 'places of sin', believing that such attacks harmed the innocent along with the guilty.

The solution he offered was simpler. He wrote: 'Islam asks us to command the Good and prevent Evil. Now Good and Evil involve men and women and not objects. All we have to do is to ask followers of Evil to stop and cross over to the side of Good. It is only when our advice is not heeded that we have no choice but to take action, including the elimination of men of Evil.'[11]

During his stay in Najaf Sayyed Muhammad bought five 'very old but still usable' guns and rented an abandoned camel shed on the old caravan route in which to set up his 'school'. In a city where seminaries abounded Sayyed Muhammad's school must have attracted more than passing attention, for what he taught was not the different styles of reciting and interpreting the Qur'an but the most effective use of scarce and expensive bullets. More than a dozen young men joined him, most of them Iraqi Shi'ites. Sayyed Muhammad would bring VIPs passing through Najaf to the school for brief tours of inspection; one such visitor was Ruhollah Khomeini, the future ayatollah and architect of Iran's Islamic Revolution.[12] But the school had to be closed down before its first year was out, either because Sayyed Muhammad had run out of money to pay the rent and buy bullets or because he could not attract any new students. When he returned to Karbala to rejoin his family, less than a year later, he did not have a single follower and, according to his own writings, did not feel 'too unhappy about it'.[13] On the outbreak of World War II he tried in vain to organize a pro-Nazi guerrilla group to murder British citizens in Iraq; he had corresponded on the subject with Grand Ayatollah Abol-Qassem Kashani in Tehran before the latter's arrest and exile by the British forces which invaded Iran in August 1941. But no matter how vehemently he hated the British, Sayyed Muhammad could not help feeling grateful to them for having forced the hated Reza Shah out of Iran and into exile in South Africa. As a descendant of the Prophet, Sayyed Muhammad was firmly convinced that the government of Islam was the privilege and the responsibility of the *sayyeds*. Reza Shah's exile had created an opportunity to hand over the reins of government to the descendants of the Prophet. But the Allies, and Stalin in particular, had insisted that the Pahlavi Dynasty should continue.

Reza Shah's exile did not put a stop to the movement for the modernization of Iran; on the contrary, it stimulated it by allowing the intellectuals to express their views without censorship for the first time in nearly two decades. Much to their horror, Sayyed Muhammad and other mullahs quickly realized that the abolition of the veil, the independence of the judiciary from the mosque and the creation of a state-run educational network, all initiated by Reza Shah, had over the years attracted genuine support among the people and would be defended by the intellectuals. In other words Islam, as Sayyed Muhammad interpreted it, had many more enemies than the mullahs imagined.[14]

Reza Shah's departure offered vast new opportunities for self-expression, but, contrary to the hopes of people like Sayyed Muhammad, they were not quickly seized on and turned to good use by the mullahs. Instead, countless new political parties and organizations were created, all advocating the further secularization of society and greater respect for individual liberties. Unlike Egypt's fundamentalists, who were fully prepared to meet the modernizers of both Left and Right on the battlefield of ideas, those who dreamed of a fully Islamic Iran had nothing to match the impressive output of secular intellectuals. The communist Tudeh (Mass) party was producing five dailies and several weeklies, in addition to publishing dozens of books every year. A variety of nationalist parties, some bordering on fascism, were also active, as were gatherings of liberals such as the Iran Club.

One of the most militant and at the same time popular advocates of the full secularization of Iran was Ahmad Kasravi. Born into a family of *sayyeds* in Azerbaijan in northwestern Iran, Kasravi had attended a seminary in order to become a mullah and wear the black turban that advertises descent from the Prophet. His contact with the Holy Book and the Hadiths, however, produced unexpected results: the young *talabeh* (seeker) quickly concluded that Islam was a religion fit for 'nomadic and barbarous Arab tribes in a state of pre-civilization'.[15] Anxious to know how and why Islam had managed to conquer Iran, Kasravi concluded that the successful Arab invasion of the country in no way proved the validity of the Islamic message. Sassanid Iran had been bled white by intermittent civil wars and the corruption of the ruling elite, and could not effectively defend itself; once the Arabs had conquered Iran they imposed their Faith on the people by force. Kasravi dreamed of a return to Iran's pre-Islamic glories, including its moral ideals.

Kasravi was especially critical of Shi'ism, which he described as a big 'swindle'.[16] The mullahs, he submitted, were a bunch of layabouts who wanted a good life at the expense of the illiterate poor who feared Allah's Hell and were tempted by His Paradise. Kasravi wrote with authority, for he knew all that any mullah could hope to know; in addition, he had the advantage of having been a brilliant student at the Tehran Law Faculty and the Sorbonne in Paris. His books sold by the thousands despite his prose, which was rather inaccessible because he insisted on purging the Persian language of as many Arabic words as possible.[17] He did not confine himself to writing books, but also addressed countless meetings attended by a growing number of young men and women who described themselves eagerly as Kasravists, meaning supporters of a de-Islamicization of Iran. The fact that the mullahs reacted by ordering the faithful to ostracize the Kasravists did not stem the tide of support for the renegade *sayyed*'s ideas.

Kasravi took no heed of 'friendly advice' aimed at putting him back on the right path. One mullah had tried to meet him on the battlefield of ideas, but had failed disastrously; he was Sayyed Ruhollah Khomeini, whose *Kashf al-Asrar* (*Key to the Secrets*) was written with the sole purpose of refuting Kasravi's ideas. That pamphlet, couched in vitriolic language full of words and phrases such as 'son-of-a-bitch', 'stupid', 'bastard' and 'cow dung', was totally ignored by Kasravi's audience of young urban intellectuals. But Sayyed Muhammad read it with great care and interest. Khomeini's pamphlet included this key passage addressed to Kasravi, who was, however, not directly named:

> The rules of Islam do not provide a cure for your diseases, which are the love of debauchery and fornication as well as compulsive lying and cheating. The rule of Islam declares your blood to be worthless and shall cut off your thieving arms. This is why you are fighting [Islam]. The mullahs want to block your path to treachery. They want to remove from behind the desks those

beautiful women who are, as we all know, used for certain purposes, so that they return to their veils. . . .[18]

That passage contained the macabre invocation of the rule by which an Islamic *qadhi* or judge can declare someone's blood to be 'worthless', virtually a death sentence for the person in question. Khomeini, using his religious authority as an Islamic judge, had in fact ordered Kasravi's assassination. Sayyed Muhammad now had the necessary permit to take action, and he wasted no time. Kasravi was to become the first of Islam's many 'enemies' to be murdered by his tiny group of 'soldiers of Allah'.[19]

The group, formed probably in 1942, was in regular contact with Khomeini, at the time a junior mullah in Qom but already developing an ambitious view of his own future role in Islam. It was probably with Khomeini's knowledge that Sayyed Hussein Emami, a founding member of Sayyed Muhammad's group, which did not then have a name, was chosen as Kasravi's executioner. It was decided that he should be put to death in the Palace of Justice, where he worked as a secular judge. The choice of venue was symbolic, for the mullahs considered the secular system of justice created by Reza Shah the 'single most tragic blow' that Islam had suffered for centuries.[20]

Kasravi was murdered in his office in the presence of more than half a dozen witnesses. Sayyed Hussein Emami, who used a knife for the purpose of 'shedding the miscreant's blood', was assisted by three other fellow-strugglers in 'Jihad'.[21] The idea was that if several people participated in the crime it would be difficult for the government to obtain multiple death sentences when the assassins came to trial.

Kasravi's murder came as a timely morale booster to the mullahs, while Sayyed Hussein and his partners in crime became instant heroes in the holy cities of Mashhad and Qom. 'It was the most beautiful day in my life,' related Ayatollah Shaikh Sadeq Khalkhali, one of Khomeini's closest friends and associates. 'We all knew that the miscreant had been struck by the hand of Allah, so that Islam could begin to live again.'[22] It was then that Shaikh Sadeq decided to join Sayyed Muhammad's group.

In high spirits over the first successful strike by his group against 'the pillars of impiety', Sayyed Muhammad quickly baptized his secret organization the Fedayeen of Islam; he also began preparing a list of other miscreants who had to be eliminated. Sentenced to death, Sayyed Hussein kept sending pathetic letters to leading mullahs, and Khomeini began pressurizing the grand ayatollahs of Qom to step in and save him from execution. But only the Shah could quash a death sentence duly passed by state law in a murder trial; he finally agreed to use his royal prerogative and Sayyed Hussein's life was spared, much to the dismay of urban intellectuals and some members of the middle class: the Fedayeen of Islam, having killed with impunity, could now proceed with the elimination of others on Sayyed Muhammad's blacklist.

By the end of 1944 Sayyed Muhammad's Fedayeen of Islam had some seventy members, of which no more than a dozen were to act as 'executioners of Allah's will'. They had all received special *noms de guerre* from Sayyed Muhammad, who from then on was referred to as Ostad Nawab (Master Nawab) or simply as Nawab. The name 'Nawab' was to become the terror of politicians and middle-class reformers throughout the 1940s and 1950s, during which the Fedayeen murdered more than a dozen 'enemies of Islam', including the Prime Ministers Abdul-Hussein Hazhir[23] and General Haj-Ali Razmara, and the Education Minister Ahmad Zangeneh. In the meantime, one of the Fedayeen's sympathizers, Nasser Fakhr-Ara'i, who had not yet been fully 'ordained' and was therefore not allowed to kill in the name of Allah, tried to assassinate the Shah in February 1946. The attempt, quickly blamed by the authorities on the communists, was used as a pretext for banning the Tudeh party. Fakhr-Ara'i himself had been put to death within seconds of firing at the Shah, and was therefore unable to deny any connection with Tudeh.[24]

Between 1941 and 1945 Iran's fundamentalists, among them the Fedayeen of Islam, had enjoyed the tacit approval of Great Britain, which did not wish to see Soviet influence spread to Iran through the expanding Tudeh party. In the 1950s, however, the fundamentalist movement began to devote the bulk of its energies to fighting British interests and influence. Nawab and his followers became powerful allies of Dr Muhammad Mossadeq, the nationalist leader who in

1951, as Prime Minister, pushed a bill nationalizing Iranian oil through a Parliament dominated by conservatives. It could be argued that fear of being gunned down by Nawab's Fedayeen played a role in persuading at least some of the parliamentarians not to oppose the bill. Enjoying the patronage of Ayatollah Kashani, by 1951 the Fedayeen were a tightly knit clandestine organization of over three hundred men; their influence was so great that they succeeded in persuading Parliament to pass a bill quashing the death sentence pronounced against Khalil Tahmassebi, Premier Razamara's assassin. Tahmassebi, a carpenter by trade, used the *nom de guerre* of Abdullah Mowah'hed Rastgar, literally the Monotheist and Redeemed Slave of Allah. A parliamentary resolution even went as far as designating the killer a 'national hero' and a 'soldier of Islam'. Tahmassebi, however, did not make much of the official honours bestowed on him and simply returned to his trade until his eventual rearrest and execution in 1953.

The success of the Fedayeen showed that the tradition of political murder in the name of religion, erroneously believed to have died after a brief reappearance during the Constitutional Revolution of 1906–11, was very much alive. Nawab had no difficulty in finding people who, told that a religious judge had passed a death sentence on a 'miscreant' or an 'infidel', would volunteer to kill and risk their own lives as well. Who were these men? Shaikh Hassan al-Banna had founded his Muslim Brotherhood movement on the educated elite and recruited his secret terrorist group from well-to-do families. Nawab, however, sought his Fedayeen among small shopkeepers, bazaar apprentices and those who were, in his own words, forced 'to the edge of society where they might at any moment fall out'.[25] It was to the same section of society that Khomeini was to appeal years later to launch his Islamic Revolution.

The speed with which the Fedayeen extended their activities throughout the country, and the ease with which they carried out their terrorist acts, were in part the result of the political and administrative weakness of the Iranian state. Post-war semi-anarchy prevented the government from devoting its resources to curbing the activities of what seemed for a long time to be little more than a romantic attempt at returning to 'the source'. But the success of the Fedayeen was mostly due to the deep understanding of their leadership, especially Nawab himself, of the psychology of traditional Iran. A 'magnetic speaker with mesmerizing eyes', Nawab always began by frightening his audience before reassuring it and pointing towards 'the blood-covered path of courage'.[26]

A typical Nawab speech would begin with lamentations concerning the decline of Islam and the 'threat of its imminent disappearance'.[27]

> Islam is encircled by its enemies. The Cross-worshippers of the West and the Jews who really guide them have only one objective: to eliminate Islam, which is the last true religion revealed to Muhammad. They are blind people and want to blind us, too. . . . They have among us a number of agents, political whores who work for them, spreading their heathen beliefs. What would happen to us if Islam – may Allah never allow it – were to fade? Foreigners would be everywhere, promoting prostitution, alcoholism, gambling and sodomy. They would take our wives and daughters away and lead our young sons and brothers to the path of perdition. We have seen what the foreigner has to offer in the way their soldiers behaved during the occupation of our country. We have seen what the domination of our society means by visiting Abadan,[28] where women have no shame and walk in the streets almost naked and where the frontier between *halal* and *haram*[29] has been effaced by sexual lust and pleasure-seeking. Open your eyes, brothers! Open your eyes before it is too late. I have seen the light of Muhammad shine on this land. I have seen it in a dream. And I know that this dream will come true![30]

The Fedayeen's organizational set-up, unlike that of the Muslim Brotherhood which was pyramidal, consisted of a series of horizontally connected cells. There was no Supreme Guide, and Nawab always behaved like 'just another militant'.[31] This was partly the result of the strong egalitarian traditions of Shi'ite Islam, which regards any attempt at 'domineering'[32] as sinful. New members were entrusted to the care of a more senior one, who was responsible for testing them and before long assigning them to specific tasks, which varied according to each new member's abilities. The most common one was observation – keeping an eye on one's friends, relatives and neighbours to make sure they did not transgress the rules of Islam. A woman who did not wear the veil would be admonished. A young man who liked drinking beer would be encouraged to return to the right path. Evil-doers in the neighbourhood would be identified and exposed, so that believers would ostracize them. Shops belonging to non-Muslims would be marked and boycotted. But above all, a new member had to attend as many religious ceremonies as possible; he had to be seen to be an exemplary Muslim.

The Fedayeen never used violence against individual evil-doers; their wrath was directed against those who 'create conditions for doing evil'. This is why, unlike their successors of the 1980s in Iran and Lebanon, they never threw acid at unveiled women nor murdered homosexuals and other deviants. Also worth mentioning is the fact that they murdered no foreigners, and took no hostages. Their victims were chosen from among high-ranking politicians and 'leaders of wrong ideas'.

Many members of the Fedayeen were also active in charitable organizations for orphans, widows and other vulnerable members of society. They believed that the force of example would strengthen their cause. Some members spent considerable time going around each district to search out non-Muslims, who would then be invited to a debate on the merits of conversion to Islam. Nawab himself, however, was opposed to 'devoting energy to converting the infidel while we have so many who are born Muslims but do not know how to live as Muslims'.[33] The issue of proselytism was to split the Fedayeen shortly before the police crackdown against them in 1953: those who believed that the conversion of non-Muslims should be a priority broke away to create the Hojatieh Society.[34] They thus escaped the ensuing repression, and were even able to secure a measure of support from the Shah's security police, SAVAK, for their ideological work against the communists.

The fate of the Fedayeen was sealed when Ayatollah Kashani sided with the Shah against Mossadeq in 1952. Mossadeq's overthrow in August 1953 was followed by a massive purge of both communist and fundamentalist militants: over a thousand were arrested, a quarter of them Fedayeen. This time no grand ayatollah was ready or able to intercede on their behalf. Nine leading members of the Fedayeen were hanged after being found guilty of anti-state activities by a military tribunal. Among them was Nawab himself, as well as Khalil Tahmassebi and Hussein Emami, who were both sentenced to death for the second time. Only the more junior members of the organization succeeded in escaping the police net and went into hiding in their native villages. They were to resume some activity in 1956, and kept the Fedayeen's name alive by a number of assassination attempts, including one directed against Prime Minister Hussein 'Ala, who, although seriously wounded, managed to survive. Among those who got away were several men destined to become key figures in Khomeini's Islamic Revolution more than twenty years later: Sadeq Khalkhali; Habiballah Asghar-Owladi, who became Khomeini's Commerce Minister in 1981; Haj Mahdi Araqi; and Assadallah Lajevardi, who was to be known as 'The Butcher of Tehran' for his role in the execution of some six thousand anti-Khomeini militants at Evin Prison. Another young member who escaped arrest in 1954 was Muhammad Abd-Khoda'i, who was to assassinate Prime Minister Hassan-Ali Mansur on Khomeini's orders in 1965.

The relative ease with which the Fedayeen organization was uncovered and smashed was partly due to the fact that since 1951 Nawab and his friends had virtually ceased to operate in a clandestine manner. Parliament's motion in favour of Tahmassebi had convinced them that no government would ever again dare dream of opposing 'the legitimate struggle of the faithful'. But the loss of the advantages of secrecy was not compensated for by the advantages that open mass organization could bring. Nawab distrusted large groups, as has already been seen, and preferred to remain within the Persian tradition of coming together in small *dowrehs* or circles of carefully selected members. More important, the defeat of the Fedayeen was largely the result of their failure to appeal to any major section of Iranian society. The peasantry, then some 75 per cent of the population, remained largely apolitical, while the urban working class was only in its infancy and in any case more interested in what the communists had to offer. The middle class was frightened by the Fedayeen's dour political face and dry attitude to Islam. Thus it was mostly only people on the fringes of these echelons of society in the urban areas who could provide the Fedayeen with recruits. But because they were isolated from the nation's mainstream politics these people could be – and in the end were – easily cast off by those who manipulated them. The successors of Nawab, and Khomeini more than anyone else, learned at least one lesson from the debacle of the Fedayeen: power cannot be shared for long, and a political partnership always benefits the stronger party.

5

The Imam Who Rose from the East

> He was like the sun: he
> rose from the East and went
> down in the West.
>
> Islamic Jihad statement[1]

'Pray for me! For I am going to the City of War.' The man who spoke these words back in 1967 was a young mullah coming to bid farewell to a grand Ayatollah in the Iranian holy city of Qom.[2] Wearing a black turban that announced his descent from the Prophet, the young mullah had at the time little claim to distinction except his illustrious name. For Mussa Sadr belonged to a long-established and highly respected family of Shi'ite theologians who had for some four centuries taught and preached 'the true version of Islam' throughout Iran and Mesopotamia. Tall, elegant and permanently suntanned, Mussa Sadr could have been quickly adopted by the fun-loving high society of Tehran. Instead, he had chosen the life of a *talabeh* or seeker in Qom and Najaf, and now that he could claim some authority in matters of religious law, he was going abroad in the service of the Faith.

The country he had chosen for this purpose was, however, no alien land, for Lebanon was one of only three Arab countries in which Shi'ite Islam had a large number of adherents.[3] In addition, going to Lebanon was for Sadr something of a return to his roots: his ancestors had been brought to Iran from the Jabal region of Lebanon in the sixteenth century when the Safavid monarchs assumed the task of reconverting Iran to Shi'ism. Sadr's ancestors, together with scores of other mullahs imported from Lebanon, had done a splendid job of conversion: by the mid-twentieth century more than 95 per cent of Iranians were Shi'ites. Now it was Iran's turn to export mullahs to Lebanon, and Mussa Sadr was to prove an outstanding one.

At the time of Mussa Sadr's arrival in Beirut at the end of 1961, Lebanon was regarded as a happy accident of history. Proud of being described as 'the Switzerland of the Middle East', the country had just emerged from a brief civil war which was wrongly assumed by many of its leaders to represent nothing but 'an exceptional episode in our history'.[4] It offered visitors from other parts of the Muslim Middle East all that the West, feared and envied at the same time, had to offer, plus the familiar accents of Islam. A constitutional government, a functioning Parliament, a free press, a variety of political parties and associations and the amazing fact that not a single person was in prison because of his or her political views, made Lebanon a source of perpetual fascination for intellectual elites. But what astonished most people was the fact that so many different religious communities could live together in harmony and even share the process of government. Lebanon was the only country in the Middle East in which neither of the two prevalent theories of state – as 'an expression of a nation's will' or as 'a framework of government for a religious community' – applied.[5] In other words, it was an anomaly; and as a result it had to be broken so that it could be recast in one mould or the other.

One man who wanted to remould Lebanon was Egypt's Gamal Abdul-Nasser: as a champion of *uruba* or 'Arabness', he wanted Lebanon to play a more active part in the campaign to eliminate Israel. Nasser exercised his influence through Sunni Muslims who, together with Maronite Christians, held the reins of power in Lebanon. The Shi'ites, even then the single largest community, played a peripheral role. Mostly poor and uneducated peasants, they were dominated by five or six feudal families who disliked Nasser because of his populism and calls for land reform.[6] Nasser was at the same time waging a vicious propaganda campaign against Iran, claiming Arab sovereignty over parts of the oil-rich south-west.[7]

With Lebanese Christians increasingly leaning towards the

Western powers, while Nasser consolidated his hold on the Sunni community in Lebanon, the outsiders seeking influence in the country were left with no choice but to seek that influence among the Shi'ites and the Druzes.[8] In Iran's case the choice was not complicated. Lebanese Shi'ites had always looked to Iran as a source of inspiration and moral support. Most of the Shi'ite *mara'je taqleed* or 'sources of imitation' – grand ayatollahs ruling on major religious topics – lived in Iran, which also housed several of the Faith's holiest shrines. The Iranian government, as well as the grand ayatollahs of Qom and Mashhad, had always sent 'missionaries' to Lebanon to keep the Faith alive and to look for new converts among Sunni Muslims. Thus Sadr's arrival in Lebanon on a sacred mission did not provoke any surprised comment, despite the fact that the Shah had personally approved and financed the enterprise as a favour to the leading Lebanese Shi'ite families. A few years later both the Shah and his allies among Lebanon's feudal Shi'ites were to regret their choice of Sadr.

Before leaving Tehran Sadr had called on General Hassan Pakravan, at the time the 'liberal' chief of SAVAK, and secured full support for the Lebanon mission. SAVAK agreed to finance Sadr's operations to the tune of 5 million Lebanese pounds – then around £700,000 sterling – a year.[9] The agreement was honoured until 1972, when Sadr broke completely with the Shah's regime and began supporting its opponents, including Ayatollah Khomeini.

During the 1950s Sadr had for a while flirted with the Fedayeen of Islam – without, however, joining their secret terrorist organization. He later became related to Khomeini through the marriage of his niece to Ahmad, Khomeini's second son. But there was much that separated him from Khomeini. Sadr was no revolutionary and quite obviously wanted to progress along the traditional path of the Shi'ite clergy to power, prestige and pre-eminence, which included a detour via the imperial court. That the Shah liked Sadr personally is an open secret.[10] But the future 'Imam' of Lebanon may have used the traditional tactic of *khod'ah* – tricking one's adversaries in order to profit from them – in his dealings with the Shah.

Once established in Beirut, Sadr began to make a thorough personal study of the condition of the Lebanese Shi'ites. It did not take him long to realize that he had only two alternatives. He could either become something of an official mullah, serving as part of the decor for the big landowning families, or he could plunge into the unknown and risk a direct appeal to the poor peasant masses. He chose the second path, and in so doing rediscovered the intrinsically revolutionary substance of Shi'ism. Starting with the organization of *hayat* or mission groups modelled on those in Iran, Sadr – who assumed the title of Imam or 'leader of the community of the faithful' only in 1968 – quickly developed new organizational formulas. He gave the religious concepts of *mustazaf* (he who is unable to decide on matters of religion on his own) and *mustakbar* (the rich and the powerful) new political meanings to suit his analysis of the local situation. The Lebanese Shi'ites were described as *mustazaf* in the sense of 'having been dispossessed of their rights', while Lebanon's ruling elites were presented as *mustakbar*, interpreted to mean 'those who impose their rule through tyranny'. The Manichean division of the world was thus complete. Imam Mussa Sadr was the leader of the Good in their Holy War against the forces of Evil. The first organizational expression of Sadr's new doctrine of revolt came in the shape of his Harakat al-Mahrumeen, or Movement of the Deprived. The fact that the original leadership of the Harakat consisted entirely of the educated children of rich families did not prevent it from attracting the poorest peasants of the south and the Bekaa Valley as well as the working-class slum dwellers of West Beirut.

Sadr's immense charisma and his talents as a mesmerizing orator filled the mosques once more and encouraged the construction of dozens of new mosques as well as Qur'anic schools. It was almost impossible to escape his charm, even when one did not share his view of the world. He was either a perfect actor, or he had genuinely accomplished his own *tazkieh* (self-purification) in Lebanon. For by 1971 the personal ambition that had hitherto shown in every word and gesture seemed to have gone. The once arrogant and aristocratic mullah, who always chose the finest material for his turban and *abaya* (mullahs' long coat), had become a humble servant of the poor, living a simple life and fasting at least one day a week. He spoke of love, fraternity, human solidarity and quiet piety in tones befitting a Sufi or a Christian monk rather than a man who was, perhaps unwittingly at the time, fathering one of the most violent and brutal religious movements in the history of the Middle East. Sadr's vocabulary and manners convinced Christian and Sunni leaders in Lebanon that he was only aiming at improving the living conditions of the Shi'ites, but as early as 1970 Sadr had ordered the training of 'volunteers' as 'armed guardians of the Faith'.[11]

The creation of a military force in the service of the Shi'ite community was almost inevitable, given that Lebanon was increasingly divided into several armed camps. The Palestinians, numbering nearly a quarter of a million, boasted more than thirty thousand armed men – nearly four times the size of the Lebanese army. Over the years Palestinian guerrilla groups had established bases in the south, on the border with Israel, and by 1971 were virtual masters of the region, which is inhabited almost exclusively by Shi'ites. The Maronite enclaves in the south were also equipped with their own armed groups, and the stage was set for future massacres inspired by both political and religious motives.

Sadr's representatives participated in the conference held by Palestinian guerrilla organizations in the Badawi refugee camp on Nahr al-Bared in 1972. It was then that Georges Habash, the Christian-born leader of the Popular Front for the Liberation of Palestine (PFLP), agreed to train a number of Lebanese Shi'ites at centres controlled by his group. Habash was unwittingly helping Israel to implement one of its most cherished plans: the arming of Lebanese Shi'ites so that they would drive the Palestinians away from the border regions of the south. When Habash stopped training guerrillas for the Shi'ite Imam, his place was instantly taken by Yasser Arafat, who offered the services of his al-Fatah organization. The various Palestinian guerrilla groups had already trained a number of Iranian Shi'ites in the art of urban guerrilla and 'commando activities', and some of these revolutionaries began to make themselves available to Sadr from 1970. But Sadr, still hoping to keep his links with Tehran intact, refused until he was forced into an open break with the Shah.

Conscious that he was acting from a position of weakness, Sadr had constantly tried to maintain cordial relations with the Shah's ambassadors in Beirut. But the arrival of Mansur Qadar as Ambassador to Lebanon in 1971 began to change all that. Qadar, a brigadier-general, was a high-ranking official of SAVAK and a firm believer that mullahs should be kept in their place. Once in Beirut, he ignored the tradition according to which the Iranian Ambassador and Imam Mussa Sadr met at the home of a local Shi'ite notable. When Qadar summoned Sadr to the Embassy he was, as he should have foreseen, politely refused. Sadr was neither a SAVAK agent nor a functionary of the imperial Iranian state, and Qadar had no right to treat him as such. But the Ambassador interpreted Sadr's refusal to come to the Embassy as 'an insult to His Imperial Majesty' and sent a report to that effect to Tehran, recommending that the government should stop the subsidy for the Imam's operations in Lebanon. By that time Sadr could easily make do without the Shah's annual donation, but he was nevertheless anxious to prevent a rupture in relations – the Shah was still popular among Lebanese Shi'ites, who saw him as the 'protector of the Faith'. In a bid to clear the air, Sadr visited Tehran in September 1972 and had an audience with the Shah, at which the two men apparently agreed to patch things up. But Qadar had already begun to support a number of groups opposed to Sadr's domination of the Shi'ite community in Lebanon.

The final break came before the end of the year, when Qadar refused to renew Sadr's passport, giving the excuse that the Imam had abandoned his Iranian nationality by becoming Lebanese.[12] From then on Sadr knew that he could not include Iran among his supporters as long as Qadar was in Beirut. He began negotiations with Syria, at the time one of the Shah's bitterest enemies, and also increased his contact with Khomeini – then in exile in Najaf – despite the fact that almost no one among the Lebanese Shi'ites followed the Ayatollah as a 'source of imitation'.[13] Sadr underlined his opposition to the Shah – without naming him in public – by attacking in his sermons those whom he described as 'Satanic rulers of the East'.

The Imam's anti-Shah posture attracted a number of left-wing and fundamentalist Iranian students attending universities in Europe and the United States. Among them was Mostafa Chamran Savehi, who had been a brilliant student at the universities of Berkeley and San Jose in California.[14] Giving himself a sabbatical in 1964, Chamran, then thirty-two, left his American wife and two children in California and went to Nasser's Egypt, where, besides learning Arabic, he studied the rudiments of urban guerrilla warfare. Chamran was at the time a follower of Muhammad Nakhshab, an Iranian thinker who propagated a synthesis of Islam and Trotskyism.[15] Returning to California in 1965, Chamran created a secret organization named Tashayu Sorkh (Red Shi'ism) for the purpose of training 'soldiers for our future struggle'.[16] The group, consisting of five men including Chamran's younger brother Mahdi and an Afghan student named Hussein Forqani, organized target practice sessions in a car park outside San Jose.

It was probably to extend his field of recruitment for Red Shi'ism that in 1968 Chamran set up the Muslim Students' Association of America, which attracted a large number of militants including Ibrahim Yazdi, who was to become Khomeini's Foreign Minister in 1979. But Chamran did not succeed in recruiting many more fighters for his urban guerrilla group, and in 1971 he decided to leave the United States for Lebanon, which he saw as a more suitable base for launching his pan-Islamic Shi'ite revolution. Once in Lebanon, Chamran was easily charmed by Imam Mussa Sadr, and it was on the Imam's orders that he settled in Tyr, where he ran a technical school for Shi'ites which he used as a cover for his guerrilla activities. Here he enjoyed 'technical support' from a pro-Syrian group of Palestinian *fedayeen* led by Nayef Hawatmah.

By 1973 Chamran's Muslim Students' Association was something of an international organization, with branches in half a dozen countries in which young Iranians attended university. Yazdi was in charge of the US branch, which boasted some seven hundred members, most of them Iranian or Afghan.[17] The United Kingdom end was run by Kamal Kharazi and Abdul-Karim Sorush, while Muhammad

Gharazi, who was to become Khomeini's Petroleum Minister in 1981, led the organization in France. The main task of the Association was to identify those young men and women whose passion for Red Shi'ism was strong enough to persuade them to cut short their studies and travel to Lebanon to learn the art of guerrilla warfare.[18] By 1975 the association was dispatching scores of volunteers to Lebanon. The PLO continued to give a helping hand, either directly or through one or more of its member organizations. In 1979 Hani al-Hassan, a high-ranking PLO official, claimed that his organization had trained 'more than ten thousand anti-Shah guerrillas' in Lebanon.[19]

The Lebanese civil war that broke out in 1974 engaged the country's main armed groups – the Maronite Falangists, the PLO and the Druzes, led by the Jumblatt clan – in a bloody struggle that prevented them from even noticing the speedy rise of their future deadly rival, the Amal (Hope) Shi'ite organization created by Imam Mussa Sadr and gradually shaped into a fighting force by Chamran. The new organization attracted a number of young educated Lebanese Shi'ites, many of them with an American background. Two of them were to become especially prominent: the Sierra Leone-born lawyer Nabih Berri, and Hussein al-Husseini. Both were close associates of Chamran and regarded him as something of a *primus inter pares*. While the other communities shed each other's blood, the Shi'ites built up their strength. Thanks to Sadr's leadership they enjoyed support from almost every foreign power interested in Lebanon – from Israel to Syria. Sadr wanted to drive the Palestinians out of southern Lebanon and away from the Israeli borders. As for the Syrians, they saw in Sadr a leader capable of counter-balancing the influence of the pro-Egyptian Sunni Muslims in Lebanon.

From 1976 onwards the Lebanese Shi'ites were assured of most of their training needs as far as the creation and enlargement of their fighting force was concerned. Before that they had used the facilities in two Palestinian camps, ar-Rashidiyah,[20] near Tyr, and the site of the city's ancient Roman racecourse, which was used for mock battles; it was there in 1974 and 1975 that Ayatollah Khomeini's two sons, Mostafa and Ahmad, learned how to handle a gun. The

Palestinians who trained the Shi'ite guerrillas could not at the time have had any idea that they were teaching their own future assassins how to use guns; nor is it likely that the Shi'ites knew then that one day they would turn their weapons against their teachers. The PLO still enjoyed high prestige, and it was automatically assumed that Palestinians themselves must act as the vanguard in the struggle to liberate their 'usurped land'. It was not until 1980 that the Shi'ites, by then heavily influenced by Khomeini's propaganda, began to see themselves as the true leaders of an Islamic revolution that would not only liberate Palestine but also conquer the whole world for the True Faith. But it is almost certain that Imam Mussa Sadr was from the very start determined to push the Palestinians out of Lebanon's Shi'ite-inhabited regions. He did not approve of the PLO's socialist attitudes and close ties with the USSR, which he considered to be Islam's 'worst enemy in the long run'.[21]

Sadr's experience with the Shah had taught him that the patronage of foreign governments could not be counted on in any long-term calculations. He was therefore careful not to put all his eggs in any one basket. While continuing to consider Syria's President Assad as an ally, he was fully aware of the Alawite leader's lack of scruples in reversing alliances. Assad's troops had originally entered Lebanon supposedly to protect the PLO against the Falangists, but had ended up siding with the latter against the former. Also, Syria had been traditionally regarded as the protector of Sunnis in Lebanon, but was now trying to play the Shi'ite card, while Sunni fundamentalists in Tripoli were beginning to attack Assad as 'an enemy of Islam'.

The search for a reserve ally, in case Syria changed its policy, took Imam Mussa Sadr to Libya, where he met Colonel Gaddafi for the first time in 1975. Gaddafi had for some time been trying to gain a foothold in Lebanon in the hope of filling, in the name of Arab nationalism, the void left by Egypt's continuing withdrawal from the Arab scene. To this end he had created the so-called Mourabitoun (Contacts) armed bands in Beirut and Tripoli, which confined their field of recruitment to Sunni Muslims, largely because Gaddafi did not trust the Shi'ites and the Druzes – he doubted the authenticity of Shi'ite Islam – while considering the Christians as traitors because of their refusal to convert to Islam.[22]

Gaddafi had been investing in anti-Shah individuals and organizations since 1971, and it was probably through his Iranian contacts that he learned of the rising fortunes of Sadr in Lebanon. Two of these contacts, Ali-Akbar Nateq-Nuri and Muhammad Gharazi, were frequent visitors to Lebanon and had strong connections with Chamran's Red Shi'ism group as well as the Amal organization itself. Another contact was Muhammad Montazeri, who was dividing his time between Najaf, where he was close to Khomeini, Beirut, where he was received by Sadr, and Tripoli, where he was a frequent guest of the Libyan colonel.[23] An alliance with Gaddafi had obvious advantages for Sadr. Libya was too small and too far away ever to exert a real influence in Lebanon, and at the same time it was rich enough to offer gifts that a country like Syria would never be able to afford. Sadr, aware too of Assad's long-term plans for the domination and – somewhere along the road – possible annexation of Lebanon, wanted the country to remain independent so that his own resurgent Shi'ite community would in time control it. His alliance with Syria could only be a tactical one.[24]

Sadr and Gaddafi never succeeded in establishing a warm personal friendship. Gaddafi was an Arab nationalist and could not forgive Sadr for his Iranian origins. The colonel also disliked all mullahs, Sunni or Shi'ite, and at times saw himself as the only authority on true Islam; he liked to debate matters of theology with mullahs in order to expose their ignorance. There were also rumours that in certain moments of mystical delirium Gaddafi, who had assumed the title of Guide, presented himself to his friends as the Mahdi.[25] He must have disliked Sadr's cool nerve, air of self-assurance and total disdain for any form of nationalism – Arab or not. Nevertheless Gaddafi proved as generous as he had always been towards other revolutionary movements fighting against imperialism and Zionism; he considered Libya's oil fortune as a gift from Allah, to be spent on fighting the enemies of Islam, and Sadr was doing precisely that by training anti-Shah guerrillas and at the same time preparing a Shi'ite force to stand up to the Christians in southern Lebanon.

The association between Sadr and Gaddafi, however, was to end in tragedy for the Imam and in total exclusion from Lebanon for the colonel. Sadr's last visit to Libya – in fact his very last anywhere – was organized in August 1978. The Imam had two reasons for insisting on a visit at that particular time, despite an evident lack of enthusiasm on the part of the colonel. First, Sadr had just been chosen for a nine-year term as President of the High Council of Shi'ites in Lebanon, and wanted official international recognition. His first visit in his new capacity had been to Syria, where he was received almost as a head of state; his next stop had to be Libya, his strongest ally and principal source of finance. The second reason was that he wanted to ask Gaddafi to put under his command the various Libyan-financed Iranian terrorist groups that were active in the Islamic Revolution in Iran. Sadr could not have imagined at the time that Khomeini could – or even wanted to – assume direct leadership of the revolutionary movement, and already saw himself in the role of leader of the opposition to the Shah, whose regime seemed increasingly threatened. Sadr had contacted the grand ayatollahs of both Najaf and Qom, and was thinking of visiting Iraq after Libya.[26]

Accompanied by one of his advisers, Muhammad Shihata Yaqub, and the journalist Abbas Badreddin, Sadr arrived in Tripoli aboard an Alitalia jet from Rome on 25 August 1978. It was Ramadan, and the fact that the Imam had decided to travel at a time when Muslims should stay at home and fast was seen as a sign of the visit's urgency and importance. Sadr and his companions were greeted at the airport by the Lebanese chargé d'affaires, Nizar Farhat, who gave a dinner in their honour two nights later. Told that he could not meet the colonel until 28 August, the Imam was already angry at the delay when he was informed that the meeting had been further postponed, this time until the morning of the 31st. On that day the Imam and his adviser were taken from their hotel to the Bab Zarbatiyah barracks, where Gaddafi lived in a luxurious, Gucci-decorated 'Arab tribal tent'.[27]

The meeting got off to a bad start. Sadr protested at the fact that he had been kept waiting for six days before meeting the Guide of the Revolution; Gaddafi apparently retorted by saying that he was not in the habit of explaining his decisions.

The discussion then moved on to the situation in Lebanon, and Gaddafi asked in a rude tone what the Imam had done with the resources that the Libyan people had put at the disposal of Amal; it was now Sadr's turn to say that he had no accounts to give to anyone. Gaddafi then proceeded to develop his favourite theme of 'growing strong through fighting', and asked Sadr why his Amal gunmen were not joining battle against the Falangists or launching any operations against Israel. Sadr commented that such expectations were based on a lack of understanding of the situation in Lebanon. The remark angered the colonel beyond measure, for he has always liked to consider himself the foremost expert on all Arab and Islamic political issues.

The meeting ended in total confusion as the two men traded insults. Gaddafi accused Sadr of being a coward, and Sadr found he had no choice but to leave. Part of the strange scene was witnessed by Captain Bashir Saad, Gaddafi's military secretary, who had never seen his boss in such a state of agitation.[28] Shaking his fist in rage, Gaddafi uttered the Arabic word '*Khalas!*' This was unfortunate as far as Sadr was concerned, for '*khalas*' could mean a number of things, among them 'Eliminate him!' It is almost certain that Gaddafi intended another meaning – 'I am through with him!' But Captain Saad decided that the colonel had the first one in mind, and instantly arranged for the disposal of Sadr and his companions.

The three guests, now waiting to be driven back to their hotel, must have thought it odd when Captain Saad emerged from the gate of the barracks to accompany them. The car did not head for the hotel but went instead in the direction of the Janzur firing range, nine kilometres west of Tripoli. There, Sadr and his companions were made '*khalas*'. On hearing Captain Saad's 'good news' concerning the end of the quarrelsome Imam, Gaddafi was both surprised and angry – he was sure he had never given an order for Sadr to be murdered. But there was no time for remonstrations. Informed of the disaster, General Mustafa Kharrubi, Gaddafi's security chief, decided to act before news of the Imam's disappearance got out. He ordered three of his agents to dress up as mullahs and take Alitalia flight 881 of 31 August to Rome, using the passports of Sadr and his two companions.[29] The Libyan news agency, JANA, reported the same evening that Sadr had decided to cut short his visit because of 'grave developments in Lebanon', and had flown from Tripoli to Rome. Needless to say, no trace was ever found of the missing men in Rome or anywhere else. And numerous missions to find out what happened to Sadr, including one sent by King Hussein of Jordan in 1978, produced no results.

Many Lebanese Shi'ites comfort themselves with the fiction that Sadr is still alive and a prisoner in Libya, and still consider him their living Imam. This is why no successor has been chosen, although Sadr's nine-year term as President of the High Council of Shi'ism in Lebanon ended in September 1986. Sadr is present through his absence. His photographs are everywhere in the Shi'ite regions of Lebanon, and more than six years of Iranian efforts to push him into oblivion, in favour of Khomeini, have produced little result.

It is difficult to imagine what Imam Mussa Sadr would have thought of the path taken by the Lebanese Shi'ites since his disappearance. He would, perhaps, look with satisfaction on the success of the Amal militiamen in imposing themselves as the main paramilitary force in Lebanon. He would also approve of the current policy of the Shi'ites to aim at direct control of Lebanon's destiny by insisting on the creation of a 'numerical' democracy in the country. But when it comes to the fact that in the 1980s Lebanese Shi'ism has become the main breeding ground for terrorism in the Middle East, it is difficult to imagine Sadr's reaction. The Shi'ites, discovery and use of terrorism is, in a sense, the inevitable result of Sadr's radicalization of his constituency. Radical Islam is bound to end in terrorism, as the experiences of Hassan Sabbah, the Muslim Brotherhood and the Fedayeen of Islam had already proved. All Sadr did was to confirm the results of those experiments.

The Amal organization created by Sadr has split into two: the mainstream group is led by Berri and supported by Husseini, while the breakaway faction, Islamic Amal, is led by Hussein Mussawi, a Khomeinist militant financed by Iran and in charge of the city of Baalbek in the Syrian-controlled Bekaa Valley. The two rival versions of Amal are, however, used chiefly as political covers for clandestine terrorist organizations. All the main leaders of Lebanese Shi'ism are on the death list of this or that clandestine terrorist group. Berri, for example, has already written and sealed his will, knowing that the man charged with his assassination may at any moment be ordered to carry out his mission.[30]

The religious leadership is also divided. The High Council is run by Ayatollah Shaikh Muhammad-Mahdi Shamseddin, a traditional doctor of theology in the conservative mould. His election as Vice-President of the Council in 1978 was decided by Sadr himself, who wished to reassure the moderate ayatollahs of Najaf and Qom while keeping his Saudi option open. Shamseddin, who is respected by the Sunni Muslims as a man of wisdom and moderation, has always enjoyed good relations with Riyadh as well. His rival and the idol of the radicals is Ayatollah Sayyed Muhammad-Hussein Fadhl-Allah, who is the spiritual leader of the Hezb-Allah, the sinister Party of Allah.

6

The Party of Allah

> Islam is not Christianity. . . .
> Islam is the religion of
> agitation, revolution, blood,
> liberation and martyrdom.
>
> Shaikh Morteza Motahari[1]

Hadi Ghaffari is a young mullah who smiles with genuine pride and satisfaction when referred to as Hojat al-Islam (The Vicar of Islam).[2] He owes his highly prized title not to any serious theological studies but to the role he played in the Islamic Revolution of 1978–79 that swept Khomeini to power. Not being a *sayyed*, a descendant of the Prophet, Ghaffari cannot wear a black turban and green belt, but he has inherited from his father, Ayatollah Mahmoud Ghaffari, a very special turban. Carefully preserved in a transparent glass container, this turban is made of ordinary white cotton but is stained with dried blood. It is one of the most important ikons of the Hezb-Allah (The Party of Allah), which was founded by Hadi's father in Qom in 1973. Ayatollah Mahmoud Ghaffari died in prison under torture. 'His body was washed in a sea of blood,' related one historian of the fundamentalist movement, Ali Davani.[3] His last words were: 'There is only one party, the Party of Allah!' Police records show that Ayatollah Ghaffari was at the time of his death the only member of the party he had founded.

Today, however, the Party of Allah boasts a membership of more than a million in the Islamic Republic alone. Its offshoots in Lebanon, Iraq, the Gulf States, India, Pakistan, western Europe and the United States act as vanguards for the export of the Islamic Revolutionary movement to the whole world.

The Party of Allah is not a political organization in the classical style. It is a way of life, an 'army of civilians', a semi-secret fraternity and, last but not least, a 'clearing house for mankind', where those who will be admitted into Paradise are separated from those destined for Hell.[4]

Ghaffari, who is said to keep his Kalashnikov rifle with him day and night, has neither a central committee nor a politburo, nor is he expected to appear in front of any party congress. 'The Party of Allah is an ethereal organization,' he explained. 'It is everywhere and yet nowhere. It is everywhere *because* it is nowhere. All I need to do is to pick up the telephone and half a million people will be on the streets in less than an hour.'[5] His headquarters is housed in a building in south Tehran which before the revolution was used as a training school for nurses. Throughout the day it teems with people – ferocious-looking bearded men with automatic machine guns, women in the *chador*, black- and white-turbaned mullahs, and crowds of children and teenagers wearing crimson headbands on which one can read the slogan 'Seeker of Martyrdom'.

The Party of Allah's ideology is simplicity itself, and it is therefore immediately accessible to the audience it favours above all: the illiterate poor in the towns and cities. This ideology, despite its Islamic pretensions, is in fact Manichean and is based on the division of all phenomena into good and evil. Mankind is also divided, between the Partisans of Allah and those who support Shaytan or Satan; the war between the two must continue until the complete victory of the Partisans of Allah. Every aspect of Satan's presence must be removed, by violence if necessary, so that divine society[6] can become a reality. Satan appears in millions of ways. He could be seen in 'a lock of woman's hair emerging from under a head-scarf'[7] or in the presence of the American University in Beirut. Satan could manifest himself in the shape of 'the bare arms or legs of a young man' or 'the occupation of Palestine by the Jews'.[8] Thus the struggle against Satan is 'a full-time occupation of the Partisans of Allah'. 'Our religion is not a mere part-time hobby, like Cross-worshippers who go to church on Sunday to bribe their God,' says the manifesto of the Party of Allah. 'It is not religion that was created for Man, but the other way round. So we cannot close our eyes even to the seemingly insignificant signs of Satan's presence around us.'[9]

The Party of Allah was revived in 1979 on Khomeini's orders as a means of confronting the political enemies of the mullahs on the streets of Tehran. Originally armed only with kitchen knives, chains, clubs, boxes of matches and cans of acid, the Partisans of Allah established their reputation by murdering opposition spokesmen, setting fire to the offices of newspapers which criticized the government, and disfiguring unveiled women activists with acid and razors. Recruited in the slum districts of Tehran among the unemployed, the downtrodden and the petty criminals, the Partisans of Allah received a modest weekly stipend for their participation in revolutionary activity.[10] They became the popular arm of the regime and, by 1981, had succeeded in smashing almost all opposition organizations from liberals to Maoists. 'We occupy every inch of Tehran's streets,' Ghaffari boasted with justice in September 1981. But it was only from 1982 that the regime began to organize the Party of Allah properly. At that time Khomeini ordered the twenty-five or so Islamic terrorist organizations that had been active before the revolution to merge into the Party of Allah.[11] The war cry: 'Only one party, the Party of Allah! Only one leader, Ruhollah!' was adopted as a motto by virtually the whole of the Islamic regime.[12] The official ruling party, Hezb Jomhuri Islami (Islamic Republic party), was reduced to a ceremonial role acting as a mere branch of the Party of Allah. This development was almost inevitable, as the IRP imitated communist parties in its method of organization, while the Party of Allah used traditional Iranian forms of grouping.

The party's set-up is based on local mosques or *takiyehs*, in which ceremonies marking the martyrdom of Imam Hussein are held in the lunar months of Muharram and Safar. Every *takiyeh* is headed by a *mass'ul* (he who is answerable), who is usually a mullah. The *mass'ul* is assisted by a team of volunteers, who ensure that the party's messages are directly received by its members. The first task of these volunteers, recruited from the ranks of those who have 'suffered from Satan' in some way – such as having served prison terms under the old regime or being orphaned at an early age – is to make sure that everyone under the jurisdiction of their *takiyeh* regularly attends the Friday noon prayer sessions. In the big cities at least, a *takiyeh* is responsible for up to three thousand people.[13] The inhabitants of every house and apartment, and those who work in every shop, office or factory within the jurisdiction of a *takiyeh*, fall under the responsibility of one or more persons who report directly to the *mass'ul*. The *mass'uls* in any given district of the city also have their own direct contacts – through weekly meetings – and are answerable to a Namayandeh Imam or Imam's Representative – usually, but not always, a mullah appointed by Khomeini himself. Nojat al-Islam Hadi Ghaffari has the task of coordinating these representatives throughout the country as well as in the Middle East.

There are two key concepts in the organization of the Party of Allah. The first is leadership. The supreme leader, Ayatollah Khomeini, is no political leader in the ordinary sense of the term, but represents Allah's will on earth. He does not have to convey his orders through any official party hierarchy; if he makes his commands known in a radio or TV broadcast he will be instantly and blindly obeyed. He does not have to be specific in giving his orders; it is sufficient for him to give a hint, and the rest will be explained by his representatives and the *mass'uls*. Early in October 1983, for example, the ayatollah called on the Party of Allah to 'put an end to the shameful occupation of Lebanon' by American and French soldiers serving in the Multi-national Force (MNF). It took the Party of Allah in Lebanon, with help from both the Syrian and Iranian governments as well as the special services of both states, some three weeks to make a move in that direction. On 23 October two volunteers for martyrdom each drove a truck full of explosives into the headquarters of the American 8th Battalion of Marines and the command post (Drakkar) of the French 1st Regiment of Commandos. The Americans lost 241 soldiers, while the French dead numbered 58.[14]

The second important concept is martyrdom. Contrary to what is generally assumed in the West, Islam expressly forbids any form of suicide, and killing in the service of the Faith is certainly more meritorious than getting killed for it. Even within Shi'ism the majority view is that Hussein, when entering the fateful and for him fatal battle of Karbala, had no desire to become a martyr but was chosen for the role by Allah because of his 'special merit'.[15] Thus all a member of the Party of Allah can do is to enrol as a Volunteer for Martyrdom; the rest is up to Allah and his representatives on earth, who will decide who has enough merit to assume the honour and who does not. Members of the party are constantly urged to be humble and not to jump the queue, as it were, in seeking the lofty position of a martyr. This is partly why the mullahs and members of their immediate families seldom figure among martyrs unless they are slain by the enemies of the movement.

Those who deserve to become martyrs, and are thus assured of a place among the Owlia al-Allah or Friends of Allah, are picked by the *mass'uls* from the most enthusiastic militants. Priority is given to young male members of poor families with numerous children. In 1981 a movement launched with the slogan 'Offer one of your children to the Imam' attracted more than a million volunteers within two weeks. Most were teenagers, who provide the backbone of the Party of Allah's organization in the Islamic Republic as well as in Lebanon.

The choice of children and teenagers is justified by Khomeini on the grounds that those over twenty already have been contaminated by 'the corruption of Satanic civilization'. Party of Allah theoreticians believe that the division of a human lifetime into distinct periods is a Western 'Satanic' invention aimed at preventing mankind from assuming its responsibilities towards the Creator. Dr Muhammad-Ali Bani-Hashemi, one such theoretician, wrote:

> Some dishonest scholars in the West invented the system that divides human life into artificial categories. They invented childhood, then adolescence, then youth. The purpose of this division is to shut out as many people as possible from society [and put them] into age ghettos in which [they] can neither vote nor assume their own destiny because they are supposed to be too young. Children are expected and made to act childishly, while young people are forced to go out and have fun and become corrupt or run after a silly ball on the football field instead of cutting down the forces of evil on the battlefield.[16]

In any case, Islam recognizes only one important dividing line in life – *tam'yeez*, or the ability to distinguish right from wrong. Girls cross that line at the age of nine, when they are considered complete women and can marry; boys cross it at sixteen, from which moment they are fully responsible in the eyes of the Almighty. All duties incumbent on every Muslim must therefore be performed from the age of nine in the case of women, and the age of sixteen for men. Waging Holy War or Jihad is obviously among the most important of duties; and the Party of Allah, in the words of Khomeini himself, is a 'vehicle for Jihad'.

The sight of twelve-year-olds brandishing their Kalashnikovs was at first something of a shock to most people in Tehran or Beirut. But by 1982 it had become clear that Children's Power was there for some time – thanks to the Party of Allah. All children must, in theory at least, receive military training. But the Party of Allah cannot cope with the numbers. Regular courses on the use of various firearms as well as techniques of guerrilla warfare, kidnapping, the seizing of hostages and the execution of designated enemies of Islam are offered on radio and TV networks by the party experts.

It is only those selected for martyrdom who benefit from full training in these skills. They become the Children of the Imam and no longer belong to their respective families. They swear a simple oath: 'In the name of Allah the Avenger and in the name of Imam Khomeini I swear on the Holy Book to perform my sacred duty as a Child of the Imam and a Soldier of Islam in our Holy War to restore to this world the Light of Divine Justice. May Allah be my Guide on the Path of Jihad and of *qital*.'[17] Once notified of their selection the Children of the Imam are sent to one of the three hundred or more camps set up throughout the country for the training of future Soldiers of Islam. Initial training lasts between two weeks and six months, at the end of which each graduate receives the crimson headband that identifies him as a Volunteer for Martyrdom. The organization which runs the training programme is called Baseej (Mobilization), and acts as an offshoot of the Party of Allah. In 1980 Baseej officials claimed that they had plans for training an army of 20 million people within five years, but most experts agree that by 1986 a maximum of 2 million of both sexes had undergone periods of military training ranging from two weeks to six months.

Most of those trained by Baseej are quickly dispatched to

the Iran–Iraq war front. In 1982 some Children of the Imam were used for running onto minefields to clear a path for a Revolutionary Guards' attack on Iraqi positions in the Chezabeh sector of the front. Accounts of young bodies being blown to pieces sent a tremor into some hearts in Tehran, but the Party of Allah defended the strategy by announcing that thousands of other teenagers had put their names down to perform the same self-sacrifice.

Some opponents of the Party of Allah claimed that the astonishingly large numbers of Volunteers for Martyrdom were due to the fact that the government offered attractive financial and other benefits to bereaved families. It was argued that some poor parents in fact forced some of their numerous children to sacrifice themselves in exchange for money and household goods such as refrigerators, sewing machines and oil heaters. Until the summer of 1981 the government also offered an interest-free loan of 2 million rials (about £2600 sterling) to every bereaved family, but these loans as well as other cash and goods incentives were stopped in 1982 as the government began facing serious financial difficulties.[18] And yet the number of volunteers did not show any appreciable decline until the summer of 1986.[19]

In seeking the bulk of its supporters among children and teenagers the Party of Allah, in addition to its advertised belief that 'the newer generations are purer', has taken into account one of the central demographic realities of the Muslim Middle East. The whole region is teeming with children whose educational and career prospects are dim even in the oil-rich countries. Even the wealthiest of these economies could not cope with a 3 per cent annual increase in population within a classical framework of economic policymaking. Egypt is sinking under the weight of its expanding population, while Turkey just manages to get along – thanks to emigration. Iran and Algeria have the added advantage of a ready source of cash from crude oil exports. But with oil prices declining at the same time as a fall in demand for crude, even countries such as Saudi Arabia, with relatively small populations, were beginning to feel the pinch in 1986.[20]

Inside Iran, the Party of Allah mobilizes Children's Power with remarkable success. Elsewhere in the region, children and teenagers constitute primary targets for the Party of Allah message of revolution. Through adherence to the party, tens of thousands of children and teenagers who would otherwise be pushed by poverty and illiteracy onto the outer fringes of society feel themselves wanted, respected and powerful. They begin with simple tasks such as keeping an eye on the behaviour of local people, so that, for example, women who do not fully respect the rules of *hijab* can be identified, admonished and, if unrepentant, suitably punished. It is also the duty of future child soldiers to make sure that men in their neighbourhood do not adopt the 'Satanic habit' of shaving their beards and wearing ties. One of the war cries of the Party of Allah throughout the Muslim Middle East is '*Marg bar rish-tarash!*' which means 'Death to him who shaves [his beard]!' Militant children have both the right and the duty to command the good and prevent evil.[21] They can, and often do, ring people's doorbells in order to demand 'a friendly exchange of views'. And who can refuse? At any objection the child could call up a club-wielding mob ready to set the house of 'the heathen' on fire or throw acid on their women. Child moralists tell grown-ups how they ought to dress as well as how to behave at home or at work. They are the eyes and ears of the Imam, on permanent guard against the emergence in their City of Faith of the slightest sign of the City of War.

It is partly thanks to the efforts of these child revolutionaries, no doubt with support from the Revolutionary Guard, the *komiteh* police[22] and other official organs of repression, that more than two-thirds of Tehran has been totally cleared of 'all Satanic traces'. It is only in the remaining one-third, mostly in the northern suburbs, that clean-shaven men wearing European suits and ties can still be spotted occasionally. But even there no woman dare appear without the mandatory veil, or wearing clothes made of any fine or colourful material. In the winter of 1986 the child soldiers of the Party of Allah organized a massive campaign of 'purification' in northern Tehran against the fans of the American black singer Michael Jackson. Hundreds were beaten up, dozens had their T-shirts torn off and burned, and many were thrown into prison for up to three months. Shops selling 'the miscreant's filthy discs' were closed down or burned, and a bonfire was made of the hundreds of Jackson video-cassettes seized during raids on 'evil-harbouring homes'. The daily *Jomhuri Islami* (*Islamic Republic*), published by the President of the Republic, Hojat al-Islam Ali Hassani-Khamenh'i, devoted several editorials to the campaign, which he described as 'an Islamic counter-attack against a conspiracy hatched by Reagan to lead our God-fearing youth astray'.[23] Friday prayer leaders congratulated the young members of the Party of Allah on their 'splendid victory'. 'You have shown that you have understood the fact that belief in Islam means readiness for perpetual Holy War,' said Ayatollah Abbas Va'ez-Tabassi in Mashhad. 'Satan appears in all forms and guises. One of his latest manifestations is in the shape of that sodomite black boy from America whose senseless wailings can have no place [in our land].'[24]

Child militants are found in almost every government office; often they have no official title and just sit next to the person in charge to 'supervise' his activities. Their task is to be on guard against bribery, laziness. bureaucratic delays and 'bad behaviour towards the people'. Their presence has in some cases considerably speeded up the country's notoriously lengthy bureaucratic procedures. It is not unusual for a child militant to insist on having the last word on an official decision, over-ruling high-ranking officials. Since 1982 these guardians of the official consciousness have been increasingly picked from war-disabled teenagers, many of whom now arrive daily at their 'place of work' in wheelchairs. They receive no salary, but civil servants under their 'moral supervision' are expected to offer them 'an adequate gift of cash' at the end of every month. The Party of Allah itself also helps by offering additional rationing coupons that fetch a handsome price on the flourishing black market.[25]

In 1986 it was estimated that 75,000 Children of the Imam had received special combat training.[26] It is from among these elite fanatics that the soldiers of Holy Terror are selected for the ultimate phase of training that makes them effective instruments of Allah the Avenger. The necessity to train special units of hit men, known as Goruh Zarbat (Strike Unit), was first mentioned in 1980 by Khomeini himself as a means of dealing with the regime's opponents. He had begun thinking about the problem on the basis of a report submitted to him in September 1979 by his friend and former pupil Ayatollah Sadeq Khalkhali. In the report Khalkhali, then acting as an Islamic revolutionary judge, complained that a number of people considered *mahdur ad-damm* (those whose blood must be shed) had escaped punishment and were plotting against the Imam's rule from hideouts in Europe and the United States. He listed seventy-nine individuals who should be invited to return to Iran to stand trial or face being 'executed' abroad.[27] Five former Prime Ministers, more than thirty generals of the Shah's army, the former Empress, the Crown Prince and a number of businessmen in exile figured on the ayatollah's death list. At the time, however, the new Islamic regime did not have any special assassination squad to send on the type of mission Khalkhali suggested. His own Fedayeen of Islam gunmen were little more than shadows of Nawab's dreaded fighters, and were certainly incapable of operating abroad.

Another development that contributed to Khomeini's decision to set up specialized hit squads was the assassination of several of the Imam's closest confidants in the first half of 1979. Ayatollah Morteza Motahari, who had acted as Khomeini's operational commander inside Iran while the Imam was in exile, was murdered by a mysterious group called Forqan, dedicated to the elimination of the mullahs.[28] Motahari's murder was followed by the assassinations of Ayatollah Muhammad Mofattah, and of the businessman Haj Mahdi Fateh, who had partly financed Khomeini's operations in exile.

To cope with the situation Khalkhali, in consultation with Khomeini, had to accept an offer of cooperation by the dozen or so Marxist-Leninist groups then trying to secure a share of power in revolutionary Iran. All of them believed that the mullahs would be pushed back to the mosques within a few months, and were therefore prepared to curry favour with them. The names of three men sentenced to death by Khalkhali were given to a Marxist-Maoist group calling itself the People's Fedayeen Guerrillas. The potential victims were former Prime Minister Shapour Bakhtiar, a former martial law administrator of Tehran, General Gholam-Ali Oveissi, and the young Rear-Admiral Mostafa Shafiq, alias Shahryar, a nephew of the Shah. All three lived in France at the time and were putting together some form of an opposition to Khomeini's regime, then at the peak of its popularity. In the event, the terrorists succeeded in assassinating only Shafiq, on 7 December 1979. Bakhtiar was being well protected by the French Minister of the Interior, Michel Poniatowski, while Oveissi had left for New York.[29] After Shafiq's death Khalkhali issued a statement on Khomeini's behalf, crowing about 'the just punishment of a runaway criminal'. The murder was claimed by a fictitious Islamic Liberation Front, but subsequent investigation by the French police showed that the Marxist-Maoist group was involved, presumably helped by local comrades in Paris.

The assistance offered by left-wing guerrilla organizations to the Islamic regime in disposing of its monarchist enemies was soon to prove too expensive in political terms. Even then the mullahs were planning the elimination of all Marxist organizations in Iran, and were in no way prepared to offer them any share of power or indeed any form of recognition. Early in 1980 two other ways of dealing with the regime's opponents in exile were put to Khomeini. One solution came from Syria, which was quickly becoming the Islamic Republic's closest foreign ally. The Syrian government offered to order some of the Arab terrorist groups working for it to carry out a number of missions; Sadeq Ghotbzadeh, then Iranian Foreign Minister and closely linked with the Syrians, was an enthusiastic supporter. It was agreed that an attempt to assassinate Bakhtiar should be made by a pro-Syrian group headed by Anice Naqqash, a Lebanese member of the pan-Syrian Socialist Nationalist party.[30] The second suggestion came from a Washington DC carpet merchant, Haj Esmail, a man of Iranian origin who had become a naturalized US citizen in the 1960s. Esmail had already devoted part of his fortune to the promotion of Islam among black Americans and of Khomeini's cause among Iranian students in the United States, and his idea now was that the Islamic Republic should hire the services of professional killers.

Haj Esmail received the green light from Khalkhali in April 1980, and less than two months later he was able to report his first success to Tehran. Ali-Akbar Tabataba'i, a former

Director General of Information under the Shah and then one of Khomeini's most active opponents in exile, was gunned down at his own front door by a black assassin wearing a postman's uniform.[31] The assassin, who had converted to Islam a few years earlier and adopted the name of Davoud Muhammad, left the United States immediately and arrived in Tehran, where he was received by Khomeini and thanked for his 'important contribution'.[32]

The Islamic leaders, however, were not satisfied with using Syrian-controlled terrorists or hired killers. To be sure, Syria did not demand any favours in return for its role in plotting the attempt on Bakhtiar's life. And Davoud, too, had not acted solely for money: he had played a part in the seizure of the Washington DC Islamic Centre by the Hanafi militants in 1977, and thus had a certain reputation as a fundamentalist militant. Nevertheless, Khomeini was anxious to have an independent force of his own. He had at his disposal several dozen trained and experienced terrorists capable of effective action within the borders of the Islamic Republic, but he was already thinking of his 'universal mission' that required a force capable of striking anywhere in the world.[33] A few weeks later Khomeini set up a three-man committee charged with creating one of the largest terror groups in the Middle East.

The man chosen to head the committee was an unassuming, soft-spoken, totally unmilitary mullah by the name of Hojat al-Islam Fazl-Allah Mahalati.[34] At the time of his appointment he was just under fifty, and was responsible for a library of theological books in central Tehran. Khomeini chose him first, perhaps because Mahalati had been his pupil in Qom and then in exile in Najaf for more than ten years. Mahalati's loyalty to his former teacher was total and unquestioned. He was not a member of any of the various factions which were already competing for power and influence in the entourage of the Imam.[35] Equally important, Mahalati possessed a reputation as a disciplined worker and, unlike many other mullahs, had an impeccable, almost ascetic, lifestyle: he had not housed himself in one of the many palatial villas abandoned by Tehran's fleeing rich businessmen, nor had he appropriated any of the bullet-proof Mercedes 600s that the mullahs had inherited from the imperial regime. He was known as 'the incorruptible'.[36]

Assisting Mahalati in his task were Chamran, whose experience of guerrilla training and terrorist organizational work in Lebanon was to prove crucial to the success of the new enterprise, and Ayatollah Ali-Akbar Mohtashami. Mahalati had chosen Mohtashami for his contacts with the Syrians. He had been a pupil of Khomeini's in Najaf, and during the 1970s had served as a courier for his master between Najaf and Damascus. It was in the pursuit of his work for Mahalati's committee that Mohtashami was later appointed Ambassador to Syria, a post he retained until 1985 when he was brought back to Tehran to become Minister of the Interior.

But Mahalati, who deeply suspected the motives of the Syrian leaders in seeking a firm alliance with the Islamic Republic, was quite obviously determined not to put all his eggs in the Syrian basket. The Alawites who ruled the country were considered by many mullahs as 'Muslims of doubtful sincerity', while President Assad's advocacy of socialism and close ties with Moscow disturbed the turbaned rulers of Islamic Iran. Mahalati began, therefore, by assessing local talent and experience. He consulted Ayatollah Muhammad Montazeri – known as Ringo because of his gun-toting antics – about the possibility of cooperating with Libyan-based terrorist groups. Montazeri, a personal friend of Colonel Gaddafi, had himself undergone guerrilla training in the 1970s. Ayatollah Ali-Akbar Nateq-Nuri, who was also close to the Libyan leader, was another expert whom Mahalati contacted, as were three militants of Afghan origin – Jalaleddin Farsi, Hussein Forqani and Abdul-Karim Akhlaqi – who all had strong connections with the Palestine Liberation Organization and had received guerrilla training at PLO camps in Lebanon during the 1970s. Finally, Mahalati had several long sessions with Ghaffari, the man who had to provide the volunteers needed. By February 1981 Khomeini's international terror organization was already in existence, although only in embryonic form. Its first training camp was quietly inaugurated on 11 February, the second anniversary of the Islamic Revolution.

7

I Kill, Therefore I Am

> If I refuse suicide, you treat
> me as a coward; and when I accept
> dying in this way, you treat me as
> a barbarian. You cannot make up your
> minds which manner of death suits
> me best so that I can escape my
> oppressors. Do you, gentlemen
> specialists in genocide, wish to deprive
> me even of the liberty of
> choosing my death?
>
> Mahmoud Darwish[1]

At first glance, the north Tehran suburb of Niavaran is a most unlikely site for a military camp of any kind. Its tree-shaded avenues, elegant villas and luxuriant orchards, all set against the backdrop of the eternally snow-capped Mount Towchal, give it the appearance of a quiet, peaceful resort. At the heart of Niavaran stand the three palaces that the Shah and his family occupied before the revolution. A modernistic park, complete with a theatre, a library and a centre for experimental film-making, used to draw large crowds of young people. Today, Niavaran houses the first and one of the largest revolutionary camps, where Volunteers for Martyrdom from some thirty countries learn how to kill and to die in the name of the Imam and in the service of the Party of Allah.

The camp is situated inside the vast and beautiful Manzarieh Park, created in the eighteenth century, which in the Shah's time was the site of national and international boy scout jamborees. At the gate stood a stone statue of Lord Baden-Powell, founder of the movement. The last international jamboree, held at Manzarieh in the summer of 1977, brought together more than twelve thousand scouts from all over the world. The park covers the gentle southern slopes of Mount Towchal over an area of some 1½ thousand square kilometres and contains some of the oldest and best oak, yew and cedar trees in the country. Until 1955 the only buildings were a pair of wooden cottages, in which two wardens and their families lived. Then others were added, including a 300-room hall of residence for the Empress Farah University for Girls, which was to have been inaugurated in 1981. But by then the Islamic Revolution had changed everything in Iran, and Ayatollah Mahalati, given the task of creating an international force to export the Imam's revolution, was able to take over the park and the hall of residence at its westernmost end. Since 1981 Manzarieh has been closed to the public and cordoned off with barbed wire. The three avenues leading to it are all sealed and permanently guarded by units of the Baseej. Electrified barbed wire fencing also separates the park from the mountain behind it, while mountaineers are not allowed to come within three kilometres of the camp.

The camp was officially inaugurated in the autumn of 1980 as a 'recreation centre for wounded Revolutionary Guards', but it was never used for that purpose. Its first courses in the art of urban guerrilla warfare and terrorism began in February 1981 with 175 hand-picked students, including nine Afghans and fourteen citizens of various Arab countries.[2] Commanding the camp at the time was Shaikh Abbas Golru, a man of Irano-Iraqi Shi'ite descent who had been a member of the pro-Syrian Palestinian commando group as-Saiqah (Lightning) between 1973 and 1975. Golru did not seem to know what kind of force he was meant to produce: the syllabuses he worked out, in consultation with Chamran who also taught there, put greater emphasis on ideological studies than on practical military training.

One of the first students described the early courses as 'a mixture of theology and target practice. . . . We could not become good in either discipline.'[3] Five prayer sessions a day, an afternoon recitation from the Qu'ran by a mullah and special sermons several times a week left little time for the art of war. Golru, whose work with as-Saiqah had consisted of forging passports and other official documents, had never gained any combat experience and seemed convinced that 'by learning the Qur'an plus a few pseudo-Marxist slogans we would conquer the world'.[4]

Golru was dropped before the end of the year and the camp was put under the joint administration of the Revolutionary Guard and the Baseej. The new commander was Nasser Kolhaduz, another former graduate of Palestinian camps in Lebanon and then a commander of the Revolutionary Guard.[5] He persuaded Mahalati, with Chamran's support, to accept a plan for inviting Syrian, North Korean and Palestinian experts to come and teach at the centre, which was now referred to as a *moassesseh* (institute). Mahalati agreed, and the plan was approved by Khomeini, though with one change: he would have no Palestinians. The Imam had been persuaded that the various Palestinian groups were working for different Arab or communist powers and could pose a security risk to his Islamic Republic. The North Koreans then sent in a team of three commando experts, plus an interpreter named Mr Lee; the officers were never named, and no one saw them outside school hours. The Syrian delegation consisted of nine men, who never appeared in military uniform, headed by a Major Adnan who was supposed to be close to President Assad's brother Rifa'at.[6] But most of the instructors were Iranians trained before the revolution by the PLO, the Amal organization or the Iraqi government.[7] Some used Palestinian-style *noms de guerre* – 'abu' this or 'abu' that – but many used their own names, among them Rahmat-Allah Yazdi, Shaikh Jaafar Razizadeh, Habib-Allah Araki, Abbas Douzdouzani[8] and Hussein Hojati.

All the students, aged between eighteen and twenty-five, had already served between six months and two years with the Revolutionary Guard or the Baseej. Each had been recommended either by influential local mullahs or, in the case of non-Iranians, by the leaders of the various Islamic liberation fronts created to export the revolution to the rest of the Muslim world. Selected from among more than a thousand applicants, all had been carefully interviewed by Mahalati, Chamran and Golru – before he was transferred – either individually or in groups. Everyone was genuinely committed to the cause of exporting the revolution. Most of the Iranians were children of peasant families, with a surprisingly large number from the central province of Isfahan.[9]

Also present, however, were some twenty young men from well-to-do Iranian families, who had been studying in western Europe or the United States at the time of the revolution. At that point they had abandoned their studies and flown back to Iran to fight for Khomeini. Most had already fought in the Iran–Iraq War and were considered veterans. Some also served as interpreters for the Syrian instructors, who for the most part spoke English. Those who had spent time in the United States were often invited by the mullahs who served as 'moral instructors' at the camp to tell the rest about 'the filth under which the Great Satan America is sinking'.[10] The picture they painted was of a civilization on the verge of collapse and incapable of resisting the challenge of resurgent Islam.[11]

Almost all the students were under the impression that they were attending an ordinary military course; they asked no questions about the future, but assumed that they would form commando units to act behind the Iraqi lines in the Gulf War. At the time there was no hint of the role the trainees might be expected to play in terrorist activities abroad. Mahalati told them: 'Our aim here is to break you. For you have been shaped by this earthly life for the purpose of performing ordinary deeds. We mean to put you back together again in a totally new form, so that you can serve your Creator and be fit for entry into Paradise.'[12]

All the students were housed in the hall of residence, where the theoretical lectures were also given. The instructors lived outside the camp and where whisked in and out under heavy armed escort provided by the Revolutionary Guard. The day began with pre-dawn prayer sessions in the hall of residence, turned into a mosque for the purpose. A mullah led the prayers, which were followed by a twenty-minute recitation from the Qur'an. Then followed ninety minutes of physical exercises, at the end of which students could shower but not shave, and be ready for breakfast at seven. Formal classes or training in the use of different weapons, mostly AK guns, RPGs, the Israeli-made Uzi automatic sub-machine gun and the Soviet-made Kalashnikov, began at eight and continued until noon, when another prayer session facing Mecca was organized. Weather permitting, these prayers took place in the open air among the park's beautiful trees. Fridays were devoted to rest, prayer, meditation and personal matters, but no one was allowed to leave the camp.

Most evenings were taken up by informal discussions, led by invited mullahs, on various points of Qur'anic law and Islamic history. A popular speaker was Ayatollah Mahdi Shahabadi, who told the students about the glorious days of Islam in Spain, promising a return to those times. The students felt as if they were meant to spearhead the 'liberation of Islamic Spain'. Some evenings were devoted to following the Imam's speeches on videotapes, followed by open discussion about the points raised in each one. After late evening prayers the students retired to their rooms where they were allowed to read books – but no newspapers or magazines – until 10.30 p.m.

The camp's library contained very little besides Persian textbooks, all prepared and printed by the regular army under the Shah. Among the few books available were Ayatollah Khomeini's works, the *Nahj al-Bulaghah* (*The Way of Eloquence*) by Imam Ali, the Persian translation of Henri Masse's *Le Prophète*,[13] the collected works of Ayatollah Morteza Motahari, several pamphlets signed by Ayatollah Muhammad-Hussein Beheshti, the Persian translation of Gorgi Zaydan's *Conquest of Andalusia*[14] and several volumes of *Documents from the Nest of Spies*.[15] The only book of military interest, apart from the textbooks mentioned, was the Persian translation of Sun Tzu's *The Art of War*.[16]

A few weeks after the course began, those cadets with previous military experience were invited to volunteer for a variety of operations within specialized units of the Revolutionary Guard. Presented as 'practical training', these missions could consist of raids against suspected hideouts of anti-regime guerrillas or serving as one-man firing squads in the Evin and Qasr Prisons.[17] Almost everyone took part in one or more 'volunteer' missions as a matter of course. Very soon it became apparent that the sole purpose of the course was not to train the cadets in the art of guerrilla and sabotage work, but to test their characters. The mullahs wanted men dedicated to

Khomeini, who were ready to kill and to die in his name. After a few weeks Mahalati and Chamran came to know every cadet personally. Chamran would, for example, select a group of twelve to accompany him during his frequent visits to the war front, while Mahalati would include some cadets in his bodyguard for periods of up to ten days. The aim was to acquire an intimate knowledge of those cadets singled out by their instructors for their Islamic zeal as well as their military abilities.[18]

More than a dozen cadets were killed on the war front or in armed clashes with Islamic-Marxist guerrillas or fighting Kurdish and Baluchi tribal insurgents. A dozen others were withdrawn from the course and assigned to protect leading ayatollahs in the provinces. Four, including a Tunisian, were sent to Damascus to protect Mohatashami, who by this time had been appointed Ambassador to Syria.[19] Seven more, including two Afghans and one Moroccan, were sent to Lebanon to help train pro-Khomeini groups in the Bekaa Valley.

So by the time graduation day came on 30 July 1981, a ceremony attended by Mahalati and the top brass of the Revolutionary Guard, fewer than 150 'blessed ones'[20] were declared 'fully ready for the service of the Imam'. A few days beforehand the cadets had been asked to write, sign and seal their wills and hand them over to a young mullah, Hojat al-Islam Naqi Sa'idi, sent by Mahalati. At the ceremony every graduate received a framed coloured portrait of Khomeini, a copy of the Qur'an and a *ta'awidh*,[21] but no certificates were handed out and no publicity surrounded the occasion. It had been understood all along that no one outside the camp was to know anything about what went on inside. On 15 August came the moment the 'blessed ones' had been waiting for all along: an audience with Khomeini himself. The Imam, appearing on the balcony of the Jamaran *takiyeh* near where he lived, spoke for less than ten minutes before waving goodbye. From what he said, it seemed that he was fully aware of the purpose of this embryonic force.[22] At the end of the audience a small square of cloth from the Imam's turban, protected by a plastic cover, was given to each graduate as a sign of special favour from Khomeini.[23]

Many of the graduates were assigned almost immediately to units fighting the remnants of Islamic-Marxist guerrillas in Tehran and half a dozen other major cities; they played a crucial role in putting down the insurrection. But Mahalati had also kept some of the 'blessed ones' to form an Iranian corps of instructors for the other training centres he had already planned. After his mysterious death in 1985 Mahalati was succceeded as 'coordinator for exporting the revolution' by Hojat al-Islam Mahdi Hashemi, a charismatic mullah related to Khomeini. He described his role as one of putting together 'the vanguard of liberating armies for all Arab and Islamic countries'.[24]

Before he died Mahalati had set up at least fifteen other camps of varying importance for training the commandos needed to carry out terrorist activities in the service of the Islamic Revolution. Accounts by former instructors and cadets at some of these camps, as well as information gathered by western, Arab and Soviet bloc Intelligence organizations, have enabled specialists to pinpoint some of them, and at the end of June 1986 the following were in operation. Manzarieh, with an estimated nine hundred cadets, remains the largest; it offers a varied range of military and paramilitary skills, some of which can be used in terrorist operations. The camp at Saleh-Abad, 45 kilometres north of the holy city of Qom, is a stronghold of the Revolutionary Guard; special training in terrorism is given in one section of the vast complex. At Parandak, 30 kilometres west of Tehran, the camp is situated on the site of the former National Railways Training Centre. Over five hundred cadets receive instruction there at any one time. Beheshtieh lies 20 kilometres northwest of the capital. It is one of two camps known to offer terrorist training to women from a number of Muslim countries. Irish, American and Lebanese women married to Iranians are also reported to have received training there.[25] Eram Park, on the outskirts of Qom, was once a hotel but is now used for training militants from the Middle East and the Indo-Pakistani subcontinent.[26] In the Gorgan Plain, 600 kilometres east of Tehran, lies Bojnurd, under the nominal supervision of the 77th Infantry Division of the regular army but in fact entirely run by the Revolutionary Guard. Tariq al-Qods,[27] northwest of Tehran, is used exclusively for training guerrillas belonging to the Iraqi ad-Da'awah party.[28] Ghayour-Asli Base, near Ahvaz, 910 kilometres southwest of Tehran, is also used for training Iraqi guerrillas, and instruction is given in Arabic. According to French Intelligence the camp at Vakil-Abad near Mashhad, 1000 kilometres east of Tehran, used until 1984 to accommodate Iraqi prisoners of war, has since been converted into a centre for training 'specialists in hijacking civilian aircraft', especially Boeing 727s and 707s.[29] The camp at Val-Fajr, near Ramhormoz in Khuzestan, was the scene of rioting in 1984 when Arab and Iranian students quarrelled about what the official media described as 'trivial matters'.[30] Shahid Chamran (Martyr Chamran), in the Bushehr peninsula, is used for training Enteharis or 'suicide-attackers'. It includes a section for training pilots, whose task would be to organize kamikazi-style raids on US warships if and when the latter try to attack an Iranian target in the Persian Gulf.[31] Beheshtieh, at Kharg, is a branch of the training centre of the same name for women near Tehran. According to French reports, at any given time it houses up to three hundred Volunteers for Martyrdom.[32]

What exactly goes on inside these camps is not known for certain, but many clues exist, often provided by disenchanted Soldiers of the Imam. Colonel Taqi Barmaki, a special forces officer who taught at the Saleh-Abad camp until the summer of 1985, talked of 'a regular sort of commando training' but admitted that the skills gained there could be used for terrorist operations.[33] The mullahs who ran the camp seemed to attach as much importance to indoctrination as to the military aspects of the course. They wanted devoted fighters who would not think of acting outside 'the normal and universally accepted rules of war'.[34] The cadets were constantly told that they would be used as 'the spearhead of the Islamic conquest of the world'. One of the ideological booklets used at the camp gave twelve priorities for the Islamic revolution,[35] and the trainees were told that it was up to them to achieve those goals. They were almost certainly prepared to do whatever was required of them. There was no doubting their determination to realize the Imam's plans.

Regular army officers like Colonel Barmaki who served at

the camps continue to justify their role by citing the Iran–Iraq War. To them the commandos trained in 'terrorist' camps could serve behind enemy lines in Iraq or carry out acts of sabotage against the Iraqi regime. This has, indeed, been the primary task of the 'blessed ones' graduating from Khomeini's schools of terror. Attacks of a terrorist nature inside Iraq are seldom reported by the international media, as opposed to those carried out against the enemies of the Imam inside Iran or in Lebanon. But more than three hundred terrorist attacks in Iraq have been recorded since January 1982. They range from the assassination of individual members of the Ba'athist regime to the blowing up of power stations and fuel depots. More than a thousand people have died in these raids.[36] But there is no doubt that throughout the 1980s graduates of the special schools of Holy Terror have also been directly or indirectly involved in dozens of terrorist outrages in the Middle East, western Europe and countries such as Turkey, Greece, Pakistan and Malaysia.

The numbers and the effectiveness of the soldiers of Holy Terror trained inside Iran have often been exaggerated, largely because of the Iranian opposition in exile's desire to score easy points against Khomeini. Newspaper reports have spoken of thousands of 'suicide attackers' getting ready to wreak havoc in the West.[37] Distorted accounts have even crept into official reports in the United States and various western European countries.[38] Two persistent fictions must be dealt with. One is that the Islamic Republic has devoted an annual budget of more than 2 billion US dollars to 'terrorist operations'.[39] The fact is that this sum, originally mentioned in the government budget for March 1983–March 1984, was earmarked for a wide variety of purposes ranging from publishing newspapers and books in more than twenty languages for the propagation of Islam to the construction of mosques, Islamic schools and an Islamic university.[40] Part of the money was to be spent on over twenty Islamic liberation movements based in Tehran. It is almost certain, too, that some was devoted to training terrorists in Iran as well as in Lebanon. It is difficult to know how much, but an estimate made by Captain Hamid Zomorrod, an expert in what is known as 'low-intensity operations', suggests under 200 million US dollars over the five years up to the time of writing.[41] He also puts the number of 'individuals capable of taking part in acts of terrorism after being trained in Iran since 1981' at around three thousand.[42] Thousands of others who have been trained at the special camps are either being used as auxiliaries in the war against Iraq or are taking an active part in the Lebanese civil war.

The second persistent fiction in studying the terror network created by the Islamic Republic concerns its leadership. Ayatollah Hossein Ali Montazeri, Khomeini's designated heir as Supreme Guide, is often called the ringleader of the network of Holy Terror. The fact is, however, that Montazeri knows next to nothing about what is going on in Khomeini's terror camps. Montazeri's son Muhammad was intimately involved in the project until his death in 1981, but he was never close to his father, who by all serious accounts has been critical of the use of terror as an instrument of domestic and foreign policy. The confusion about Montazeri's role, when not deliberate, stems from the fact that he is the nominal head of the Vahdat or Islamic reunification movement, which is aimed at creating a pan-Islamic pact some time in the future. But Montazeri, who until the autumn of 1986 lived in Qom in virtual isolation from affairs of state, was unlikely to have been informed about the activities of the terror network.[43] Montazeri is the spiritual head of that faction in the Islamic Republic's leadership which opposes attempts at exporting the revolution by force or terror. Exporting the revolution remains one of the declared objectives of the republic, and no one in the leadership dares openly reject it. But unlike Khomeini, who believes that the employment of every conceivable means is justified in the service of Islam, Montazeri emphasizes the force of example. Opponents of the regime claim that Khomeini and Montazeri, by stating diametrically opposed views on the use of terror in the service of the Faith, are offering no more than a Shi'ite version of the 'tough-cop, soft-cop' show designed to confuse the enemy. This may or may not be true. But Montazeri has consistently opposed the use of violence except for Islamic self-defence, as in the case of the war with Iraq.

Another important point concerns the degree of effective official control that the Islamic Republic exercises on the soldiers of Holy Terror. It can be total and absolute, as in the case of units directly attached to the Revolutionary Guard in Iran and Lebanon, but sometimes the Islamic Republic exercises practically no authority over the activities of trained terrorists once they have left Iran. In such instances Tehran can only exert a degree of influence on Islamic terror squads by using its ideological and financial powers as well as Khomeini's prestige, which remains supreme among radical fundamentalists. Hojat al-Islam Ali-Akbar Hashemi-Rafsanjani, the Speaker of the Islamic Parliament in Tehran, was not trying to be evasive when he said that the Islamic Republic did not have responsibility for the many terrorist organizations in Lebanon. 'Only the Party of Allah listens to us,' he said. 'Other Islamic groups in Lebanon have close ties with us, but take their own decisions.'[44]

The various Arab Islamic liberation groups working to overthrow the governments of their respective countries also enjoy an unusual measure of autonomy, despite the fact that most of them have been created and totally financed by the Islamic Republic. One example of this independence was the kidnapping of the Syrian diplomat Zyad al-Mahmoud by the Iraqi ad-Daawa guerilla group in Tehran in October 1986. The diplomat was released after twenty-four hours and ad-Daawa made it clear that the kidnapping was a warning to Damascus not to think of improving ties with Baghdad as long as Saddam Hussein remained in power. The incident greatly embarrassed Tehran in its relations with Syria, the Islamic Republic's closest Arab ally.

Khomeini seems to be content with his ideological control of these terror organizations; he does not care about the detail of their activities – such as the holding of hostages – as long as they show that they are moving in the direction indicated by the Imam. Thus the terrorism inspired and financed by the Islamic Republic differs fundamentally from that used at various times by certain Middle Eastern states, ranging from Nasser's Egypt to Libya, Iraq and Syria. The government in Tehran is telling the truth when it vehemently denies being in charge of the Holy Terror network. Government ministers can influence the terror groups set up in Iran and financed by the Iranian Treasury only through Khomeini and the twenty or so mullahs who run the network for him. This is an important fact to take into account in diplomatic negotiations concerning the threat of terrorism in the Middle East. Government officials may promise anything; but they can hardly ever deliver. In the Islamic Republic, the government itself is terrorized by the Party of Allah and totally incapable of developing an independent policy on any major issue. Repeated attempts at bringing the Party of Allah and its terrorist offshoots inside and outside Iran under some form of government control have failed because of Khomeini's constant opposition.

The Imam wants to address his holy warriors directly and to make them feel that it is their individual effort that would 'humble the Reagans of this world and hoist high the banner of Muhammad'.[45] He knows that it is by making the 'downtrodden' feel powerful that he can continue to persuade them to kill and to die for his cause. A great believer in the merits of having multiple centres of power, he has systematically prevented the creation of a central command for the revolutionary organizations which fight in his name. He seems to think that the creation of any central command would lead the movement towards negotiation, diplomacy and compromise. It is with the same logic that he has been urging the destruction of the PLO and its replacement by 'dozens of fighting groups, all going the same way but not in the same vehicle'.[46] This taste for unity in diversity has led the Imam to endorse and support several liberation movements in a single Islamic country at the same time. It is the individual duty of every Muslim to take up arms in the service of the Faith; thus no one can impose on other believers a single organizational pattern of struggle. Inside Iran, Khomeini has consistently refused to invite people to join the government-run Islamic Republic Party (IRP). And in the Muslim world at large he favours a policy of distributing his financial and moral support among as many groups as possible.

The Ayatollah's idea of helping the 'downtrodden of the Earth' fight for their 'usurped rights' does not limit itself to Muslims. His Islamic Republic has offered bases, arms and financial resources to a number of non-Muslim organizations, such as the Armenian Secret Army for the Liberation of

Armenia (ASALA), which is dedicated to the destruction of the Turkish state. Until the end of 1984[47] ASALA maintained two camps in the Iranian province of West Azerbaijan, plus offices in the city of Rezaieh.[48] 'We cannot but feel close to all those who are ready to fight for a just cause,' Khomeini said in a Christmas message addressed to 'the followers of Jesus' in 1983.[49] It was also on his orders that some of Tehran's central streets have been named after men and women who are considered terrorists elsewhere: the IRA's Bobby Sands (the street named after him was formerly Churchill Street and opposite the British Embassy), Khaled Ahmad Showqi al-Islambouli,[50] Suleiman Khater,[51] Sumayah Sa'ad,[52] Leila Khaled,[53] Muhammad Abd-Khoda'i[54] and many others.

In 1983 and 1984 the Ayatollah's representatives in Europe contacted a number of terrorist organizations, including the Basque ETA and the Corsican National Liberation Front, for 'exchange of information and ideas with a view to future cooperation'.[55] The meetings, arranged through Libyan intermediaries, led nowhere, however, as the Basques and Corsicans showed no interest in the Islamic Revolution and its leader's scenario for 'the universal struggle of the downtrodden against the oppressors'. The Ayatollah has also been singularly unsuccessful in the export of his own version of revolution to Latin America, despite the establishment of close ties with the Sandinista government in Nicaragua as well as Castro's Cuba.

8

The Waiting Room of Paradise

> It now matters none where life
> may take me from here. For I have
> been to the ante-chamber of Paradise,
> I have seen the Imam. . . .
>
> Shaikh Ragheb Harb[1]

According to an old Shi'ite tradition, those destined for Paradise will learn of their happy fate by catching a glimpse of that 'garden of pure joy' here in this world. The experience is usually associated with visits paid to the shrine of one of the various imams in Iraq, Arabia and Iran.[2] Since the Islamic Revolution, however, a glimpse of Paradise is said to be experienced by militant fundamentalists during their visits to the Islamic Republic, where, if they are lucky, they are received in audience by the Living Imam.[3]

The excitement created in the Muslim world by the unexpected success of the Islamic Revolution in 1979 attracted hundreds of fundamentalists from all over the world. 'Our brothers come here from the four corners of the world to see the miracle of Islam in action,' wrote an enthusiastic fundamentalist in the first days of the Imam's rule.[4] Since then the revolutionary regime has developed its own version of 'holy tourism'. Companies have been set up in Britain, the United States, France, Germany, Austria, Italy and many of the Islamic capitals for the purpose of offering inexpensive guided tours to the Islamic Republic. Applicants must be Muslim, young and prepared to spend a minimum of two months there. Tens of thousands had accomplished these 'pilgrimages of revolution', as they are described, by 1986. Most visitors have been students, and many stayed to train either as propagandists of the Faith or soldiers of Holy Terror.

The idea of recruiting future terrorists and activists from among Muslim students and workers in the West had been raised by Mostafa Chamran as early as 1978, shortly before the success of the Islamic Revolution. Dozens of members of the Lebanese Amal organization, as well as commandos sent by the PLO, had taken part in the revolution against the Shah in Iran and proved particularly effective in carrying out sabotage missions and selective assassinations. It was now the turn of the Islamic Republic to do its duty towards other 'downtrodden Muslims'.

The creation of a propaganda organization which also arranged guided tours of revolutionary Iran was considered a priority by Mahalati soon after he had completed his plans for the creation of an international network of revolutionary activity. From 1981 almost all the Islamic Republic's embassies were used as covers for revolutionary activities, often aimed against the host countries. By 1983 the twin embassies to Italy and the Vatican, both in the centre of Rome, were identified by Western Intelligence as the nerve centres of the network of Holy Terror in Europe.[5] The 600-room Rome Embassy, at 361–363 Via Nomantana, became no less than a revolutionary base. According to the Italian police, Mahalati's agents had succeeded in 'smuggling' great quantities of arms into the Embassy building,[6] which housed more than a hundred people with diplomatic status, plus dozens more said to be on business. In January 1984 the Italian Prime Minister, Bettino Craxi, ordered a special inquiry into the activities of the two embassies.[7] The full text of the inquiry was never published, but dozens of Iranian diplomats were quietly asked to leave. The Vatican Embassy was run by Hojat al-Islam Hadi Khosrowshahian,[8] who set up a publishing company registered in Jersey for the purpose of 'pursuing Islamic cultural activities'. In 1984 alone more than £4 million sterling was credited to the company's account by the London branch of the Islamic Industrial Bank.[9] Several diplomats serving at one or other of the two embassies defected in 1983 and 1984, and offered information about the strange activities of the Imam's representatives.

In Paris, between 1982 and 1986 the French police expelled

more than seventy Iranian diplomats or 'students' for alleged involvement in terrorist activities. Among those thrown out in 1985 was Massoud Hindi, a nephew of Ayatollah Khomeini. Gaston Deferre, in 1983 Minister of the Interior, accused Khomeinist agents of involvement in workers' violence in various French car factories employing Muslim immigrant workers. In a series of raids in 1983 the Paris police discovered quantities of arms and propaganda material in nine safe houses belonging to the Islamic revolutionary movement. Some of these safe houses were in luxurious apartment blocks in the most fashionable districts of the city.[10] The covers used varied from that of the Islamic Cultural Association, set up by the ayatollahs, to an expensive Persian restaurant-cum-carpet shop in the Champs Elysées. In 1984 the Cultural Association was disbanded on police orders and more than thirty of its members expelled.

In Britain in 1984, Scotland Yard raided a safe house used by agents of the Islamic Republic in Draycott Place, Chelsea, and expelled a total of twenty-three Muslim militant fundamentalists linked with Tehran. A mosque in Holland Park in West London, and three *takiyehs*[11] – in Hendon in north London, in Tooting in south London and in Bradford in the north of England – have also been used as points of contact between Islamic revolutionaries and future recruits among Muslim students and workers in Britain. In 1985 alone more than 1700 Muslim students from nineteen Islamic countries put their names down for summer courses in the Islamic Republic through the various associations and travel agencies set up in the United Kingdom by the ayatollahs.

In West Germany more than a dozen *takiyehs*, plus a mosque in Hamburg, have been used as propaganda centres for the Islamic Revolution. Here, too, expulsion measures have been taken against Khomeinist militants during the five years up to 1986. But the Party of Allah has been careful to limit its activities in the Federal Republic, largely because of Bonn's exceptionally close ties with Tehran. In 1984 the West German Foreign Minister, Hans-Dietrich Genscher, became the first high-ranking Western diplomat to visit Tehran since the revolution. Relations between Bonn and the Islamic Republic suffered a set-back in October 1986 when a Party of

Allah mob attacked and ransacked the Federal German embassy building in central Tehran.

Austria and Switzerland are used essentially for handling the Party of Allah's financial transactions. But regular indoctrination sessions were also organized at *takiyehs* in Vienna, Graz, Geneva and Zurich during 1984 and 1985. Muslim students and workers in both countries have also benefited from inexpensive group tours of the Islamic Republic.

Between 1981 and the summer of 1986 more than 150 Party of Allah propagandists, including some seventy ayatollahs, visited Britain, France, Italy, Belgium, Spain, Switzerland, Austria, West Germany, Denmark and Sweden for stays of up to eight weeks, during which they addressed meetings of Muslim students and workers. Among the visiting ayatollahs were such high-ranking members of the revolutionary apparatus as Hadi Ghaffari, President of the Party of Allah, Muhammad Mussavi-Khoiniha, the leader of the 'students' who took the American diplomats hostage in 1979, Mehdi Karrubi, President of the Martyrs' Foundation, and Ahmad Azari-Qomi, a former Islamic Prosecutor-General. The programme under which revolutionary propagandists visit European countries to address Muslim students and workers is called Jihad Tanvir (The War of Enlightenment) and is financed from the special fund for 'exporting the revolution' that Montazeri supervises in name only.[12] The result has been impressive. Between 1981 and 1986 more than half a million Muslim students and workers in ten western European countries have been directly reached by revolutionary propagandists during special indoctrination sessions. In the same period the publication division of the Party of Allah, with its headquarters in Rome, published over three hundred books and booklets in English, French, Italian, Persian, Turkish and Arabic, representing a total circulation of more than 5 million copies. A sound and video-cassette division, operating from London until 1986, also boasted impressive production figures. It turned out more than a million sound cassettes plus around a hundred thousand video-cassettes in Arabic, Turkish, Urdu, Persian and English.[13] Although some of the books and cassettes were exported to or smuggled into

Muslim countries as far away as Malaysia, the bulk was destined for Muslim students and workers in western Europe.[14]

The Party of Allah also publishes a weekly newspaper which is printed in the Netherlands, Britain and the United States and distributed in more than thirty countries.[15] In addition, the party finances an English-language monthly in London, a bi-weekly in Toronto and a weekly in Lille in northern France. The funds made available for the War of Enlightenment are also used for totally financing or subsidizing a number of Islamic institutes and associations, mostly run by Pakistanis who are used as cover, in western Europe and North America. In addition, various Islamic liberation fronts, financed by the Party of Allah and controlled from Tehran, maintain offices in London, Paris, Bonn, Brussels, Rome and Madrid.[16] One of these 'fronts' was used in 1984 for planning a bomb attack on a Saudi Arabian civilian aircraft on a flight out of Madrid. The discovery of the plot led to the expulsion of some twenty people, including diplomats from the Iranian Embassy. An arms cache was also discovered in a safe house rented by the Embassy in a suburb of the Spanish capital.

Between 1980 and 1983 the United States was considered off limits as far as direct propaganda efforts by the Party of Allah were concerned, because the Islamic revolutionary leaders saw in President Reagan a tough adversary who ought not to be provoked. They decided to test Reagan's resolve through a series of tests outside the USA, beginning with the sporadic kidnapping of American citizens and culminating in the blowing up of the Marines' dormitory in Beirut. Reagan's refusal to retaliate against either Tehran or Damascus, which were behind all these attacks, was instantly interpreted as the green light for a resumption of propaganda activity among Muslim students, as well as black Muslims in the United States. It is worth recalling that the USA had been one of the most important breeding grounds of the Islamic Revolution outside the Middle East itself. American-educated men and women played a central role in the creation of the Shi'ite Amal organization in Lebanon, and later provided the Islamic Revolution in Iran with some of its militant cadres. The 'students' who seized the US Embassy in Tehran on 4

November 1979 were led by a group of graduates from various American universities. In 1986, American-educated militants were strongly represented in the second echelon of revolutionary leadership in the Islamic Republic. In fact the Islamic Revolution and its offshoot, the network of Holy Terror, can be described as a joint venture of radical mullahs and the alumni of various American universities.

Between 1984 and 1986 the Party of Allah steadily extended its activities in the United States. The various Muslim students' associations that had lain dormant since the hostage crisis were reactivated, and some of the militants who had temporarily withdrawn to Canada or western Europe returned to resume their activities. The branch of the Party of Allah that deals with the United States is headed by Ayatollah Muhammad Nasiri, an Iraqi-born former guerrilla trained at the PLO camp in Tyr in southern Lebanon in the 1970s. It was his close personal friendship with Khomeini's late son, Mostafa, that won him a special place in the entourage of the revolutionary leader from 1978 onwards. He entered Iran, via Turkey, illegally in the summer of 1978 and played 'a modest role' in the Islamic Revolution.[17] Between 1984 and 1986 the ayatollah visited the United States and Canada five times, ostensibly to address religious meetings, each time staying between six and nine weeks. The US authorities found nothing illegal about his visits, despite allegations by a French newspaper that Nasiri was on 'a mission to reorganize the infrastructure of terrorist operations in the region'.[18] Nasiri's time, however, was mostly taken up by his efforts to take the message of the Party of Allah to Muslim students and black Muslims. He has delivered passionate sermons to audiences of Iraqi, Iranian, Egyptian, Moroccan, Saudi, Afghan and Malaysian students in New York, Washington DC, Houston, Los Angeles, San Francisco, Chicago and Boston. His main theme is that only the Islamic Revolution can end racial discrimination and solve global economic problems.

An important contribution to the Party of Allah's propaganda efforts and recruitment of militants in Canada and the United States is made through Afghan individuals or associations. Because of the Soviet occupation of Afghanistan, citizens of that country enjoy a certain measure of sympathy as well as a variety of administrative advantages in both Canada and the United States. Afghans can thus be used to give the Party of Allah an acceptable face in countries where Khomeini has been exceptionally unpopular since the hostage crisis. The fact that most Afghan militants speak the same language as Khomeini is ignored by many Americans, who seem easily persuaded that almost any ideology is acceptable as long as it is anti-Soviet.

The Party of Allah is present in almost all Islamic countries, where embassies and consulates as well as students' associations, mosques, *takiyehs* and special schools serve as channels for its propaganda and recruitment activities.

One important base is Turkey which, because of the immense profits it made from trading with the Islamic Republic between 1981 and 1986, has been prepared to turn a blind eye to the presence on its soil of scores of Khomeinist militants serving the network of Holy Terror as informers and operatives. In 1983 agents who had entered Turkey from Iran murdered Haj Muhammad Yalfani, an Azerbaijani bazaar leader opposed to the Party of Allah and living in exile in the eastern Turkish town of Erzerum. In 1985 another group of hit men sent by the Ayatollah 'executed' Colonel Hadi Aziz-Moradi, a former officer of the Shah's army, in Ankara.[19] In the summer of 1986 two other former officers working for Bakhtiar's opposition group were murdered by 'unknown individuals' in Istanbul. One of the officers died when a bomb exploded in his hotel room. The same tactic was used when a bomb exploded in a bookshop in London's Kensington High Street, killing a young Iranian, in August 1986. The victim, Bizhan Fazeli, was the son of Reza Fazeli, a militant monarchist and opponent of Khomeini. Bizhan's 'execution' was claimed by a group calling itself 'Fedayeen of Imam Khomeini or 'Fakh'.

In Pakistan, police investigation of 'suspicious movements' in and out of the Iranian Embassy in Islamabad led to the discovery of an arms distribution network among Shi'ite groups and tribes opposed to the central government. More than ninety people, including diplomats and employees of the Embassy, were expelled between 1983 and 1986, and the Ayatollah quietly recalled his Ambassador, Commandant

Abbas Zamani, one of the founding fathers of the Revolutionary Guard and a former PLO guerrilla using the *nom de guerre* of Abu-Sharif. Between 1983 and 1986 Iranian embassies and consulates were either closed or had their activities drastically curtailed by a number of Muslim countries, among them Morocco, Egypt, Sudan, Somalia, Tunisia and Oman.

Not all the foreign activities of the Party of Allah can be directly linked with terrorism. The main objective remains propaganda, which includes intensive indoctrination courses for promising would-be militants. Once a militant has shown enough zeal and taste for action he is invited to visit the Islamic Republic, at which time the second stage in the selection process takes place. Only those who get through are offered a place on one of the many courses in practical Holy War, which range from straightforward theological studies in Qom, Mashhad and Tehran to training for guerrilla and terrorist activities in the camps described in Chapter 7. In 1986 an estimated seventeen thousand theological students from more than thirty countries, including the USSR, were attending courses of varying lengths in the Islamic Republic.[20] The vast majority of these future mullahs may never become revolutionaries on their return to their respective home countries,[21] but some at least are bound to become ardent partisans of Khomeini's message of Holy War.[22]

In 1982 a new map of the world produced by the Cartographical Society in Tehran on Mahalati's orders was presented to Khomeini. It divides the world into three regions, each shown in a different colour. The green areas, which include Soviet Central Asia, southern Spain, the islands of Malta, Lampedusa and Cyprus in the Mediterranean, Albania, parts of Yugoslavia, northeastern China, parts of Thailand, Burma, the Philippines and most of Africa, as well as the forty-one member states of the Islamic Conference,[23] represent the realm of Islam or the City of Faith. The areas in red and black depict the two versions of Dar al-Harb or the City of War – the first covers the rest of the USSR and its European satellites (except Albania), plus the rest of China, Vietnam, Laos, Kampuchea, Cuba and Ethiopia; the second, the rest of the world, is the specific realm of Great Satan America. The Iranian holy city of Qom is singled out as the 'shining heart of Islam', and Muslim countries and regions inhabited by Muslims are given their old Islamic names. All the frontiers between Muslim lands have been effaced, representing the hope that one day all Muslims will unite under Khomeini's banner, creating the third superpower to stand up to the other two, which are 'Satanic', and finally defeat them both.[24]

In the meantime, however, the Party of Allah has established its own hierarchy of priorities. The first country in which the Partisans of Allah expect to extend the rule of the Islamic republic is Iraq. In March 1986 plans for the establishment of a single government for the whole of Iraq – in the event of the latter's defeat in the war – were apparently abandoned in favour of a new scheme for dividing the country into three 'fraternal Islamic republics'.[25] A coalition of Shi'ite parties would seize control of predominantly Shi'ite southern Iraq, while the central regions, inhabited by Sunnis, would be handed over to a pro-Syrian wing of the Ba'ath party.[26] The northern regions, where the Kurds live, would be turned into a Kurdish republic under Massoud Barzani, the son of Mullah Mostafa Barzani, the great Kurdish guerrilla leader who died in 1976.[27] In the summer of 1986, however, prospects for the implementation of such a plan in the foreseeable future remained dim. The plan even divided the Iraqi mullahs opposing the Ba'athist regime in Baghdad. Hojat al-Islam Mahdi Hakim-Tabataba'i was among those who opposed the plan. He was removed as President of the High Council of the Islamic Revolution in Iraq on Khomeini's orders. His younger brother, Muhammad Baqer, replaced him. Mahdi was forced into exile in London.

The Party of Allah's hopes of success remained high, however, in the second country on its list of future conquests for the Islamic Revolution: Lebanon. Here, an exceptional coalition between Shi'ite and Sunni fundamentalists began to take shape from the beginning of 1986, with a view to mobilizing the country's Muslim majority for what Tehran believes to be 'the last stages of our Holy War to end the domination of Lebanon by Cross-worshippers and their Crusader masters'.[28] But Lebanon is not only a testing ground for the ideas of Khomeini; it also serves as a major base for

Holy Terror – in fact the single most important such base outside the Islamic Republic itself. Lebanon is also one of only two countries – the other is Syria – in which the Islamic Republic maintains military forces under its own direct command. These forces, totalling 2200 Revolutionary Guards, are camped at Zaynabiah, near Damascus, and in Lebanon at Shaikh Abd-Allah near the Syrian border and the al-Darak garrison outside Baalbek in the Bekaa Valley.[29] All these forces are under Commandant Mahmoud Kanaani, who is directly responsible to the Commander-in-Chief of the Guard in Tehran, Mohsen Reza'i; politically, however, it is the local representative of the Party of Allah who is responsible for the forces. Mohsen Rafiqdust, Minister of Revolutionary Guards, Hojat al-Islam Ghaffari and other high-ranking officials of the Party of Allah are frequent visitors to the three bases. All three are used for 'the training of Muslim revolutionaries both for Lebanon and other afflicted countries of Islam'.[30] Two smaller camps, Zebdani and the gendarmerie garrison of Baalbek, were formally handed over to local militia groups early in 1986, but remain under the political control of Tehran.

The Party of Allah's theoreticians see the 1980s basically as 'an era of sowing the seeds of tomorrow'.[31] What is important is to take the message of the Islamic Revolution to as many Muslims as possible. This message, offered on tapes and in books, newspapers and radio programmes in many languages, is backed by the financial, political and military might of Iran, which is emerging as 'the new superpower of the Persian Gulf', according to some Western analysts.[32] In an Arabic booklet,[33] the Party of Allah states its objectives as follows: (1) To teach Muslims that Islam and impiety can never coexist. (2) To mobilize the forces of Islam for Holy War unto victory. (3) To teach every Muslim that his duty towards his Creator includes readiness to kill and to die. (4) To make sure that all the rules of Islam are obeyed in Muslim countries down to the minutest detail.

The Party of Allah is not the party of the meek and faint-hearted, nor is it a gathering place of those who look on war as an abomination to be eliminated from human existence. In an address to fundamentalist militants from more than thirty countries gathered at his house in Jamaran on the birthday of the Prophet Muhammad, Khomeini himself summed up the message of the Party of Allah.

> If one allows the infidels to continue playing their role of corrupters on Earth, their eventual moral punishment will be all the stronger. Thus, if we kill the infidels in order to put a stop to their [corrupting] activities, we have indeed done them a service. For their eventual punishment will be less. To allow the infidels to stay alive means to let them do more corrupting [activities]. [To kill them] is a surgical operation commanded by Allah the Creator. . . . Those who follow the rules of the Qur'an are aware that we have to apply the laws of Qissas [retribution] and that we have to kill. . . . War is a blessing for the world and for every nation. It is Allah himself who commands men to wage war and to kill. The Qur'an commands: 'Wage war until all corruption and all disobedience [of divine law] are wiped out!'
>
> The wars that our Prophet – blessed be his soul – waged against the infidels were divine gifts to humanity. Once we have won the war [against Iraq] we shall turn to other wars. For that would not be enough. We have to wage war until all corruption, all disobedience of Islamic laws cease [throughout the world]. The Qur'an commands: 'War, war unto victory!'[34] A religion without war is a crippled religion. Had Jesus – Allah bless his soul – been allowed to live a little longer, he too would have acted as Moses did and used the sword. . . . It is war that purifies the Earth. Those courtier mullahs who say [war] is contrary to the rules of the Holy Book are enemies of Islam. But Allah be praised, our young warriors are putting his command into effect and fighting. They know that to kill the infidels is one of the noblest missions Allah has reserved for mankind.[35]

One of the many revolutionary sermons available to Arab Muslims on cassette tapes sold throughout the Gulf States deals with the theme of fear.

> The basis of the power of those who rule you is fear. Your kings frighten you. Your prime ministers and presidents frighten you. Your army jackboots frighten you. Your fat, rich bosses frighten you. Your bejewelled whores imitating Western whores inspire in you a sense of awe. You are scared even of looking at those luxurious palaces where every single imaginable act of lust is practised day and night. You dare not cross the road when those huge, expensive limousines appear on the horizon. You are scared

> of asking where all that money comes from – all that money which is gambled or spent on voluptuous blonde women. You do not find enough courage to demand what war those jackboots who call themselves commanders and marshals and such things have ever seen – except on their colour TV sets. Yes, you are scared to death. They have taken your guts away. They tell you that Islam means nothing but praying five times a day and fasting during Ramadan. They tell you that Islam means obedience to authority even when that authority consists of decadent filth. They tell you that if you protest, America, the Great Satan, will come and puff fire on you and all will vanish! The so-called wise ones, wearing ties and spectacles and putting themselves forward as doctors of law and of philosophy, tell you that only this or that Western idea can cure your ills, and for that you have to be patient. You have to be patient while those who say these things to you lick the boots of kings and presidents to be invited to their Sodom and Gomorrah parties. . . . But all you have to do is return to the Qur'an, to the very source of your existence, to the reason for which God created you in the first place. You are the downtrodden of this Earth. Does not Allah command you to kill those who rebel against His will? Are you incapable even of using a simple knife or a simple shotgun? Think! Act! Think and act before fear eats you all up, turning you into an empty shell of a man. . . .[36]

Pilgrims to the 'waiting room of Paradise' start their guided tour of the Islamic Republic with a visit to the Behesht Zahra (Paradise of Flowers) graveyard south of Tehran. There they are invited to stand for a minute's silence in front of the Fountain of Blood, a 4.5 metre-high fountain out of which surges a blood-red liquid, symbolizing, in the words of the guide, the essence of Islam's message. At the end of the minute's silence, a choir of child warriors recites a revolutionary song whose refrain is '*Khomeini Mi Razmad! Amrika Mi Larzad!* ('Khomeini fights! America trembles!'). Many visitors have tears in their eyes, tears of joy and determination. Some end up as Volunteers for Martyrdom, keeping the camps of Holy Terror busy.

9

The Brides of Blood

Child: Mother dear! When will I be old enough to drive a truck?
Mother: Why do you ask, dear one?
Child: Because I long to fill a truck with explosives and drive it into one of the strongholds of the infidel in our country!

Al-Amal[1]

25 March 1986. The ar-Raza mosque, in southern Beirut's Bir-Abed district, is teeming with people: mullahs with black or white turbans engaged in what look like passionate discussions; bearded militiamen in khaki caressing their Kalashnikovs while keeping an eye on everyone else; teenage Volunteers for Martyrdom, distinguished by their crimson headbands; bearded men, young and old, everywhere, playing with their worry beads or chatting the moments away in what seems a relaxed gathering of friends. Every now and then *sakis* serving a sherbet made of rosewater, sugar and a hint of cinnamon pass among the rows of seated believers, all facing the pulpit, to offer them goblets of the delicious mixture. This is a special occasion and the audience has been waiting for more than an hour to hear a special sermon. There seem to be no women around, and yet today's gathering is being held to honour a group of young women who bear the awesome title of Arous ad-Damm or the Brides of Blood.

Who are these Brides of Blood who have secured a unique place in Shi'ite mythology? Not every female could aspire to so distinguished a position: one has to be marked out for it by divine will. The Brides of Blood are pure virgins who have decided to embrace death in order to avenge the blood of Hussein, who fell – a martyr – on the battlefield of Karbala on 10 October 680. The Brides of Blood are considered to be daughters of the Prince of the Martyrs[2] and, once in the next world, will have their husbands chosen for them by Hussein from among 'the most pious and shapely of young men, free of all blemish'.[3]

A hush falls on the congregation as a group of women, all veiled and wearing black, arrive in the hall. They are led to the harem part of the mosque, a section of the hall cordoned off by thick grey curtains. There they will hear the sermon, but will neither see the men nor be seen by them.[4] They are women of every age group, but all wear an expression of grim determination. Some are mothers, sisters, grandmothers or cousins of those Brides of Blood who have already fulfilled their heroic destiny. Others are young women who have put their names down for martyrdom.

Today's congregation has assembled more specifically to pay its respects to two Brides of Blood who in 1985 accomplished 'the highest duty of every Muslim', which is 'to kill and to die for the Faith'.[5] Both were still in their teens at the time they embarked on their *me'eraj*.[6] They did not know each other, but both were children of uprooted Shi'ite families from southern Lebanon and had grown up in the sprawling, rat-infested slums of West Beirut. They belonged to two different political groups, but were both considered to be 'daughters of the Party of Allah'.

The first, Sumayah Sa'ad, had joined the Party of Allah's Sayyedah Zaynab Brigade – named after Hussein's sister and the first of several female Shi'ite commando groups – in 1983 when she had just turned sixteen. Longing to die and to kill, she had volunteered for the Entehari (suicide) operation against the American Marines' dormitory in Beirut, and had at first been accepted and trained for that mission. At the last moment, however, her commanders decided that the mission should be carried out by a man. Sumayah's chance to become a Bride of Blood came more than two years later, when on 10 March 1985 she was allowed to drive a car loaded with dynamite into an Israeli military position in southern Lebanon. The fifth confirmed Entehari attack on Israeli positions in southern Lebanon since 1982, it killed twelve Israeli soldiers and wounded fourteen others.[7] Two months later Sumayah's widowed mother and her brother were invited to the Islamic Republic, where they were received by Ayatollah Khomeini. A major street in Tehran was named after Sumayah, 'the heroine of Islam'.

The second Bride of Blood to be honoured was San'ah Muheidli, who had just turned seventeen on the eve of her Entehari mission. She left her home in the Mussaitabah suburb of West Beirut on 25 March, ostensibly to do some shopping. But she never returned. On 9 April she drove a Peugeot loaded with TNT into an Israeli military convoy in southern Lebanon, killing two enemy soldiers and wounding two more. Her own body was 'scattered all over the place'. San'ah had been a native of the south Lebanese Shi'ite village of Aqnun, which for years had suffered from both Israeli and PLO military incursions. Before going on her mission San'ah conformed to the rules governing all volunteers for martyrdom and prepared her will. Instead of pen and paper she chose a videotape, which has become 'a cherished part of Islamic history'.[8] The teenage Entehari told her mother, and through her the entire community of the faithful, to 'be merry, to let your joy explode as if it were my wedding day'.[9] She was instantly declared a 'national heroine' in Lebanon, and has since been the subject of many poems and short stories praising her deed.[10] To the Algerian fundamentalist writer Hamzah Kaidi, what she and Sumayah did amounted to 'acts that elevate war to the level of love'.[11]

Neither of the two Brides of Blood had given their families the slightest hint about the kind of destiny they were planning for themselves. Both knew the art of keeping a secret, one of the highest virtues extolled by the Prophet himself.[12] Perhaps only the leaders of the Party of Allah know exactly how many Brides of Blood the martyr Hussein has in Shi'ite Lebanon; but even the most sanguine observer of the Lebanese saga of desolation and death must realize that the number of 'chaste and pure maidens' aspiring to join Sumayah and San'ah is more than Khomeini needs to fulfil his dream of fighting what he considers 'the last stage of the historical Crusades' in Lebanon. For to the Party of Allah and its Supreme Guide the Crusades never came to an end. The Crusaders left behind the Lebanese Christians – referred to as Nazarenes by Muslims – to guard a bridgehead for the 'infidel' West. Lebanon must be reconquered by Islam and ruled in accordance with the rules of the Qur'an. 'We cannot prepare for the liquidation of Israel without restoring the rule of Islam to another, equally important, portion of the Muslim homeland, which is Lebanon,' states a Party of Allah editorial. 'Christians can, of course, continue to live in Lebanon and benefit from full protection in accordance with the law of the Qur'an. They will be treated fairly, as are all minorities under Islam.'[13]

The idea of ending the domination of Lebanon by Christians had preoccupied Shi'ite leaders long before the invasion of that country by Israel in 1982. During the 1958 civil war in Lebanon, for example, several grand ayatollahs called for volunteers from all over the Islamic world to take arms against 'the Cross-worshippers of Shaam and their foreign backers'.[14] In fact one of the declared objectives of Mussa Sadr, at the start of his mission to Lebanon in 1961, was to put an end to the sequels of the civil war that had dealt Lebanese Muslims a serious blow, largely because of the intervention of US Marines invited by Camille Chamoun, the Maronite President of the Republic. But it was not until Khomeini's revolution in Iran that the prospects of an 'Islamic' government of some form or other in Lebanon came to be taken seriously.

Between the 1958 civil war and Khomeini's revolution in 1979, Lebanese Shi'ites experienced a dramatic transformation. Thanks to an exceptionally high birth rate they emerged as the single largest confessional community in the country.[15] They also came into direct contact with the Palestinian revolution. At first it fascinated them: they saw, for the first time in generations, that the ability to wage war was not the exclusive prerogative of either the Christians or the dreaded Druzes of the mountains, and that they too, inspired by the Palestinian example, could one day take up arms. But that contact ended in deep hostility between the Shi'ites of Lebanon and the Palestinian fighters who, together with their families, were imposed on Lebanon as 'guests' by Egypt's President Nasser. Yasser Arafat's men proved to be rather relaxed about their Islamic duties and spoke of socialism, of Marx and Lenin and other alien concepts, and of 'heroes'. They also felt under no obligation – especially when crates of whisky, all gifts from friendly embassies in Beirut, arrived in the south – to respect the women in the Shi'ite villages. Young Shi'ites learned to fight from Palestinian guerrillas, but their leaders secretly cooperated with Israel. Both Israel and the Shi'ites wanted Arafat's men out of southern Lebanon, though for different reasons. 'Shi'ites are our best friends in Lebanon,' Israeli officials liked to boast, and still do in private. The 1982 Israeli invasion of Lebanon was initially welcomed, and to a certain extent helped, by the Shi'ites.[16]

With the Palestinian 'state within the state' eliminated from Lebanon as a result of the Israeli intervention in 1982, prospects for the creation of a new Lebanese national entente began to be discussed by the leaders of all faiths in the country. Perhaps not quite all – for a strong Shi'ite undercurrent was already making itself felt against the conservative leadership of the community. This contested leadership was symbolized by two men. On the religious side it was Shaikh Muhammad Mahdi Shamseddin, who did not share Khomeini's dream of removing all frontiers between Islamic countries. Shamseddin, an eminent theologian who has been teaching Shi'ite law for over thirty years, is not a descendant of the Prophet – hence his white turban – but has all the other qualities required for claiming the mantle of the missing Imam Sadr.[17] As Vice-President of the High Council of Shi'ism in Lebanon he was Sadr's heir-apparent until the wind of the Islamic Revolution changed everything. In an astute manoeuvre aimed at preventing Shamseddin from being declared Imam, the pro-Khomeini faction spread the myth that the missing Sadr was still alive and would in time return to resume leadership. Those who know Shamseddin well often compare him to the late Iranian Grand Ayatollah Sayyed Muhammad-Kazem Shariatmadari, who could not persuade himself that the ends justify the means and was therefore crushed by Khomeini in the course of the Islamic Revolution.[18] By all accounts, Shamseddin is the most erudite and authoritative of Lebanese Shi'ite theologians and one of the few to enjoy approval from the traditional grand ayatollahs of Najaf and Qom.

But by 1986 Shamseddin, who seems to hate talking and prefers to spend as much time praying as he does on anything else, was simply in the wrong game. To win the mantle of Sadr, the supreme turban of authority, he was required to use the entire arsenal of tricks authorized in Shi'ite strategy – but he would have none of that. He seemed to have missed his chance for ever, remaining in the game, so to speak, only thanks to his association with Nabih Berri, the politico-military leader of the Amal (Hope) militia.

Berri's emergence as an internationally recognized political leader of the Shi'ites in Lebanon was at least partly due to a strong helping hand from both the United States and Israel. Berri, born in Sierra Leone and educated in the United States, had to divorce his American wife in order to silence criticism fomented by the Khomeinists. Berri, no pan-Islamist, is interested in seeing Lebanon reorganized as a republic in which the Shi'ites would enjoy political power in proportion to their numerical strength. In other words, he sees no reason why Lebanon should not one day have a Shi'ite president. What distinguishes him from the Party of Allah in Lebanon is that he is prepared to consider the Christians and the Druzes the full equals of Shi'ites as far as political rights are concerned. This is anathema to the Party of Allah which, as already noted, wants to establish an Islamic republic.

Will Berri one day have to choose the fate either of Sadeq Ghotbzadeh or of Abol-Hassan Bani-Sadr?[19] The question remained topical in 1986 despite Berri's success in staying at the head of Amal for nearly four years.[20] In any case, the Party of Allah has already designated a 'volunteer' who would, when the time comes, try to assassinate Berri; more than twenty other moderate Shi'ite leaders are also on the Party of Allah's death list in Lebanon.[21] The man designated to kill Berri could be any one of his personal bodyguards, or he could be an Entehari sent down from Baalbek to carry out the sentence of death.

The split in Lebanese Shi'ism and the subsequent emergence there of the Party of Allah came in 1982 after a three-man delegation of Khomeinists visited the Islamic Republic on a special 'revolutionary guided tour'. The three were Shaikh Ragheb Harb, a firebrand mullah who advocated the declaration of Lebanon as a province of the Islamic Republic, Hussein Mussawi, an adjutant of Berri's and Amal's official spokesman, and Sayyed Ibrahim al-Amin, who had once served as private secretary to the missing Imam Sadr.

In Tehran they met Ayatollah Mahalati, whose title at the time was Representative of the Imam in the Revolutionary Guard, and were told that it was only by organizing a branch of the Party of Allah that they could hope to benefit from Tehran's financial and political support. A compromise was finally reached, under which Mussawi would create a breakaway branch of Amal in order to keep alive the memory of the missing Sadr and use it for political purposes, while Harb would create the first secret groups of the Party of Allah.

Returning to Beirut, the extremist trio encountered little difficulty in finding a mullah of sufficient stature to endorse their project. Sayyed Muhammad-Hussein Fadhl-Allah was an eminent scholar hiding his revolutionary fervour behind an appearance of enigmatic calm, and by 1986 he was established as the spiritual guide of the Lebanese branch of the Party of Allah. Born in 1936, in the holy city of Karbala in Iraq, to a Lebanese father and an Iraqi mother, he decided at an early age to become a mullah and move to the holy city of Najaf, where he became a pupil of several grand ayatollahs with conflicting visions of Shi'ism and the political role it should play.[22] A brilliant *talabeh* or seeker, he began writing and publishing learned essays on the lives of the Twelve Imams and their respective interpretations of the doctrine long before he could claim the title of Hojat al-Islam (Vicar of Islam). Returning to Lebanon early in 1960 – almost at the same time that Sadr was settling down in Beirut – Fadhl-Allah inaugurated an informal club called Usrat al-Ta'akhi (Circle of Fraternity), in which a group of some twenty young mullahs, including Harb and al-Amin, studied and debated the main problems of the Faith.

Two major currents of influence can be detected in Fadhl-Allah's thinking. The first is that of the Pakistani Mawlana Abul-Ala Mawdoodi who, writing in Arabic, was the first to develop the idea of an Islamic state. The second belongs to Muhammad Nawab-Safavi's Fedayeen of Islam, who developed the practice of clandestine work in the service of the cause. Fadhl-Allah's Usrat possessed no weapons and its members did not train for missions of political assassination, but the cabbalistic style of their organization and its militant fundamentalism recalled the Fedayeen, at least in their earlier days.

Fadhl-Allah constantly denies being a leader of the Party of Allah. In saying this, however, he is taking advantage of the Shi'ite tradition of *taqiyah*, by which the faithful can conceal the truth in order to protect the higher interests of the community. Strictly speaking, Fadhl-Allah is not a leader of the Party of Allah for the simple reason that the party does not exist in the generally accepted meaning of the term. No membership cards are issued, and no annual conferences are held. There is no central committee, no politburo and no general secretary. The Party of Allah is as much of a mood in Lebanon as it is in the Islamic Republic. Fadhl-Allah, basing himself on Khomeini's pronouncements in Tehran, sets the course for a certain type of action by Shi'ites in Lebanon. Those who take that line are considered members of the Party of Allah, while those who act differently are described as 'misguided'.

Members of the Party of Allah are free to organize themselves in whatever way they deem best. Some are members of circles that meet once or twice a week for Qur'anic studies and discussions. Others create clandestine terrorist cells to eliminate the enemies of the Faith. Still others belong to fairly large militia groups, the largest of which is called al-Amal al-Islami (Islamic Hope) and is headed by Hussein Mussawi. Operating from its headquarters in Baalbek, in a part of Lebanon under Syrian military occupation, the Islamic Amal trains members of smaller militias or secret cells and coordinates their activities.

Mussawi, a former chemistry teacher in his early forties, has no more than 1200 armed men under his command, but he knows that he has the weight of the Islamic Republic behind him. Sitting under a huge portrait of Khomeini, Mussawi makes no secret of his total devotion to the Imam. Years of Syrian efforts to woo him away from Iran have failed, and Mussawi speaks with confidence of the 'imminent emergence of an Islamic state' in Lebanon.

Western Intelligence has traced many of the terrorist attacks in Lebanon since June 1982 to Mussawi and other militia groups or secret terrorist cells linked with the Islamic Republic. Mussawi has made no effort to deny these charges. On the contrary, he has shown a curious taste for announcing

The 'Imam'. Ayatollah Ruhollah Khomeini addresses a crowd at his residence in north Tehran. The Party of Allah considers him as the 'Imam' or the leader of the entire Moslem community in the world (*P. Ledru/Sygma: John Hillelson Agency Ltd*).

LEFT *The heart of the revolution.* Believers gather in the holy shrine of Maasoumah at Qom, south of Tehran, to mourn a grand ayatollah. The city is the heart of the revolution launched by the partisans of Holy Terror to conquer the world (*Frank Spooner Pictures*).

FAR LEFT *Commander of the 'Enteharis'.* Hojat al-Islam Muhammad Taqi Mudarressi makes a point in a sermon. He is the head of the suicide squads ready to kill and die for the Imam (*Jeune Afrique/Gamma/Frank Spooner Pictures*).

RIGHT *Spiritual leader of Holy Terror.* Sayyed Muhammad Hussein Fadhl-Allah leader of the Shi'ite hardliners in Lebanon delivers a sermon (*Camera Press*).

ABOVE *Soldier of Allah.* Hussein Mussawi, leader of the Islamic Amal (Hope) Organisation controls the largest armed group of the Party of Allah in northern Lebanon. He describes himself as a disciple of Khomeini and admits that his group participated in 'acts of war' against Westerners in Lebanon (*John Hillelson*).

RIGHT *Getting ready.* Theological students at Qom seminary. Most study the Qur'an and the sayings of the Prophet. Some, however, use Islam to achieve the goals of the revolution launched by Khomeini (*Gamma/Frank Spooner Pictures*).

LEFT *Forest of the Martyrs.* Two mourners walk through the graveyard at Behesht e Zahra, near Tehran, which is reserved for the martyrs of the Party of Allah (*John Hillelson*).

Hostage-holders. Party of Allah gunmen pose for a photograph somewhere in Lebanon. They took part in the hi-jacking of an American passenger aircraft. A portrait of the missing Imam Mussa Sadr is in the background (*Magnum/John Hillelson*).

BELOW LEFT *Iranian in Lebanon.* Imam Mussa Sadr, an Iranian Mullah who became the architect of the Shi'ite revival in Lebanon, is still considered by the Party of Allah as a 'leader'. Eight years after his disappearance during an official visit to Libya at the invitation of Colonel Gaddafi, his supporters believe he is still alive (*AP Wire photo*).

ABOVE RIGHT *Seeking the missing Imam.* Fundamentalist women demonstrate in Beirut, Lebanon, to demand the return of their 'missing' Imam Mussa Sadr, believed to have been murdered in Libya in 1978 (*John Hillelson Agency Ltd*).

The army of 'twenty million'. A group of female soldiers of Allah march in a Tehran street. They form part of the nucleus of 'the army of twenty million' which Khomeini hopes to raise before the end of the decade in order to 'liberate the whole of Islam' (*Frank Spooner Pictures*).

Women's day in Tehran. Armed women belonging to the Zaynab Commando Squads march through the streets of Tehran. They are not allowed to remove the chador even on the battlefield (*Gamma/Frank Spooner Pictures*).

He brought a message. Father Lawrence Jenco, an American priest who was held hostage by Holy Terror in Lebanon, was freed in July 1986 with a message for the American government. In the publicity that followed revelations concerning the message, the hostage-holders denied having sent any message at all and hardened their position vis-a-vis their other captives (*Gamma/Frank Spooner Pictures*).

Holy Terror hostage. American journalist Terry Anderson is one of several western journalists kidnapped and held hostage by the network of Holy Terror in Lebanon (*AP*).

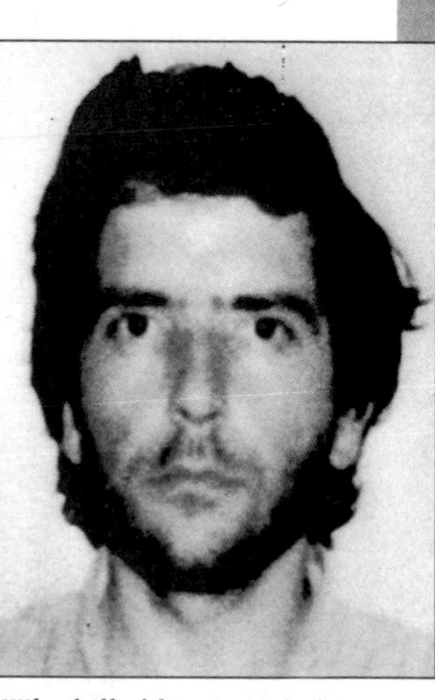

Who killed him? Michel Seurat, a French researcher in Lebanon, was 'executed' by his captors in 1986. According to some reports he died under interrogation attended by members of Syrian Intelligence (*AP*).

Murdered by Holy Terror. British journalist Alex Collett was murdered by the Partisans of Allah in Lebanon. He was 64 at the time of his murder (*AP*).

They killed the 'Pharaoh'. Members of an Islamic Jihad group that organised and carried out the assassination of Egyptian President Muhammad Anwar Sadat on the first day of their trial in Cairo. They attended the trial in a huge iron cage (*Sygma/John Hillelson Agency Ltd*).

Mourning the Prince of Martyrs. Lebanese Shi'ites performing a mourning ceremony in memory of Imam Hussein, the third Imam of Shi'ism who has the title of 'the Prince of Martyrs' (*Magnum/John Hillelson Ltd*).

After the explosion. Marines rescue one of their comrades after the terrorist attack on the US military base in Lebanon in 1983. The attackers, driving two trucks laden with explosives into the building, caused what is described as 'the single biggest non-nuclear explosion in the world since World War II' (*AP*).

Repaid in kind. A young Shi'ite helps the survivor of a bomb blast in Beirut. Opponents of the Party of Allah at times use its own tactics against it (*AP*).

some of his most dramatic intentions. In spring 1983, for example, he announced the launching of a campaign to force both Israel and the United States, together with Britain, France and Italy, to withdraw their troops from Lebanon. The threat was summarily dismissed by Western and Israeli Intelligence, but Mussawi was to prove true to his word.

In April a two-man commando of Enteharis drove a car loaded with explosives into the chancellery of the United States Embassy in Beirut. Sixty-nine people died, including several high-ranking agents of the CIA in the Middle East who had gathered in the Lebanese capital for a secret seminar. Beirut had apparently been chosen as the venue because the CIA thought that the presence of US Marines automatically assured the safety of the participants. A few months later it was the turn of the Marines themselves to be directly targeted in a suicide attack. This time the French paratroopers who formed part of the so-called Multi-national Force (MNF) also figured on the Entehari hit list. In two simultaneous attacks on 23 October 1983 the suicide men killed 241 American Marines and 58 French paras.

The explosion caused by the suicide attack on the Marines' headquarters in Beirut has been described by American experts as 'the single largest non-nuclear blast on Earth since World War II'.[23] According to FBI forensic scientists, more than six tons of explosives were used in what was instantly characterized as 'the single most effective terrorist attack in Middle East history'.[24] The driver of the yellow truck loaded with dynamite smiled at a Marine guarding the gate before slamming the deadly vehicle into the massive four-storey building, turning it into a pile of rubble mixed with human flesh and bone. This was the so-called *bassamat al-farah* or 'smile of joy' which, according to Shi'ite tradition, the martyr wears at the time of accomplishing his duty.

The epidemic of suicide attacks continued on 4 November with another Entehari commando destroying the headquarters of the Israeli forces in Tyr, in the south, killing sixty-seven people, including thirty-two Lebanese prisoners of war. The Reagan administration in Washington, badly shaken by the attacks but unable or unwilling to retaliate directly, encouraged the Israelis and the French to 'punish the terrorists'. On 16 November an Israeli raid on Mussawi's stronghold claimed sixteen lives, mostly women and children. The following day it was the turn of the French to act. Fourteen Super-Etendard heavy bombers, taking off from the aircraft carrier *Clemenceau* just off Beirut harbour, roared into the sky above the Bekaa Valley in a show of force. Two of the planes launched clusters of rockets over the Shaikh Abd-Allah garrison buildings, which housed Mussawi's militiamen together with some Iranian Revolutionary Guards. More than thirty people lost their lives in the attack. The forces of 'Satan' were playing their part in the drama by giving the Party of Allah the martyrs it so badly needed in order to legitimize its own use of terror in Lebanon. The American media gave the Israeli and French attacks a generally favourable reception, which encouraged Reagan to order a punitive operation of his own. On 14 and 15 December the giant battleship *New Jersey*, wallowing near the Lebanese coast like a sea monster, bombarded parts of the Bekaa Valley controlled by the Party of Allah.

The attacks were greeted in Tehran as a sign of Allah's special favour for Khomeini's dream of extending his rule to Lebanon, since they instantly transformed what had hitherto been regarded as a hotch-potch of extremist groups into the main force of opposition to the presence of foreign forces in the country. 'Only we can force the infidel out of this land,' boasted Mussawi.[25] In accordance with the tradition created by the revolutionary mullahs of Tehran, Mussawi, accompanied by Harb, Amin and another turbaned militant, Subhi Tufeili, visited the relatives of the martyrs to 'congratulate them on the honour that has descended upon their house'. There was to be no mourning, and the burial of the martyrs was accompanied by shouts of joy from the members of Sayyedeh Zaynab's Brigade, brought in for the occasion. Suddenly the rivals of the Party of Allah, from Berri to Sayyed Hussein al-Husseini, the rising star of centrist Shi'ites, appeared as dwarfs compared to the giants within the Party of Allah who had proved capable of provoking not only Israel but Presidents Reagan and Mitterand – both described as 'the main chiefs of Crusaders in the world'.[26]

Since the first suicide attack on the US Embassy building in

Beirut, the Party of Allah has used the term Islamic Jihad or Holy War as a signature in claiming each action. This has led to the assumption in the West that Islamic Jihad is a structured terrorist organization distinct from the Party of Allah. In reality, however, the term covers a variety of operational terrorist groups within the Party of Allah. A study of some of the most important terrorist attacks against Western interests since 1983 shows that at least eight different groups have been involved, most of which do not seem to have any structured and regular relationship with one another beyond a deep ideological affinity. With the exception of some key operations which involved Syrian and Iranian Intelligence services, at least at the planning level and in providing necessary logistical support, the groups in question seemed to have almost total operational independence. For guidance on important political and ideological questions, as well as to obtain the religious authority needed for any act of Jihad or Holy War, the various commando groups look to an informal High Council of Islamic Jihad for Lebanon.

The High Council, often referred to as Majlis al-Shawra or Consultative Assembly, met in full only on very rare occasions between February 1983, when it was first constituted on Mahalati's orders, and 1986. But smaller meetings take place frequently, and telephone contact among members can occur daily. It is quite possible that members of the High Council have never had detailed information about every individual operation carried out in their name by the commandos of Holy Terror. The most senior theologian on the Council is of course Fadhl-Allah. He has at his side five other Lebanese mullahs: Subhi al-Tufeili, Ibrahim al-Amin, Abbas Mussawi (a cousin of Hussein), Muhammad Yazbeq and Hussein al-Khalili. Shaikh Ragheb Harb was also a member of the Council until his murder, almost certainly by the agents of the Israeli secret service, MOSSAD, in 1984. Other members of the Council are Hussein Mussawi, Abd-Allah Nasr-Allah (in charge of the military services of the Party of Allah), Haj Muhammad Emad (who looks after security problems), Muqaddar Hilwan and Abdul-Fattah Kamal. The Islamic Republic is represented by Hussein Ahromi-Zadeh, military attaché at the Iranian

Embassy in Damascus, and Nasr-Allah Nurani, Iranian chargé d'affaires in Beirut.

Until 1985 the Iranian Embassy in Damascus was the nerve centre of Tehran's campaign to export the Ayatollah's revolution. The Ambassador, Ali-Akbar Mohtashami, who enjoyed direct access to Khomeini, orchestrated the operations of the Party of Allah in Lebanon, Syria and Jordan. The Syrians had given him virtual *carte blanche* in the use of his diplomatic privileges, and during 1983 thousands of tons of goods, including arms as well as propaganda material, arrived at the Embassy in containers labelled 'diplomatic mail'. A Bulgarian trucking company, carrying the Ayatollah's 'diplomatic mail' from Tehran to Damascus via Turkey, must have made a good profit. The Damascus Embassy also enjoyed the biggest budget ever allocated to any Iranian mission abroad. In 1983 alone, the ayatollah-ambassador had at his disposal the equivalent of 400 million US dollars.[27] The number of people listed as Embassy employees topped two hundred. Most of these 'diplomats', bearded and going around with submachine guns hanging from their shoulders, spent much of their time in Lebanon.

The Syrians, who had gone out of their way to help the Islamic Republic export its revolution to Lebanon, began to have doubts about the wisdom of their policy as early as the autumn of 1983, at a time when they were still quietly celebrating their success in forcing the United States to withdraw from Lebanon. The suicide attacks that forced the Multi-national Force out of Lebanon could not have been planned without the direct participation of Syrian Intelligence services. The Party of Allah, offering more passion than intelligence, would have had no means of finding out the necessary details about the buildings to be attacked, the way those buildings were guarded and the time schedules observed by their victims. Only Syrian Intelligence, with its vast and well-entrenched network in Lebanon, could have done that. Syrian help was also essential in securing, transporting and storing the type of explosives required for the operations.[28]

The Syrians, however, would have been unable to carry out such operations through their traditional terror groups, which, consisting of regular agents of General Ali Dibbah's secret service, were effective only in murdering President Assad's political enemies in the dark – and that only when assured of being able to get away safely. Syria could also use the services of contract killers in Beirut.[29] But it could not find anyone prepared to give his life for President Assad – that type of person, the Entehari, could be supplied only by Khomeini. The joint venture made sense for Syria as long as it remained the main and more immediate beneficiary of every suicide attack while the Islamic Republic, lacking diplomatic and Intelligence experience, failed to reap all it had sown.

The situation began to change towards the end of 1983. Mohtashami, by then aware of the real power he wielded, began keeping more and more of his secrets to himself. The Party of Allah, on the other hand, manifested a momentum that clearly worried the Syrians. Tehran began speaking openly of the need to create an Islamic republic in Lebanon, while Assad, who describes himself as a socialist, based his policy on the creation of a broad coalition of groups from various faiths practised in Lebanon under Syrian suzerainty. But Mohtashami's most serious mistake was, perhaps, the secret contact he established with Sunni fundamentalists dedicated to the overthrow of Assad's Ba'athist regime. These links were at first assured through Shaikh Sa'id Sha'aban, leader of the Sunni fundamentalists in the northern Lebanese city of Tripoli. But very quickly Mohtashami felt confident enough to establish direct ties with the Syrian branch of the Muslim Brotherhood which, unlike the Egyptian branch, advocates policies similar to those defended by Khomeini.[30]

Assad decided that Mohtashami must go. Demanding his recall from Tehran, however, could lead to an open diplomatic rift. Mohtashami, strongly endorsed by Mahalati, was the key man in Khomeini's first successful attempt at exporting his revolution. Damascus had to communicate its message in a different way, which it did the following year when Mohtashami received a special gift – a precious, illuminated edition of the Qur'an – through the mail. The ayatollah opened the parcel personally and began leafing through the book. Within seconds, a charge of dynamite in the binding exploded. The ayatollah was seriously injured and had to be flown to West Germany for an emergency operation. He survived though he lost the fingers of his left hand – and had to stay away from Damascus for several months. He then seemed to find the climate of the Syrian capital unsuited to his nature, and returned to Tehran where he replaced the pro-Libyan Ayatollah Ali-Akbar Nateq-Nuri as Minister of the Interior.

Since Mohtashami's return to Tehran his role as co-ordinator of operations in Lebanon has been handled by a committee whose members are frequent visitors to Damascus and Beirut. Heading the committee is Ayatollah Mahdi Karrubi, President of the Martyrs' Foundation, who is in charge of the financial aspects of Tehran's support for the Party of Allah in Lebanon. On his first mission to Beirut in 1984, Karrubi provoked much curiosity by handing out more than 3 million US dollars that he had brought with him in cash. But it did not take him long to learn more discreet methods of giving the 'downtrodden' a financial boost.

The key member of the committee as far as paramilitary operations are concerned is Commandant Kan'ani, who seems to be quietly pursuing his policy of creating a full-scale guerrilla army of Shi'ites in Lebanon. He has succeeded in gaining control of various Sunni militia groups known as the Jund-Allah (Soldiers of Allah), and in the autumn of 1986 was trying to merge them with the Party of Allah to create a pan-Islamic force.[31] The committee's liaison officer with Syria is Hussein Shaikh al-Islam, whose official title is Deputy Foreign Minister but whose real job is to export Khomeini's revolution.

'Shaikh', as he is known in fundamentalist circles, was born in Tehran in 1957 and spent some time studying at the University of California at Berkeley. As an active member of the Muslim Students' Association in the United States he was picked by Chamran as a future militant and received guerrilla training in southern Lebanon in 1977. After the Islamic Revolution he became a founding member of the group of 'Muslim Students Following the Imam's Line' who raided the United States Embassy compound and seized diplomatic hostages. During the hostage crisis Shaikh – who was referred to by the captive diplomats as 'Gap Tooth' because of a hole in his upper row of teeth – was in charge of interrogations. He later helped found the publishing firm that produced sixty-three volumes of secret or restricted documents seized at the US Embassy.

According to American Intelligence, Shaikh was intimately involved in the planning of the suicide attack on the US Embassy in Beirut as well as that on the Marines' headquarters in 1983. He was in fact in Damascus at the time, ostensibly to put the final touches to the plans worked out with Syrian participation.[32] But it seems unlikely that Shaikh would have been informed about the exact nature of such operations. Neither senior enough, nor trusted enough by the mullahs to be allowed any role that requires him to act on his own initiative, he seems to have been included in the informal committee only to reassure the Syrians that Tehran would make no move in Lebanon without consulting Syria – its 'strategic ally'.[33] The fact that Tehran used other high-ranking members of the Iranian Foreign Ministry for contact with the Party of Allah in Lebanon in 1986 may be taken to mean that Shaikh al-Islam's membership of the committee is mainly a matter of bureaucratic convenience.[34]

Relations between Syria and the Islamic Republic began to show signs of strain from the end of 1984. The decline in Tehran's oil revenues, due to falling demand and prices, prevented the mullahs from offering Damascus the kind of financial subsidy that President Assad expected from his revolutionary allies. But it was Lebanon that indirectly provided the core of the increasingly open conflict between Khomeini and Assad. The Islamic Republic rejected all Syria's attempts to stabilize the situation in Lebanon, and from the end of 1985 began ordering the Party of Allah to 'expose and depose' elements suspected of working for the Syrians. The slogan 'Only one party, the Party of Allah! Only one leader, Ruhollah!' became the war cry of Khomeinists who purged from their ranks scores of militants accused of pro-Syrian sentiments. The split between Tehran and Damascus over Lebanon dramatically reduced the ability of the two 'allies' to act against their common opponents in the war-torn country.

The rift between Tehran and Damascus over Lebanon meant, at least temporarily, a halt in suicide attacks and other spectacular acts of terrorism. In 1986 neither country was in a position to make use of such methods alone, though both were trying to develop independent facilities of their own. It is not difficult to imagine that once they have succeeded they will start using their capabilities against each other, as well as against common enemies. The stage is already being set for the next round in Lebanon, in which – unlikely though it may have seemed earlier in 1986 – Syria will be forced to ally itself with the Christian minority, as well as the Druzes and elements from the Sunni community, to stem the tide of the Party of Allah which may benefit from Israel's opportunistic support.

'Lebanon is far from being saved for Islam,' said Jalaleddin Farsi, a leading strategist of the Islamic Republic. 'Imperialism and Zionism have not stopped their plots, and they are receiving support from local enemies who hide behind the mask of friendship. We must be ready to create a sea of blood to drown these plots. And, Allah be thanked, we now have that capacity in Lebanon.'[35]

10

Daily Life Under Terror

A man who lets his womenfolk cast off their veils and wear make-up shall have his name marked in the Register of the Heavens as a cuckold before being escorted to Hell where he shall roast until the end of time.

Ayatollah Abdul-Hussein Dast-Ghayb[1]

The fundamentalist terror that has hit the world's headlines since the victory of Ayatollah Khomeini's Islamic Revolution in Iran in 1979 has not limited its choice of victims to the ill-defined 'foreign enemies of Islam'. True, many of its most spectacular attacks, ranging from the massacre of American and French soldiers in their sleep to the murder of handicapped Britons,[2] have been directed against what Colonel Gaddafi likes to describe as 'Western vampires'.[3] But the principal victims of Holy Terror are those people, mostly Muslims, who live under the direct or indirect rule of the Party of Allah. The unspoken doctrine of the Party of Allah is that terrorism cannot be used against 'the foreign enemies of Islam' until Muslims themselves have been taught how 'to fear the Creator's ire'.[4]

The use of terror as a theory of state begins with the imposition of a totalitarian ideology in which, according to Shaikh Ragheb Harb, one of the 'saints' of the Party of Allah in Lebanon, the individual is 'melted into the community', thus losing his identity.[5] It is important that not a single moment of an individual's life, nor a single act, be left to his own private initiative.

You shall begin to live once you have killed yourself. The 'you' in you is none other than Satan in disguise. Kill him and you will be saved.

Muslims are lucky because they can accomplish this self-annihilation in accordance with divine rules. For Islam has an answer to every imaginable question. All an individual needs to do is to obey the rules without posing questions, without seeking variations.[6]

The imposition of political and social uniformity is often described by the theoreticians of the Party of Allah as *towheed* or 'one-ness', the ideal of creating a society in which everyone will regain his 'lost unity' with the Creator.[7] In practice, however, it has led to the setting up of new and strange versions of the police state in Iran and parts of Lebanon controlled by the network of Holy Terror. Among the countless slogans scribbled on the walls of West Beirut, one stands out: '*Kulunna Khomeini!*' It means 'We are all Khomeini!' The Ayatollah is the model of ideal Man. All believers should aspire to achieving his degree of *taqarrub* (proximity) to Allah, and that can only be achieved if the faithful are enabled to live in accordance with the law of the Qur'an.

The first step in that direction is to expel from the community all those who may 'tempt it into trying different ways'.[8] This was to a large measure achieved in the Islamic Republic between 1979 and 1986, by a variety of means. Before the Ayatollah's revolution, more than a million non-Muslim foreigners, citizens of more than forty countries,[9] lived and worked in Iran. By 1986 their number had dropped to less than three thousand, mostly from socialist or other 'revolutionary states', and they were allowed to work in Iran mainly because their expertise was needed for the continuation of the war against Iraq. Most were forced to live in heavily guarded buildings and were denied regular contact with the local people.

Next in line for expulsion were the middle classes, described as 'the fifth column of America'.[10] By 1986 the number of middle-class Iranians who had gone into exile reached the 2 million mark.[11] But the purge has not stopped there. Tens of thousands of former allies of the Ayatollah in the revolution have been murdered or thrown into prison.[12] With large groups capable of organizing any form of resistance – even passive – physically eliminated, the society of *towheed* could be created with the assistance of an apparatus of repression unique in the contemporary world.

Beirut's experience under the Party of Allah and its captive partner, Berri's Amal organization, has not been dissimilar. In 1979 the Lebanese capital was host to more than half a million foreigners of more than sixty nationalities. By June 1986 that number had dropped to less than a hundred.[13] Also expelled from areas controlled by the Party of Allah were Lebanese Christians, Sunni Muslims known for their nationalistic or left-wing politics, the Druzes, and above all Palestinians still faithful to the PLO chief Yasser Arafat.[14]

The methods used to 'persuade' the undesired *aghyar* (aliens)[15] to leave areas inhabited by the *owlia* (Friends of Allah) vary from the use of psychological pressure to plain murder. In the Islamic Republic, part of the task was accomplished by the revolutionary *komitehs*[16] and the Revolutionary Guard. A report in January 1986 on 'the services of the *komitehs* and the Guard in uprooting counter-revolutionary forces and other deviationists' offered a number of interesting statistics.[17] Members of the *komiteh* and the Guard were said to have broken into a total of seventy-nine thousand private homes in five years, seizing 'enormous quantities' of 'objects of sin such as tape recorders, playing cards, chess and backgammon sets, devices for smoking opium, musical instruments and records, alcohol and stills, lipsticks, perfumes, indecent clothes, un-Islamic literature and paintings and sculptures that could induce viewers to have wrong thoughts'.[18] Private estimates put the number of Iranians who since 1979 have been in prison for varying lengths of time on charges of 'un-Islamic behaviour' at over a million, or one in forty of the population.[19] And at least two thousand have been executed for 'crimes' such as adultery, homosexuality, the sale or use of narcotics, the organization of 'mixed' parties of men and women, and so on.[20]

The areas of Lebanon controlled by Holy Terror began experiencing a similar 'purification' in 1983. No official statistics were available, but it was no secret that the Party of Allah was holding more than four thousand people in its unofficial prisons in West Beirut and its suburbs, as well as in the Bekaa Valley. Some of these prisons, like the notorious

Haimadi, are abandoned school buildings. It was in Haimadi, as well as the Bir-Abed central school and the Khamsa wa Araba'in (Forty-five) military command centre in Beirut, that most of the Western hostages spent part of the initial phases of their captivity from 1983.[21] Kidnapping opponents and the holding of hostages are widely practised methods of imposing the rule of Holy Terror in both the Islamic Republic and the Party of Allah's sector of Lebanon. According to Tehran's official press, an average of three thousand people a year have disappeared in the city since the revolution.[22] In Beirut in 1985 and 1986 hundreds of women could be seen demonstrating almost every day, demanding news of their 'lost ones'. Private estimates put the number of Lebanese citizens being held hostage in July 1986 by the Party of Allah at over eight hundred. The sinister running joke in Beirut, 'Make a hostage of them before they make a hostage of you', reflected a grim reality.

When night raids on people's homes, combined with the forcible eviction of 'undesired ones', do not produce results, and other methods such as assassination, imprisonment and the holding of hostages are difficult to practise on a day-to-day basis, the Partisans of Allah have recourse to other means of pressure. Brigades in charge of 'enjoining the good and preventing evil' were created in Tehran and Beirut from 1980. Their task was to impose the *hodood* or 'limits' that Islam has fixed for individual behaviour. Members of these brigades used the lofty title of Muhtasseb or 'he who holds others to account'. They patrolled all public places round the clock to make sure that women did not go around unveiled and that men were not dressed 'provocatively'. They also looked for signs of alcohol consumption and illicit relations between men and women. In July 1986 some of Beirut's most famous beaches, once the most popular in the Middle East, were divided into two sections – one exclusively for men and the other exclusively for women. Some six years previously a similar programme had been put into effect by Ayatollah Khomeini at all Iranian seaside resorts.

The Partisans of Allah are authorized, indeed commanded, by their leaders to use whatever means they think fit in combating evil before the rule of Islam is fully established. This includes burning the homes of the infidel or 'the impure', throwing acid at unveiled women and men of loose behaviour,[23] and looting or destroying shops selling illicit goods such as alcohol and videotapes.[24] Between 1979 and 1986 the Islamic Republic was more than willing to share its experience with fundamentalist militants throughout the world. In July 1986, for example, the Islamic Republic's Embassy in Beirut presented a strange gift to the Lebanese section of the Party of Allah. It was an electrical machine, developed in the Islamic Scientific Institute in Tehran, for cutting off the fingers of people found guilty of stealing.[25]

Living under the rule of the Party of Allah, whether as a theoretically free citizen, or as a hostage or prisoner, has been described as a nightmare by people of many different backgrounds and nationalities. An Iranian writer who succeeded in escaping execution in 1979 said:

> It was not until I experienced life in one of Khomeini's prisons that I understood the tragic solitude of the human individual. We were made conscious of our irreversible solitude largely because we were never left alone. All our activities, from the way we slept to the way we entered a lavatory, were watched so that we would not violate the laws of Islam. Khomeini has written that on entering a lavatory a believer must put his left foot forward first. We were taken to task for violating even that rule.[26]

Another leading Iranian intellectual, with a UNESCO background, had a slightly different experience. 'During my two years of imprisonment I was taken out of the cell I shared with thirty other people almost every day and subjected to five lashes [of the cane]. The reason was that I had naïvely admitted that I had never performed my five daily prayers, so they wanted me to pay my debt to the Creator.'[27]

Joseph André, a Lebonese Christian journalist, has written of his experience as a hostage of the Party of Allah.[28] He portrayed a Kafka-esque atmosphere in which the destruction of the human individual was the primary objective of self-appointed defenders of divine law. André was subjected to torture by electric shock before experiencing a sustained attempt at brainwashing by his captives. It began with one of the captors playing the role of a well-wisher trying his best to 'solve your problem and have you released'. The well-wisher at times even went as far as cursing those higher up who could not make up their minds. The whole thing became a sinister game, at the end of which a hostage would lose all sense of time and place.

Another hostage had to pass a written examination in 'Christian history and rituals' in order to prove to his captors that he was not a Jew. 'They kidnapped me because I had a name that sounded Jewish to them,' he said in an interview.

> I told them that I was a Christian, but they kept insisting that I was a Jew and an agent of Israel. My misfortune was that I had been circumcised in childhood and, when examined by my captors, could not prove my Christian background. The fact that they themselves, being Muslims, had also been circumcised changed nothing. I was not a Muslim, so I had to be a Jew. After four months someone had the bright idea of setting an exam for me. One day I was handed a questionnaire containing over a hundred questions about Christianity and the Church to which my parents belonged. Not being a practising Christian I must have made a mess of the test. But somehow I passed and was set free.[29]

While captive he was repeatedly told that if he were in fact a Jew and an Israeli agent his capture would result in a major improvement in the fortunes of the group holding him. 'Then,' one of the captors told him, 'we would have money thrown at us from all nations!'[30]

Kidnapping people for ransom or in the hope of attracting financial support from the Islamic Republic, Syria, Libya or other states involved in terrorist activities in Lebanon is often the rule rather than the exception.[31] The two professors from the American University in Beirut who were kidnapped and later found dead in April 1986 were almost certainly victims of kidnappers working for money. They had to be murdered after Libya refused to 'buy' them.[32]

Some people are made hostage because their profession may help their captors achieve publicity. This was the case with Terry Anderson, the American journalist and Beirut veteran who headed Associated Press's Lebanese bureau. Anderson, always full of sympathy for the 'just grievances' of Muslims against Israel and the West, was soon joined in captivity in 1985 by Jean-Paul Kaufman of the Parisian weekly *L'Evénement de jeudi*. Kaufman had the added disadvantage of having a Jewish-sounding name, a fact emphasized by his captors.[33] A five-man French TV crew were seized in 1986 because of what they did for a living.[34] Teaching is also a risky career in the realm of Holy Terror. In January 1984 Dr Malcolm Kerr was murdered inside the American University in Beirut, of which he was President.[35] His predecessor, Dr David Dodge, had been kidnapped and held hostage for a year in 1983.[36] Michel Briant, a teacher at the French lycée in West Beirut, was kidnapped in 1986 but managed to escape when being taken to Baalbek, the headquarters of the Islamic Amal organization.

The most dangerous profession of all is, of course, diplomacy. Between 1980 and 1986 more than a hundred diplomats from more than a dozen countries, including some Muslim ones, were kidnapped and held hostage for varying lengths of time in both the Islamic Republic and parts of Lebanon controlled by it. While some of the kidnappings were no doubt ordered by the governments of the Islamic Republic or Syria, many of the diplomats seized were victims of excessive zeal on the part of autonomous terror groups in West Beirut or the Bekaa Valley. According to Arab sources, it was the Soviet KGB who identified William Buckley as a top CIA agent in Beirut and 'encouraged' Syria to arrange for his kidnapping. The operation was finally carried out by a commando group loyal to Ayatollah Khomeini. Buckley was taken to Tehran 'some time in 1985' and subjected to 'prolonged interrogation under torture' in the presence of Syrian Intelligence officers. He died under torture after being removed to the Caspian resort of Chalus, where he was held at the former Hyatt Hotel which had been converted into a prison for foreign hostages in January 1980.[37]

One man who was neither journalist, teacher nor diplomat, but who was nevertheless kidnapped by the Party of Allah in 1984, was a researcher named Michel Seurat, whose 'death' was announced in the name of 'the Islamic Jihad' early in 1986. Seurat, an Arabist who had lived in Beirut for years and was married to a Lebanese Christian, was at the time of his disappearance working for the National Centre for Scientific Research in Paris. The reason for his kidnapping, according to Arab sources, was that he was 'one of the most knowledgeable men in the world' on the organizational structures and activities of the Syrian branch of the Muslim Brotherhood. He was no doubt in contact with the group, which constituted the most determined opposition to President Assad in Syria while rejecting Khomeini's interpretation of Islam. Using pseudonyms as a means of protecting himself against any possible Syrian revenge, Seurat published many learned articles and a book on the activities of the Brotherhood in Syria.[38] He had an exhaustive collection of documents on the subject, and the Syrians may have wanted to extract confidential information from him. He may have died under torture while being interrogated.[39]

Seizing hostages, whether through attacks on embassies or kidnapping individuals, is one way of establishing a militant group's credentials. Contrary to widespread belief in Washington, the 'students' who seized the US Embassy compound in Tehran in 1979 did not take their orders either from the Kremlin or from Khomeini; they were making their own bid for influence and power within a chaotic situation. They won largely because both Khomeini and President Carter agreed to play their respective roles the way the 'students' wanted. In just over a year the kidnappers took over dozens of major posts within the revolutionary apparatus in addition to imposing their hard-line policies on the country as a whole.[40]

Similarly, in June 1985 the Party of Allah succeeded in upstaging Nabih Berri and his Amal group by hijacking a TWA jumbo jet on a flight from Athens to Rome. Throughout the three-week crisis that ensued Berri was on American television almost every day; but he knew, and everyone in Beirut knew, that he was just acting as a powerless spokesman for the Party of Allah, which had by then emerged as the rising star in Shi'ite politics in Lebanon. The fact that the USA chose not to retaliate in any way after the hostages were eventually freed enhanced the party's prestige even further.[41] But more important was the fact that Israel, no doubt under pressure from Washington, had agreed to release nearly five hundred Shi'ite prisoners as part of a deal to set the TWA passengers free.

'Berri talks but we act,' said Party of Allah leaders in Beirut. They could dictate their terms to both the United States and

Israel. The hijack enhanced the revolutionary careers of its authors and perpetrators beyond their wildest dreams. The mastermind behind the operation, Ibrahim al-Amin, was received in audience by Khomeini two months later, and the man who led the hijack, Haj Ali Imad, a former companion of Arafat, was named head of the movement's secret service. A second hijacker, Murad Murhaniah, was assigned to the Islamic Republic's Embassy in Paris as a 'cultural adviser' in October 1985.[42]

The various groups belonging to the network of Holy Terror are often involved in competition with one another. Each acts to prove itself more militant than the others and in a stronger position to carry out the wishes of the Imam in Jamaran.[43] Every speech by Khomeini and every commentary by Tehran Radio's Arabic programme, which is listened to by the Partisans of Allah as if it indicated divine will, might be seized upon as an excuse for a new form of violence in Lebanon and elsewhere.

In December 1985, for example, Khomeini launched an unusually strong attack on the Jews, quoting the Prophet himself in a speech to prove that the very fact of being born Jewish makes one an 'enemy of Islam'. A few days later, on Christmas Day, the murdered bodies of two prominent Lebanese Jews, Isaac Tarab and Chaim Cohen, were found. Both had been kidnapped by a Party of Allah group calling itself the Oppressed of the World, which claimed that the murders were in retaliation for Israel's raids on southern Lebanon.

The emergence of the Party of Allah as the most active terror organization in the Middle East changed many time-honoured conventions established by some fifteen years of terrorism in the region. It had, for example, become a tradition for various international airlines to make a 'voluntary' annual contribution to the PLO and its offshoots as insurance against hijacking. Among those participating in this unusual protection racket were Air France, British Airways, Lufthansa and a number of other western European airlines.[44] But in 1985 they were informed by the PLO that they could no longer be protected since the Party of Allah was an entirely independent entity – or, rather, more than half a dozen different entities.

Subjecting foreigners and their interests to perpetual violence is in itself a means of terrorizing the local Muslim community into blind obedience to the wishes of the Holy Terror network. The message was well put by Khoiniha as early as December 1979: 'Those who made Carter crawl at the feet of the Imam and beg for pardon, those who made the chief of America wag his tail and rub his nose in dust, will not be afraid of little Satans and their assistants.'[45]

Holy Terror propaganda will never admit a setback, and gives the impression that life consists of perpetual struggle against 'Satanic forces'. The Party of Allah does not hesitate to use what may seem the most trivial of subjects to mobilize its troops for Holy War. In the Islamic Republic, for example, the launching of a nationwide campaign against dogs was presented as 'a decisive battle against the heathen West'.[46] In the summer of 1984 Friday prayer leaders throughout the country began enumerating the evils that dogs can do to true believers. One of the capital's largest dailies ran a series of articles by doctors of theology to prove that dogs, being 'unclean', must be put down.[47] Imam Jaafar Sadeq, the founder of Shi'ite theology, was quoted as saying that the dog was 'a new version of the pig' and therefore considered 'unclean'. In a month-long campaign tens of thousands of dogs and 'other harmful or unclean animals' were killed by teenage boys.

In Egypt and a number of the Gulf States it was the campaign against videotapes that gave the exponents of Holy Terror an occasion for showing their strength. Preachers at mosques, especially in Egypt, spent the first half of 1986 singling out videotapes as 'the latest device of the West in its war against Islam'. 'The video is the evil work of Satan,' they said. 'It spreads immorality and vice and drives the believers away from their duty of worshipping only Allah.'[48] Some prayer leaders went so far as to describe the anti-video campaign as a Holy War, forcing President Mubarak to intervene personally and order the crackdown on video-hunters of the Islamic Jihad.

The strategists of Holy Terror are convinced that the faithful should have not a single moment of idleness lest they be led astray. It is therefore vital to keep them occupied round the clock in the service of the Faith. And to make sure that no one cheats by being idle when alone, solitude is condemned as a 'Satanic state of being'.[49] 'Good Muslims are never alone,' wrote one philosopher of Holy Terror, Ayatollah Shirazi. 'This is why the Prophet said that saying our prayers together gives us more merit. A man who sits alone is bound to be approached by Satan, who will tell him to do untoward things with his own body. A father who wants his son to become a true Muslim will not give him a separate room. A boy in a room of his own is sure to go astray.'[50]

A true believer must not allow his thoughts to be diverted for a single moment from the worship of Allah and the performance of his duties under divine law. Shi'ite theology has no fewer than 732 different prayers that can be 'murmured to oneself' throughout one's waking hours. The idea is to fill every second with thoughts of Allah, thus preventing 'other thoughts' from invading one's mind. 'A man who thinks is sending signals to Satan,' wrote Muhammad-Baqer Majlisi, one of the greatest doctors of Shi'ite theology.[51] Thinking is deemed not only dangerous but also unnecessary, since all the answers to all the imaginable questions can be found in the Qur'an and the Hadiths, while the theologians of the day, who are allowed to 'think' in a certain sense, are there precisely to clarify every issue and to guide the faithful in all aspects of life down to the minutest detail.[52]

The faithful must be on guard against the danger of vacant spaces appearing in their lives. A life worthy of a true believer is a full one, in the sense that the whole of it is taken up by the performance of one's duties towards the Creator. The faithful have a special Islamic lunar calendar in which every day of the year is marked out for a specific act of worship.[53] Four months of the year are completely set aside for prayer, mourning, pilgrimage and other acts of worship; normal activity is kept to a minimum at these times, to allow believers to devote more time to the performance of religious duties. The months are Ramadan (the month of fasting), Zul-Hajjah (the month of pilgrimage to Mecca or gatherings of the faithful in their home towns), Muharram and Safar (the months of mourning the martyrdom of Imams Hussein and Hassan).

The Islamic calendar also marks the anniversary of both the

birth and death of the Prophet, those of his daughter Fatimah and of the Twelve Imams, in addition to six special days connected with Khomeini's life.[54] Five times as many days are marked for mourning as are set aside for festivities. All these special days are celebrated in a number of ways ranging from public ceremonies and mass demonstrations to private gatherings at the homes of the wealthier believers. Every adult male must play a role in the planning and organizing of these celebrations.[55] In this way an effective method of regimentation is put at the disposal of the Holy Terror leaders. Sometimes the organization charged with making sure that everyone attends Friday prayer gatherings is in command of the special days as well. Thousands of teenage boys, wearing the headband of the Volunteers for Martyrdom and often carrying machine guns, knock on every door to make sure that no one forgets to attend to his duties. The teenage Volunteers – who never smile, because they are told that the Prophet damned those who did – spread the word in the neighbourhood: Attend the ceremony or else. . . .

One of the chief grievances of the Party of Allah concerns the alleged failure of all governments in Islamic countries – with the obvious exception of Khomeini's in Iran – to treat women in accordance with what is presented as 'true Islam'. The abolition of the veil by Atatürk in Turkey and Reza Shah in Iran, and the establishment of mixed schools in both countries, are referred to in the literature of the Party of Allah as deliberate steps aimed at turning Muslim women into 'whores' and Muslim youths into 'slaves of lust'.[56] 'Mixed schools, by putting young girls and boys together, become places of debauchery and destroy all morality and the sense of piety. They sap the very root of life.'[57] One of the most important items on the programme of the Party of Allah is to 'restore Muslim women to the proper place assigned to them'.[58]

The party's theories concerning the 'proper place' of women in society can best be described as a Middle Eastern version of apartheid based on sex instead of race and colour. Women are believed to be vulnerable, fragile and constantly open to temptation, and must therefore be protected by men. The Prophet himself is quoted as warning the faithful against the harm that women can do to Islam: 'Had it not been for women, Allah would have been worshipped in a way that He deserves.'[59]

The party's propagandists claim that leading Muslim women astray is part of a plot by 'the foreign enemies of Islam' to spread prostitution in Muslim countries and make 'our youth forget their duty of fighting for the Faith'.[60] In a statement justifying the murder of Anwar Sadat in 1981, the Egyptian Islamic Jihad spoke of the dead President's 'greatest treachery, which was the encouragement of sexual licence in the country'.[61] It also claimed that the number of 'full-time or part-time prostitutes in Cairo and its suburbs' exceeded 250,000.[62] The treatment of women as the equals of men by the government of President Bourguiba in Tunisia has for years been a source of resentment on the part of the fundamentalists.[63]

The subject of relations between men and women is treated with exceptional care and gravity in Islam. The Qur'an itself devotes more attention to it than to any other issue of earthly life.[64] The Qur'anic rules are in turn explained and elaborated through thousands of traditions attributed to the Prophet and the Imams. Leading theologians treat the subject as 'the cornerstone of social life'.[65] Any deviation from the rules, which regulate even the most intimate aspects of sexual relations between men and women, is considered as 'an act of war on Allah'.[66] Government leaders who do not please the Party of Allah are often accused of indulging in sexual deviations or of spending public funds for the satisfaction of their own 'bestial needs'.[67] These leaders are said to go on official visits to the West 'for the purpose of participating in activities of a nature that no honest man or woman would tolerate'.[68] Ibrahim Hamdi, the Yemeni President who was murdered by his opponents in 1977, was accused, among other things, of organizing what a pamphleteer described as 'an air bridge between Seoul and Sanaa, bringing Korean loose women for the President and his accomplices'.[69]

Keeping women in purdah is openly cited as one of the most important tasks of the fundamentalist movement. Women fundamentalists share the view, and go out of their way to endorse the reimposition of the veil. Even women who trained for guerrilla warfare in PLO and Amal camps in the 1970s were prepared – with a great deal of well-publicized enthusiasm – to return to the veil. One of them, Zahra Rahnavard, a graduate of several guerrilla training centres in Lebanon, said in a radio interview: 'The return to the veil must be seen as the greatest achievement of Muslim women in the past hundred years. The veil protects us from the ills of invading cultures; we feel safe behind it. As long as Muslim women retain their veils, Islam can continue to triumph. . . . Compared to our veil, America's atom bombs are nothing.'[70] Another woman militant, Aqdas Elhami-Rad, a graduate of the University of Southern California, also defended the restoration of the veil in Iran:

> Islam is for clear-cut rules and situations; there are no grey areas, no innuendos, no possibility for ambiguous relationships in Islam. The veil is a symbol of that clarity, that frankness. As a woman I am either a man's wife, in which case he has every right to acquaint himself with my physical as well as spiritual existence, or I am off limits to the men I may see or meet. In that case they have no right to know anything more about me than the strict minimum required under Islamic law.[71]

The imposition of the veil and other rigorous rules of dress, which also concern men, is often referred to as one of the key successes of Ayatollah Khomeini's revolution both in Iran and in those parts of Lebanon that have fallen under the control of the Party of Allah. Throughout the Muslim world and in Muslim communities in western Europe and North America the wearing of the *hijab*, as specified by Khomeini, has become a symbol of fundamentalist militancy. As described elsewhere in this book, physical and psychological terror are often used to force women to adopt the veil. In Istanbul, women undergraduates not covering their heads were beaten up by organized gangs of fundamentalists in 1980 and 1981. And in Egypt, women refusing to wear the veil are ostracized by local fundamentalists. In an interview given in 1983 one Egyptian student at Ain-Shams University in Cairo explained her own reasons for adopting the 'correct Islamic appearance':

> I began by receiving little notes advising me to adopt the veil. Then I was contacted by fellow-students, who told me of vague dangers

facing women who went around incorrectly dressed. I took that to mean the danger of being attacked by acid. Then men went to my father's shop and told him that I was a loose woman. That broke his heart and caused a crisis. . . . I saw more and more of my friends giving in to pressure and accepting the veil in order to buy peace. So I said: Why not me? I have one more year to go here, and then I will be free to go as I please.[72]

The increase in the number of women wearing the veil and men who grow beards is the most concrete sign of the presence of 'a truly dynamic Islamic movement', according to Muhammad Heidar, a Khomeinist militant in the Paris suburb of St Denis. This is why the Islamic Republic agreed in 1986 to offer women who adopted the 'correct Islamic appearance' a monthly subsidy of 200 francs for three months. The cheques came from the Islamic Cultural Centre in Rue Fortuny. An estimated four thousand women had joined the scheme by July 1986, but thousands more were wearing the veil without getting paid for it. Cash rewards were also offered in 1984 and 1985 by the Islamic Republic to women in Jordan, Syria and Senegal. According to Ayatollah Ali-Akbar Meshkini,[73] number three in the Islamic Republic's theological hierarchy, the first step towards the creation of the 'divine society' is to make sure that people 'look right'. The fact that Bani-Sadr shaved was a sure sign of his 'flawed faith'. Nabih Berri's opponents often refer to him as 'the one who shaves', thus emphasizing the Amal leader's supposedly incomplete conversion to true Islam.

In contrast with its iron-fisted imposition of political uniformity and conformist social and ethical behaviour, the Party of Allah allows a surprising degree of freedom in other domains. With official bureaucracy either in total disarray or frightened into inaction, individual believers can engage in a variety of economic enterprises, most of them linked with the black market. In both the Islamic Republic and the Islamicized regions of Lebanon, in the first half of the 1980s what is described as the parallel economy showed far more buoyancy than the sector controlled by the remnants of the state. In Iran, the breakdown of the imperial machinery of state created undreamed of opportunities for people, especially in the countryside, to reorganize their economic lives more or less as they pleased. Restrictions on the use of natural resources were lifted, and millions of square kilometres of forest could be cut down and sold at great profit. Prohibitions on the cultivation of certain crops, notably opium poppies, were also ignored, and in 1985 the Islamic Republic became a major producer.[74]

In Lebanon, the cultivation of hashish became a vital source of income for Shi'ite farmers in the Bekaa Valley as early as 1982. The original investment in hashish-growing in the area was made by a group of Turks who had been forced out of Turkey after the military coup d'état which brought the army to power and restored order at the end of 1980. The Turkish army then burned the hashish and opium fields as a favour to the United States, so Lebanon became a natural choice for the Turkish hashish barons. The powerful Jaafari clan, which has organized several armed groups of its own, controls the hashish trade in the Bekaa.[75] A share of the profit goes to the Party of Allah, while the Syrian military, which controls the main communication centres of the plain, also receives gifts in cash and kind.

Another dynamic sector of the economy under the Party of Allah consists of what is described as 'border trade', more commonly known as smuggling. The bazaars of Tehran and other major Iranian cities are full of smuggled goods from Iraq, despite the fact that the two neighbours have been at war since 1980. The Lebanese market is shared between Israel and Jordan, while Beirut and Baalbek also act as conduits for trade in smuggled goods deep into Syria and parts of southwestern Turkey.[76]

Perhaps the most common feature of life under Holy Terror is the general feeling of insecurity at all levels of society. The leaders of the Party of Allah live in perpetual fear of assassination. Many have escaped at least one attempt on their lives. Ayatollah Muhammad-Hussein Fadhl-Allah, for example, was the target of at least five assassination plots in 1983, 1984 and 1985. The last took the form of a booby-trapped car that exploded in Bir-Abed moments before the *sayyed* was due to arrive at an apartment block he used as his headquarters. More than sixty people were killed, but the *sayyed* was not harmed since on the day of the explosion he had decided to stay at home after consulting his worry beads.[77] The Party of Allah immediately accused the CIA and proceeded to murder more than a dozen people suspected of working for them. Fadhl-Allah and other leading members of the Party of Allah are obliged to spend each night in a different place; in 1985 they were presented with thirty-two bullet-proof cars by the Islamic Republic.[78]

The party leaders in Tehran have an even tougher time. Of the top thirty leaders of the Islamic Republic, only two have never experienced an attempt on their lives. And one of the two, Khomeini himself, was unable to leave the house in north Tehran into which he moved in May 1980.[79] Several leaders had suffered grievous injuries such as the loss of a hand or an eye or fingers, all the result of explosions arranged by their enemies.

The number of Party of Allah leaders and militants killed between 1980 and 1986 in the Islamic Republic and Lebanon exceeded four thousand, according to unofficial estimates. Rival groups, opposition parties and terrorists working for foreign governments were all involved in what amounted to a virtual war on the Party of Allah.[80] Needless to say, the party retained its initiative in political violence and killed many more of its enemies.

'Managing to stay alive is a feat in itself,' wrote a correspondent from Tehran in March 1986.

> Life here is like swimming in a lagoon filled with man-eating sharks. . . . There is no time to think of opposing the rulers, since every minute of our lives is committed in advance: two hours spent eating two meals a day, four hours queuing up to get rationed food for the next day, four hours taking part in religious ceremonies, demonstrations or the Qur'anic discussion group organized by some zealots on the block, four hours persuading the Good and Evil Brigadiers, who have invaded your apartment in the middle of the night in search of videos and whisky, that you are clean, and endless hours to get through the city's traffic. . . . Islamic days are short indeed.[81]

It is in an atmosphere of terror that the Party of Allah best thrives. It can terrorize its enemies because it is terrorized by them. It is afraid of life and thinks that by destroying it, either physically or spiritually, it will secure its own safety. The instigators of Holy Terror do not want to brainwash those who live under them; brainwashing implies persuading an individual or a whole community to think in the way one wants him or them to think. Since Holy Terror discourages all thinking, however, its method is that of 'brain-bashing',[82] not of brainwashing.

11

The Broken Crescent[1]

> Allah warned me that the day will come when nothing will remain of Islam but its name; a day when people will be Muslims in word but as far as possible from Islam in deed; a day when mosques shall be perfect while prayer leaders are flawed. On such a day, the most evil creatures under the dome of the Heavens will be the theologians. For they provoke sedition and in turn will fall victims to sedition.
>
> The Prophet Muhammad[2]

In March 1983 French, West German and Italian security services held a secret meeting in the small town of Vernon, northwest of Paris, to discuss what their political brief described as 'preparations for facing an Islamic Holy War in Europe'. The meeting was arranged two months after Pierre Mauroy, then Prime Minister of France, had received a detailed confidential report on the activities of the Party of Allah in France. It spoke of the 'clandestine network of individual agents as well as associations' created for the purpose of 'exporting the Islamic Revolution' to Europe.[3] Those present at the meeting made two sets of recommendations. The first resulted in a series of expulsions of diplomats, businessmen and students linked with the Party of Allah's network in western Europe. The second was to lead, three years later, to the creation of a unified European service for monitoring terrorist activities, as well as suggesting new laws and regulations needed to combat 'the threat of the rising Crescent'.[4]

What neither the writers of the report nor the delegates at the Vernon meeting realized was that at the time the Holy Terror network had no plans for carrying the Holy War into western Europe. The Party of Allah was only using the freedoms and facilities available in Europe for the purpose of transmitting its message to other Muslim countries. The geographical 'crescent of Islam', spanning the whole region between the Atlantic Ocean and Indonesia, was a broken one and had to be 'put together again by blood'.[5] The ideologues of the Party of Allah saw different Muslim countries as being at different stages of revolutionary development, and the presence of some 5 million Muslims in western Europe offered a unique opportunity for narrowing the gap that separated some countries from others as regards their respective 'ripeness for revolution'.[6]

Two years before the report prepared for Premier Mauroy was completed, the Party of Allah had worked out its own order of priorities in exporting the revolution. As noted in Chapter 8, Iraq was then considered the easiest target. More than six years later, the Party of Allah is still convinced that it is in Bayn an-Nahrayin[7] that the Islamic revolution will next triumph.

The Islamic revolutionary movement in Iraq is one of the oldest in the Middle East. The Muslim clergy played a key role in fighting British domination of the country throughout the 1920s. The Shi'ites, who form the majority of the population, were doubly determined to subvert the Baghdad government, which they saw as not only a tool of the British but also an instrument of Sunni rule. Nawab-Safavi's Fedayeen of Islam movement in Iran had several Iraqi members who, after the 1953 police crackdown in Tehran, returned to Iraq and settled in the holy cities of Najaf and Karbala. In 1956 they created the Hezb ad-Dawat al-Islamiah (The Party of the Islamic Call), known for short as ad-Da'awah and inspired by an Egyptian group of the same name. The brains behind the party belonged to Ayatollah Muhammad Baqer Sadr, who was then at the peak of his intellectual development as the leading contemporary theoretician of political Shi'ism. Ad-Da'awah openly aimed at the violent overthrow of the Iraqi monarchy and its replacement by the rule of the Shi'ite clergy. But the 1958 coup d'état, led by Brigadier-General Abdul-Karim Qassem, dealt a severe blow to ad-Da'awah's chances of ever winning power in Baghdad. The coup, and the revolutionary phraseology of its leaders, attracted many Shi'ite militants who were in the years to come to progress beyond Qassem's 'Marxist nationalism' and provide the backbone of the Iraqi communist party. Throughout the 1960s the Islamic discourse of ad-Da'awah was pushed into the background as the more politically aware Shi'ites went over to Leninism; it was not unusual for them to carry in their pockets small portraits of both Imam Ali and Lenin.

The return of the Shi'ites to their 'source' had to wait until 1978, when Khomeini's Islamic Revolution began to change the ideological map of the Middle East. 'We suddenly realized that we had been blind all along,' confessed a militant Leninist who returned to the bosom of Islam in 1979. 'Lenin's had been not a revolution but a putsch, and the state that resulted from it could not but become an apparatus of repression sustained by a brutal police force. Lenin attracted no crowds and had no contact with the masses. . . . It was Khomeini who showed us what a true revolution was.'[8] Many ad-Da'awah militants were smuggled into Iran in 1978 and the first weeks of 1979 and played an active role in the Islamic Revolution. Some of them died while carrying out operations such as setting cinemas on fire or trying to sabotage passenger trains. The Iraqi militants also helped to raise money for the Khomeinist movement in Najaf, Karbala and Kazemain.

The triumph of the revolution in February 1979, however, proved something of a disappointment for Iraqi Shi'ites. Khomeini insisted that only native or naturalized Iranians could hold public positions in his new Islamic Republic. As early as March 1979 he told the Iraqi militants to return home and create an Islamic republic of their own; the dream of a pan-Islamic republic was still far away. But the Iraqi militants who had helped Khomeini were not to go entirely unrewarded. In April 1979 an account was opened for ad-Da'awah at the Rahni Bank in central Tehran, with an initial payment of the equivalent of 10 million US dollars. A few months later, the newly created Revolutionary Guard began training the Iraqi party's members for guerrilla and sabotage work. The first group of these revolutionaries returned to Iraq in the summer of 1979 and began a series of terrorist attacks, including the murder of two junior officials of the ruling Ba'ath party in Basrah. A few months later they aimed higher and tried to kill Tareq Aziz, then just emerging as the regime's number three man.[9] The plot gave the Iraqi regime the excuse it needed to begin a nationwide campaign to suppress its Shi'ite opponents. Within a few days several thousand people, including hundreds of mullahs, had been thrown into prison and scores were shot without trial. Among those shot was Ayatollah Baqer Sadr, known as the Khomeini of Iraq but in reality a philosopher of the revolution rather than an activist prepared to condone in practice the violence he preached in his writings. According to Iraqi Shi'ite sources, Sadr was shot dead either by Saddam Hussein himself or by Barzan Takriti, the President's half-brother.[10]

One religious clan that suffered particularly badly as a result of Saddam's anti-Shi'ite activities was the Hakim-Tabataba'i of Najaf. Between 1961 and 1968 the clan had exercised an almost unchallenged domination of Shi'ism, thanks to Grand Ayatollah Muhsen Hakim-Tabataba'i whose learning and piety made him *primus inter pares* among the theologians of the day. He had maintained excellent relations with the Shah, and on a number of occasions had refused to receive Khomeini, then in exile in Najaf. At least two of the Grand Ayatollah's six sons were in contact with SAVAK, the Shah's secret police, and furnished occasional information concerning Khomeini's revolutionary activities in exile.[11] But in 1978 they had enough vision to realize that the Shah's regime was bound to be destroyed and that it was wiser, or at least more profitable, to side with Khomeini. Almost at the eleventh hour they too became revolutionaries, offering Saddam Hussein the excuse he needed for massacring their families. In escaping to Iran the remaining members of the Hakim family who had been lucky enough not to be arrested by Saddam Hussein's agents were in fact returning home, for the Hakims originated in Shiraz and had retained their Iranian passports.

In 1981 Khomeini ordered the inauguration of the High Council of Islamic Revolution in Iraq, with Hojat al-Islam Mahdi Hakim-Tabataba'i as its President. The Council's aim was to unite under one command the dozen or so Iraqi revolutionary groups that had sought refuge in Iran. The main group was ad-Da'awah, under Ayatollah Muhammad-Mahdi al-Assefi, who had at his side a number of veteran Shi'ite revolutionaries including Ayatollah Aamer al-Helou, Ibrahim Muhammad, Ali al-Azzawi and Abd-Allah Nesh'at, alias Abu Khalaf, who created and commanded the party's military wing in 1980. Next in importance was the Mujahedin al-Thawrat al-Islamiyah fi Eraq (The Combatants of the Islamic Revolution in Iraq), known as Mujahedin for short, who came into being in 1980 and were quickly absorbed into the Party of Allah's network of military groups. The Mujahedin are led by Hojat al-Islam Aziz Hakim-Tabataba'i, another son of the ayatollah. By July 1986 they had created three groups of specialized fighters. One of these groups, consisting of around 1200 people recruited mainly from Iraqi Shi'ite prisoners of war in Iran, fought alongside Iranian troops in the Gulf War under the command of Muhammad Ahmad al-Haydari. A second group, active inside Iraq and responsible for sabotage work and the assassination of government officials, was commanded by Muhammad Dakh'khani and believed to consist of six hundred men and women. Finally, Hojat al-Islam Jalaleddin Saghar commanded a force of around three hundred whose main task was propaganda, information gathering and occasional acts of sabotage through a network of clandestine cells inside Iraq.

Each of these three groups, as well as ad-Da'awah, claimed to have been behind scores of terrorist attacks inside Iraq between 1981 and 1986. The most spectacular occurred in November 1983 – the destruction by a suicide commando of the building that housed the headquarters of the Iraqi security police in Baghdad. By all accounts, the attack claimed more than eighty lives, including many of Saddam Hussein's top security aides. Two members of the Mujahedin, Abd al-Hussein Abu-Lahmah and Ibrahim Salman, also died in the attack, and two new suicide squads were instantly named after the 'martyrs'.

The Iraqi Shi'ite revolutionary movement, probably the strongest of its kind outside Iran, made its influence felt in other countries of the Persian Gulf between 1981 and 1986. The presence of a vast Iraqi colony in Kuwait, in addition to more than 25,000 Iranians, offered Tehran and its Iraqi allies an opportunity for putting the emirate under pressure. As early as 1981, in a report submitted to Ayatollah Mahalati, ad-Da'awah suggested that Kuwait was 'ripe for revolution'.[12] The report claimed that most of the 600,000 native Kuwaitis would either flee the country or submit to an Islamic regime in the event of an Islamic revolution in the emirate. The estimated 300,000 Palestinians living in Kuwait were, according to the report, unlikely to risk their lives in defence of the ruling family. The Shi'ites numbered fewer than 200,000, but were said to be prepared to 'overwhelm' the Sunni majority, thanks to their revolutionary zeal.[13] Special mosque gatherings addressed by Shaikh Abbas Mahri, an Iranian firebrand who had lived in Kuwait for many years, unleashed enough passion to confirm the report's conclusions.[14]

The usual scenario of an Islamic revolution began in Kuwait in January 1982 with a series of attacks on cinemas, girls' schools, restaurants and libraries. Several women wearing 'un-Islamic' clothes were stabbed, and cars belonging to pro-Iraqi businessmen were set on fire. These attacks were mainly aimed at testing the Kuwaiti government's resolve to defend itself. The Kuwaiti leaders adopted a soft attitude and began seeking a dialogue with Tehran; the veteran Foreign Minister Shaikh Sabah Ahmad al-Jaber visited Tehran to reason with the ayatollahs. The attacks ceased, but the Party of Allah dramatically increased its propaganda activity. In addition to two schools, with more than six thousand pupils, the mullahs set up over a hundred Qur'anic classes, which in reality developed into centres for revolutionary training.

By the time the Kuwaitis decided to review their policy and adopt a tough line, the Party of Allah had firmly established its local branch of Holy Terror. In December 1983 a series of car bomb attacks were carried out against American and French embassies and businesses in the emirate. At least six people died and seventy others were injured. This was followed by a fresh series of operations against 'places of sin', as well as attempts on the lives of three known opponents of Khomeini.[15] In May 1985 the Party of Allah moved a step further and approved a plan to assassinate the Emir, Shaikh Jaber al-Ahmad al-Sabah. A commando of Iraqi Shi'ites threw bombs at the Emir's car but failed to kill him. Four people died in the attempt. This was followed in July of the same year by bomb attacks on two popular cafés, described as 'wounds in the heart of Islam' because they allowed men and women to eat and drink together.[16] At least twelve people died and more than a hundred were injured.

The Kuwaiti government was considered particularly vulnerable because of its policy of allowing a more or less genuine parliamentary system to function. Pressure from the Party of Allah on some members of Parliament either forced or encouraged them to radicalize every debate and prevent the state from showing its teeth against subversive elements. The fact that Kuwait did not execute any of the seventeen members of the Party of Allah arrested after the December 1983 attacks was interpreted in Tehran as a sure sign of the emirate's fragility.

The conquest of the Iraqi peninsula of Fao by Iranian troops in February 1986 added to the pressure on Kuwait. Iranian troops, camped within only twenty-five kilometres of the Kuwaiti border, could provide logistical support for larger revolutionary operations inside the emirate. In June 1986 a series of commando attacks were launched against vital oil installations at Mina al-Ahmadi, the nerve centre of the emirate's economy only twenty kilometres from Kuwait City. It was, by all accounts, a matter of pure chance, considering the hopeless incompetence of the Party of Allah commando, that the oil installations suffered even minimal damage. But the blow was strong enough to force the Emir to give in to a government demand for the dissolution of Parliament and the adoption of a tougher security policy. But a statement published by ad-Da'awah in Tehran promised more action: 'Islam is at war against the mercenary Kuwaiti regime. . . . Kuwait is a zone of combat and will remain so until complete Islamic rule is established there.'[17]

Next on the Party of Allah's hit list in the Persian Gulf was the emirate of Bahrain, which has a predominantly Shi'ite population. Iran had maintained a claim to sovereignty over the archipelago until 1970, when the Shah agreed to recognize the independence of Bahrain on the basis of a compromise worked out by the United Nations. The Al-Khalifah ruling family repaid the Shah by accepting his leadership in the region, and in 1978 Bahrain was the first Gulf emirate to crack down on pro-Khomeini Shi'ites raising funds for sabotage operations in Iran. Thus it was natural that the Ayatollah should consider the Al-Khalifah clan 'enemies of the Islamic Revolution'.[18]

In March 1979, only a few weeks after Khomeini had seized power in Tehran, a group of 'volunteers' gathered at the port of Bushehr to sail to Bahrain and hoist the flag of Islam on the Emir's palace at Manama. A timely piece of 'friendly advice' from Britain to the new revolutionary regime in Tehran discouraged the mullahs from proceeding with a hasty invasion of Bahrain. But the emirate was not forgotten. Speaking in Qom, Ayatollah Sadeq Rouhani announced that taking part in the 'liberation of Bahrain was a sacred duty of all true Muslims'.[19] Meanwhile a young mullah of Iranian origin, Hojat al-Islam Muhammad-Taqi Mudarressi, had begun using the Manamah mosque – which had been constructed with the help of a donation from the Shah – as a centre for pro-Khomeini propaganda. Without directly naming the Emir, Shaikh Issa ben Salman, the revolutionary mullah called for the overthrow of 'the rule by the agent of Satan in these blessed islands'.[20] The Bahraini authorities were eventually forced to ask Mudarressi to leave. He returned to Iran in the spring of 1980 and was to become one of Mahalati's earliest collaborators. By 1982 Mudarressi had been promoted ayatollah at the age of forty, and designated the future President of the future Islamic Republic of Bahrain.

A charismatic orator and an extremely ambitious and dynamic man, Mudarressi quickly succeeded in attracting Khomeini's attention and in 1983 was put in charge of coordinating all revolutionary activities in the Arabian peninsula. He created a party of his own, Al-Amal al-Islami (Islamic Action) and began recruiting would-be militants from among Arab students in western Europe and the United States. The party claimed more than a hundred 'revolutionary achievements' between 1983 and July 1986, including the assassination of two customs officers and a businessman of Omani origin, and the burning of cars and shops said to belong to 'enemies of Islam'. The presence of a US naval task force off Manama, however, meant that considerable American money and effort was being poured into protecting the emirate from revolutionary turmoil. Mudarressi's vow to 'execute' the leading members of the ruling family remained an empty threat, despite two unsuccessful attempts at bombing the Emir's car in 1984.

Shi'ite agitation in Bahrain, and more specifically an alleged coup plot in 1981, in which Mudarressi was not involved despite claims by the authorities, led to a series of mass expulsions from the archipelago. The plot, as a result of which more than a hundred activists were arrested, was pinned onto the Islamic Front for the Liberation of Bahrain, which had been founded in London in 1977 before the success of Khomeini's revolution in Iran.[21] The Bahraini government had at first toyed with the idea of a massive show of force, including the execution of the ringleaders. In the end, however, a much softer line was adopted, presumably after advice from Britain. The situation was partly defused, but Bahrain was not able to return to the atmosphere of social tolerance and relative political liberty that throughout the 1970s had distinguished it from the other emirates.

The emergence of the Party of Allah and its network of Holy Terror as a day-to-day fact of life in the region quickly faced the smaller emirates with a choice between submitting to Khomeini's diktats or risking the anger of revolutionary mullahs. Dubai's Shaikh Rashed ben Sa'eed Al-Maktum was the first of the local emirs to conclude a deal with the mullahs of Tehran. Under it, Dubai has served as an entrepot for the Islamic Republic in addition to allowing the Party of Allah to use its territory for intelligence purposes. The Emir of Abu Dhabi, Shaikh Zayed ben Sultan Al-Nahiyan, has also maintained close ties with Tehran since 1980.

Only Qatar and the sultanate of Oman appeared unwilling or unable to court the revolutionary mullahs. But neither seemed particularly threatened, partly because of tribal loyalties to the respective ruling families. Both countries, as well as the smaller emirates of Sharjah, Ras al-Khaimah, Fujairah, Ajman and Um ul-Quwayn, also owed part of their relative tranquillity to the fact that the Iran–Iraq War continued to drain much of Tehran's revolutionary energy, while Khomeini's Lebanese adventure attracted most of his attention. Khomeini was at the same time confident that when the time came he could seize control of the smaller emirates through classical military operations rather than as a result of popular revolutions. Iraq and Kuwait remained his more immediate targets in the region, with Bahrain coming third.

Saudi Arabia has not yet been mentioned, for the simple reason that it is recognized by all concerned as the biggest prize in the Middle East. To the Americans, the importance of the Wahabbite kingdom lies in its seemingly inexhaustible oil reserves. To the Party of Allah, however, it is the presence of Islam's two holiest shrines – the Haram al-Sharif (Noble Shrine) in Mecca and the Masjed an-Nabi (The Prophet's Mosque) in Medina – that give Saudi Arabia its special place in the world. The Wahabbites, to which the Saudi ruling family belongs, form one of the smallest of many puritanical sects in Islam. It is estimated that no more than 15 per cent of Saudis are Wahabbites,[22] while the followers of the sect number no more than 2 million throughout the world. Leaders of rival Muslim sects, and Shi'ites in particular, have never fully accepted the idea of Mecca and Medina being controlled by the Wahabbites. In one of his books written in the 1940s, Khomeini describes the Wahabbite version of Islam as 'a distortion, a tissue of lies woven out of true elements, taken out of context'.[23] And in 1986 Ayatollah Montazeri, Khomeini's chosen heir, went one step further in claiming that Wahabbism was 'nothing more than a tribal aberration, a set of pre-Islamic rites'.[24]

The Wahabbites have repaid the compliments in kind over the years. In a series of pamphlets published between 1933 and 1974 in Saudi Arabia, and distributed among pilgrims at Mecca, Wahabbite theologians attacked every last detail of Shi'ism and described it as 'the religion of the Magus, disguised behind a thin Islamic veil'.[25] Prior to Khomeini's revolution Saudi Arabia devoted millions of dollars to the propagation of Wahabbite Islam in Iran and among Shi'ites in

Iraq, Lebanon, Bahrain and Pakistan. The mutual hatred of Shi'ite and Wahabbite theologians was one of the main stumbling blocks to the creation of a pan-Islamic defence grouping led by Iran under the Shah, and Saudi Arabia.[26]

Apart from a tradition of theological dispute, the Party of Allah was resolutely committed to the destruction of the Saudi ruling family for two more reasons. First, Saudi Arabia was a monarchy and Khomeini claimed that monarchy was by definition anti-Islamic.[27] Second, the Saudi kingdom was the United States' closest ally or client state in the region. It was therefore not surprising that in his first Haj pilgrimage message after his accession to power in Tehran, the Ayatollah indirectly called for the overthrow of the Saudi regime.[28] An attempt at fulfilling his wish was made within forty-eight hours of the message being broadcast on Tehran Radio's Arabic programme. It came, however, not from the Shi'ite revolutionaries trying to repeat his success in Iran, but from a group of conspirators belonging to a semi-secret sect founded in Egypt in the 1920s.[29]

Khomeini had counted on anti-American demonstrations in Mecca just over two weeks after the seizure of the US Embassy compound in Tehran. His agents had managed to smuggle into Saudi Arabia thousands of his portraits as well as revolutionary leaflets for distribution among the 3 million Muslims expected to gather for the Haj pilgrimage at the start of the fifteenth century of the *hegira*. But what actually took place went far beyond the Ayatollah's wildest expectations. The Saudi authorities, too, had expected trouble and had dispatched some twenty thousand troops and police to the holy city. But they too were taken totally by surprise. What happened came all of a sudden and without the slightest warning: it proved to be the biggest upheaval in the history of Arabia since the 1930s.

Shortly after dawn prayers at the Haram al-Sharif (The Holy Shrine), where the black stone of the Ka'abah represents the solid heart of Islam, fifty thousand or so pilgrims in the vast courtyard saw a hailstorm of bullets unleashed above their heads. The first of them were fired from a first-floor gallery dominating the courtyard and the Ka'abah itself. Unseen gunmen were apparently firing at policemen positioned at certain points to survey the crowd. Contrary to an explicit ban on bearing arms inside the holy shrine – a ban emphasized on many occasions by the Prophet himself – the Saudi police on duty on that fateful day were carrying small arms. The initial shoot-out, lasting around fifteen minutes, clearly demonstrated the assailants' superior numbers and type of weapons. It also claimed more than a hundred lives, including those of many pilgrims. Before the pilgrims had had time to recover from their initial shock hundreds of them were forced into the basement of the shrine by young gunmen emerging as if from nowhere. The pilgrims knew that they were both hostages and witnesses of the first armed rebellion in Mecca since the Revolt of the Negroes.[30]

The hostages were informed through loudspeakers that the shrine was now in 'the hands of true Muslims for the first time in centuries'. They were then invited to hear a 'sermon' by the leader of the rebellion, who turned out to be a young, thickset man with 'a soft, almost feminine voice' and a pair of deep black eyes 'visibly burning with rage'.[31] Talking through a microphone connected to the loudspeakers of the shrine's minarets, so that everyone in Mecca could hear, the man began with the celebrated Islamic slogan: 'There is no God but Allah!' He then introduced himself as Johaiman, son of Muhammad, son of Sayf of the al-Utaibi tribe. He continued: 'The hour promised by our Prophet – blessed be his soul – when Islam shall triumph over impiety has arrived. I and my brothers have been dispatched by the will of the Almighty to put an end to the rule of corrupt, depraved and eternally doomed princelings who have brought shame to Arabia and its Muslim people.'[32] The 'sermon', lasting less than thirty minutes, continued with detailed examples of the 'corruption, cupidity and callousness' of the kingdom's rulers. 'Believers!' Johaiman shouted. 'These princelings are interested in nothing but women, wine, money, games and music. They abandoned Islam a long time ago, as soon as they saw the golden-haired women of the West and the glittering dollars of Aramco.'[33]

Johaiman's 'sermon' proved so effective that most of the estimated six thousand pilgrims taken hostage[34] came forward and demanded to be armed in the service of the cause; and several hundred pilgrims who had succeeded in leaving the shrine at the start of the shoot-out returned to join the insurgents. Johaiman, who was to be referred to as 'Jackass Joe' by CIA experts flown into Mecca for advice a few hours after the outbreak of violence, had with him some 1500 armed men.[35] Many were members of the Saudi Royal Guard, an elite force to which Johaiman himself had once belonged.

The Saudi authorities have done their best to portray Johaiman's revolt as an isolated case of 'individual madness'. They have described Johaiman himself as 'a homosexual drunkard' who had been excluded from the kingdom's armed forces because of his 'depraved habits'. This is acceptable in so far as the Saudi authorities are repaying Johaiman's compliments; but Johaiman's revolt, ill prepared as it turned out to have been, was certainly neither an isolated operation nor the work of just one 'mad homosexual'.

At the same time that Johaiman was addressing the pilgrims a series of bombs exploded at various sensitive points in Mecca, Medina, Jeddah and the capital, Riyadh. The bomb in Riyadh, placed in the courtyard of the royal palace, killed two guards. The rebels in Mecca had with them at least 1500 weapons, including dozens of automatic rifles and sub-machine guns. They had also smuggled into the basement of the shrine huge quantities of food and drinking water that were intended to last them and their 'guests' several days. The insurgents had clearly prepared themselves for a long siege, apparently in the hope that if they resisted long enough the entire population would rise against the rulers. They did succeed in beating back several attacks of the Royal Guard as well as an attempt by elements of the elite Jordanian 91st division to dislodge them.[36]

'We are fully prepared,' Johaiman had said in his 'sermon', 'and the rest depends on Allah.' But Allah did not come down on the side of the rebels, although the kingdom was shaken to its very foundations for nearly three weeks as the Qahtan and Utaibi tribes staged two separate armed rebellions. Anti-regime demonstrations were also organized in no fewer than eighty-seven towns, especially in the oil-rich provinces of the Persian Gulf. In many cities groups of militants, often armed only with knives, attacked local mosques and tried to repeat Johaiman's adventure.

Johaiman and his companions kept fighting for fourteen days, and eventually surrendered out of physical and spiritual exhaustion. A special force of French commandos had been sent by President Giscard d'Estaing at the request of Prince Fahd, then Crown Prince, Deputy Premier and the regime's strong man.[37] Not knowing what was happening in the rest of the country, and convinced that the general insurrection they had hoped for would now not take place, the rebels stopped fighting and gave Captain Barril's task force an easy victory which the French have not ceased to brag about ever since. A parallel was drawn between the rising of the Mahdi in nineteenth-century Sudan and Johaiman's revolt in Mecca. The Sudanese Mahdi had defeated the British and killed General Gordon; in Mecca, however, Captain Barril had stayed alive and the 'Mahdi' had been captured.[38] Truckloads of corpses were carried out of the holy shrine where at least two thousand people, including hundreds of Saudi soldiers, had fallen during the long battle. Saudi State Radio was able to announce 'the end of the false Mahdi'.[39]

The Saudi royal family, encouraged by the energetic Prince Fahd, hit back hard and fast. In the weeks that followed sixty-eight members of the insurgent group, including Johaiman himself, were beheaded in public in fourteen of the kingdom's cities. Hundreds more were sentenced to long prison terms. But the Saudis nevertheless failed to secure the unanimous support of their own Wahabbite clergy for the condemnation of Johaiman and his companions. Johaiman had left the Saudi armed services to devote himself to the study of the Qur'an and the Hadiths. By the mid-1970s he had already established his reputation as a doctor of theology and, as a protégé of Shaikh Muhammad al-Baz, a leading fundamentalist teacher in the Hejaz, was held in great esteem even among the Wahabbite establishment. The two pamphlets he published in 1975 and 1976 were certainly violent in their denunciation of anti-Islamic trends in the kingdom, but the royal police had to swallow the insults, for Johaiman was upholding the same values that had initially brought the Saud clan into prominence in Arabia in the 1920s. The Islamic Revolution in Iran and the cult of 'Islamic action' preached by the Moroccan fundamentalist Muhammad Abdul-Mut'ee had persuaded

Johaiman, possibly from 1978 onwards, that words without action would not be sufficient to 'save Islam'.[40]

Johaiman's revolt and the sympathy it attracted in the kingdom – even among students who had previously been suspected of harbouring Marxist dreams – proved the failure of the Saudi system to promote itself as the exclusive custodian of strict Islamic values. Johaiman would not have been content with imposing the rules of the *shari'ah* (Islamic law) in public only; he wanted to 'extend the writ of divine law into the privacy of every home'.[41] It was not sufficient for people not to drink and gamble in public in Saudi Arabia; they had to be 'forced, if necessary' to behave in the same way at home or when travelling abroad.[42] Finally, living in accordance with Islamic values also meant waging a Jihad against the infidel. The Saudi state did a great deal to extend the realm of Islam by spending vast sums of money on missions in Africa, India and Indonesia,[43] but all its efforts were worthless as far as the fundamentalists were concerned, if only because the rulers in Riyadh were allies of the American Great Satan.

Despite the fact that Johaiman, a militant Sunni, would have put the Shi'ites to the sword had he gained power, his message of revolt found its strongest response in the Shi'ite-inhabited regions of the kingdom, notably the oil-rich coastal plain of al-Hasa on the Persian Gulf. Tension in al-Hasa remained high for weeks as scores of teachers, oil workers and small shopkeepers were arrested. The Saudis had never allowed their Shi'ites, who may number around a million,[44] to have mullahs like other Shi'ites in the rest of the Muslim world. But since mid-1979, and no doubt inspired by Khomeini's triumphant revolution, the Shi'ites of al-Hasa have begun to appoint a number of learned men among themselves as acting mullahs. At the end of 1979 private Qur'anic schools started to be set up there for the first time in more than half a century, and ceremonies marking the anniversary of Hussein's martyrdom were held at private homes in Dhahran. Though such ceremonies, abhorrent to the Wahabbites who consider them anti-Islamic, were illegal, they were tolerated by the authorities in order not to provoke a confrontation with the ayatollahs of Tehran. Johaiman's revolt, however, put an end to all that and new repressive measures against Shi'ites were initiated in earnest in 1980.

The Party of Allah responded by launching a recruitment drive among Saudi students in the United States and Europe, in addition to organizing radical demonstrations during Haj pilgrimage seasons in Mecca.[45] Up to 1980 the bulk of the opposition to the Saudi regime had flirted with the many different versions of Marxism. Since then, however, Islam has been put forward by all of them, including the Saudi communist party, as the 'ideological content of our struggle for freedom and justice'.[46] The opposition remains deeply divided, none the less. The traditional opposition groups, including the various parties of the Left, still hope to destabilize the Saudi regime through infiltration of the armed forces, which could, when the time came, stage a 'progressive' coup d'état. This would be a repeat of the classic Arab scenario for change, which has already been tested in Egypt, Iraq, Yemen and Syria. The fundamentalists, on the other hand – and the Party of Allah especially – consider the Saudi army to be nothing but an instrument of American domination. Their hopes for revolutionary change are focused on the urban masses, who they feel would rise in revolt in the name of Islam and neutralize the Saudi army and other coercive forces.

Saudi Arabia is subjected to a vast and sustained propaganda effort directed from the Islamic Republic. Huge quantities of tapes, books, leaflets and posters are smuggled into the country through its Persian Gulf coastal areas. Scores of Saudis are receiving revolutionary training, too, including courses in terrorist activities, in the Islamic Republic and Lebanon.[47] Tehran Radio's Arabic programme, which concentrates on 'exposing the crimes of America's Saudi puppets', has attracted a large audience in the kingdom.

From 1955 until 1971 the Saudis played the fundamentalist card against the neighbouring sultanate of Oman, with which they even fought a curious border war in 1956. The old Sultan Sa'eed ben Teimur al-Bu'saeedi of Oman was anything but a modernizer – his fear of the modern world was so intense that he forbade the construction of roads and schools and attempted to return his sultanate to 'the golden days of the

Prophet'.[48] And yet the Saudis were able to attack even him. The point is worth emphasizing, since it shows that even the most strict 'Islamic' rulers are not automatically invulnerable to those who preach an even stricter version of the faith. Saudi rulers, who are now the target of fundamentalist anger for being 'impious and corrupted by the West', were only a decade ago criticized for their 'too strict style of applying the rules of Islam'.

The Saudi-encouraged fundamentalist movement in Oman was led by Imam Ghalib ben Ali, who had secured a following among the Abadhi Muslims in the Jabal-Akhdhar region and preached the establishment of an 'imamate' based on the principle of Walayat Faqih[49] which was to be advanced by Khomeini more than fifteen years later.[50] The Ibadhi revolt was eventually crushed with British support in the late 1960s; Imam Ghalib, accompanied by his brother Talib ben Ali who had been the military commander of the movement, fled to Saudi Arabia.

In 1979, shortly after the victory of Khomeini's revolution, contact was made between Tehran mullahs and Ibadhi militants in exile in Dubai and Kuwait. But Tehran soon found that prospects for an Ibadhi uprising inspired by Khomeini were far from assured. In 1983 representatives of the Party of Allah met five leaders of the defeated Dhofar rebellion,[51] thanks to Libyan contacts in Tripoli.[52] Cooperation against the Sultan of Oman was extensively discussed at that meeting.

The official media in the Islamic Republic reported more than a dozen 'acts of heroism' by members of the Party of Allah in the sultanate between 1984 and 1986. These ranged from attacks on shops selling 'anti-Islamic products' to the distribution of Khomeini's portraits among schoolchildren in the city of Muscat. Perhaps the most serious was an attack on a police station in the town of Rustaq, which was carried out by the Martyr Hussein Brigade, one of the many sobriquets used by the network of Holy Terror to claim credit for its acts. Former members of the Dhofar Liberation Front were not involved in any of the operations, which aroused in the minds of the leaders of the Party of Allah lingering doubts about the sincerity of their conversion to Islam.

Oman's strategic position at the entrance to the Persian Gulf gave it a measure of protection from major acts of violence by the Party of Allah. The mullahs knew that any prolonged closure of the Strait of Hormuz would hurt them more than anyone else, and that the USA, which already had a military presence in the sultanate, would not hesitate to take limited action to protect the Sultan against any major attack backed by the Islamic Republic.[53] A plan to seize the Omani island of Beit al-Ghanam (House of the Goat), just off the tip of Ras Mussandam, was quickly shelved by the Islamic Revolutionary Guard in January 1985 after a US threat of retaliation was relayed to Tehran via Muscat and Damascus.

One of the first countries selected as especially suitable for the implantation of the Party of Allah and its network of Holy Terror was Pakistan. The fact that the country owes its *raison d'être* to Islam persuaded the mullahs and their political advisers to probe Pakistan's revolutionary potential. It was in the hope of creating a revolutionary climate in Pakistan that Abbas Zamani, alias Abu-Sharif, was persuaded in 1980 to resign his post as Commander of the Islamic Revolutionary Guard and become Ambassador to Pakistan. Zamani, a close associate of Chamran and a graduate of several PLO guerrilla schools, quickly turned the Iranian Embassy in Islamabad into a centre for revolutionary activity. Very soon, however, the Party of Allah found itself bogged down in the traditional Shi'ite–Sunni disputes that have marked Pakistani life ever since the country was created in 1947. The Sunnis, accounting for more than 85 per cent of the population, would not accept Khomeini as Imam, and the Shi'ites, traditionally engaged in radical politics, found the Party of Allah too reactionary for their taste. As a result, the party failed to make much headway in Pakistan despite the huge sums of money it spent on its activities there between 1980 and 1984.[54]

Outside Pakistan, however, the Party of Allah has depended heavily on Pakistani militants, and in some cases political mercenaries, for the purpose of infiltrating other countries or setting up propaganda units. This was particularly true in Britain, where hundreds of Pakistanis were employed by the Party of Allah as revolutionary missionaries. Through a variety of institutes, Qur'anic schools, periodicals and associations these Pakistani militants have helped spread Khomeini's message of Islamic revolution.

On 10 June 1986 the cabinet in Tehran approved allocations amounting to some 30 million dollars for 'emergency aid to revolutionary groups coordinated by the Party of Allah abroad'. More than 10 per cent of this was earmarked for Islamic revolutionary organizations run mostly by Pakistanis in the United Kingdom.[55] Pakistani militants also play a key role in the Party of Allah's activities in Canada, the United States and Australia. In 1985 an estimated 115,000 Pakistanis visited the Islamic Republic; many stayed for more than three months in order to 'acquaint themselves better with the revolution'.[56] Pakistani militants also received preferential treatment as far as employment in Iranian government enterprises abroad was concerned. In 1986 an estimated 15 per cent of all employees of banks, airline offices, companies and legations belonging to the Islamic Republic in more than eighty countries were Pakistanis. Many Pakistani militants were also employed as 'ethical inspectors' to keep an eye on Iranians travelling to Europe and North America for their holidays or on business.[57]

The idea of creating one or more Islamic republics in India was a major item in the Party of Allah's programme right from the start. Apart from the state of Kashmir, which is routinely included among 'occupied territories' in the literature of the Party of Allah, the Muslims of Maharashtra, Gujarat and Uttar Pradesh are also regularly invited to 'shake off the yoke of Hindu colonialism'. Between 1980 and 1986 the Party of Allah dispatched more than seventy thousand of its militants to India, mostly as students attending technical courses of between six months and three years. At least twenty-five thousand of these 'students' were there at any given time. Many were expelled after being found guilty of anti-state activities, and between 1983 and 1986 at least six were killed in mysterious circumstances on different occasions and in different states; some may have been victims of Hindu extremists or Sikh militants. The Muslim Students' Association, the Islamic Friendship Society and smaller clubs in seven Indian states were all used as vehicles for spreading the Khomeinist version of the True Faith. Many Indian militants were at the same time used for taking the message further afield – notably to the Philippines, Indonesia and Malaysia. Indian militants chosen to become 'missionaries of the Islamic Revolution' in other parts of Asia were given special training courses in Tehran, Qom, Mashhad and Isfahan before being sent on their missions.

In India itself, however, the Party of Allah could not report any major breakthrough in 1986 despite years of hard work and investments estimated at millions of dollars. In some universities, female Muslim students had agreed to wear the Khomeinist *hejab* in exchange for allowances varying between the equivalent of five and twelve dollars a month. Some shopkeepers were also prepared to display portraits of Khomeini and sell English and Urdu versions of his works, almost certainly in exchange for cash from local branches of the Party of Allah. Beyond that, however, the vast majority of Indian Muslims remained unsympathetic to the party's message of bloody revolution and terror against the infidel.[58]

The party discovered the Muslims of the Philippines towards the end of 1981 – largely as a result of the activities of Libya's Colonel Gaddafi who, despite his well-publicized differences with Khomeini, considered the Ayatollah an important partner in exporting revolutionary Islam to the whole world. The revolt of the Mindanao Muslims against Ferdinand Marcos's corrupt and authoritarian regime in Manila began in 1969, before Gaddafi himself had seized power in Tripoli and long before the emergence of the Party of Allah and its network of Holy Terror. But it was not until the mid-1970s that the revolt developed into a major insurrection, thanks mainly to financial and political support from Saudi Arabia, Libya, Iraq, Syria and several other Muslim countries. The Islamic Republic was the last to arrive on the scene and offer help to the Muslim insurgents, but it was both more generous in its financial assistance and more genuine in its propagation of revolutionary ideals. By 1984 the Moro Liberation Front (MLF), the principal non-communist Muslim rebel organization in the Philippines, was almost totally controlled by the Party of Allah. The MLF maintained sumptuous offices in Tehran, plus a training camp for 'revolutionary preachers' in Borujerd, west of the city.

The MLF was nevertheless not the only Filipino group to enjoy support from the Party of Allah. Agents of the Islamic Republic sent to the Philippines as students, diplomats and businessmen established contact early in 1982 with two sects of Muslim extremists. Hojat al-Islam Yahya Malakzadeh, a representative of the Party of Allah who toured the Philippines, Malaysia, Indonesia and Thailand that spring, reported in a long study published at the end of 1982 that Islam 'could sweep through Asia like a bush fire'.[59] The most important of the two Filipino sects was the Sabilyoun or People of the [Right] Path. This secret society, set up in the nineteenth century, models its organization on that of the Assassins. It is totally devoted to the murder of the infidel, especially Catholics in Mindanao. The sect is divided into numerous clandestine cells of between five and ten men – women are not allowed to join it – who meet and act under a *murshed* or guide known as *pandita*. Every member takes a solemn oath that binds him to the organization until death.[60]

The ideal of each Sabili is to put to death as many non-Muslims as possible before entering a Paradise that in its description strangely resembles that of Hassan Sabbah – complete with ever-virgin houris and the fountain of eternal youth. Once admitted into a secret cell the Sabili undergoes a period of intensive physical and spiritual training aimed at making of him a 'clear-headed madman'.[61] He will kill as only a madman can, braving all dangers, but will at the same time retain the lucidity needed for taking the enemy by surprise.[62]

It was a Sabili terror squad that carried out a grenade attack on a Catholic church in the small town of Salvador, 800 kilometres south of Manila, on 8 June 1986. Eleven members of a wedding party at the church were killed and 123 others injured. On 22 June another Sabili terror group attacked a Christian village in the same region, murdering seven people. This time, pitchforks and axes were used in the attack.

The other extremist sect to establish an alliance with the Party of Allah, known as the White Flag movement, is active not only in the Philippines but also in Malaysia and Thailand. A myth, according to which a new wave of victories for Islam will begin under the leadership of a super-*pandita* from the West, facilitated the task of the Party of Allah propagandists in claiming that Khomeini was the providential leader promised by legend.

Both the Sabilyoun and the White Flag have included in their rituals much that is evidently un-Islamic – probably a relic of the native cultures of Southeast Asia. The White Flag, for example, use in their ceremonies an alcoholic liquor derived from local fruits, while the Sabilyoun are fond of music and dancing, both of which are considered by the Party of Allah to be deadly sins.

In the Philippines, Indonesia and Malaysia, and to a lesser extent Thailand, the Party of Allah has emphasized its opposition to the United States as the principal enemy of Islam in the contemporary world. It has found a receptive audience among the tens of thousands of students from these countries who are attending university in the United States. Many of these students, often enjoying financial support from Tehran, return home during the holidays in order to spread Khomeini's message. A leaflet published in 1983 by the Malaysian Students' Islamic Association of the United States said: 'Today it is no longer sufficient to say the *shahadatayn*[63] to be a true Muslim. It is also necessary to add: "Death to the Great Satan, the enemy of Islam." '[64]

Between 1982 and 1986 all Southeast Asian countries with substantial Muslim populations experienced growing agitation on the part of the fundamentalists.[65] In 1984–85 Indonesia expelled a total of 1200 Iranians, including students, diplomats and businessmen, for 'activities harmful to the security of the state'. Several Islamic associations, financed by Saudi Arabia and therefore hostile to the Party of Allah, organized anti-Khomeini riots in Java in 1984, setting on fire a number of houses and shops belonging to sympathizers of the Party of Allah. In Malaysia, the murders in 1984 of several policemen, bank managers and local officials were claimed by Muslim extremists. The Party of Allah was believed to have inspired and financed some of the operations.

The Indonesian government ordered a crack-down on fundamentalist groups late in 1985 after a mosque gathering in Jakarta's poorest district near the docks led to riots. The gathering was addressed by preachers who described themselves as 'partisans of Allah' and reportedly incited the crowd to attack a nearby police station where two youths were being held on a charge of larceny. The attack provoked the intervention of the army and led to a veritable carnage, in which at least thirty demonstrators were killed and 700 others injured. Among the dead was one Shaikh Khalifah Muhammad, a preacher trained in Qom and described as 'the Khomeini of Asia' by his supporters.

In the subsequent raids organized against the homes of some of the preachers involved in the riot, huge quantities of Party of Allah literature, as well as arms, acid and cash, were seized by the police. A document described as 'the constitution of the Islamic Republic of Indonesia' was also seized.

In none of the countries in question, however, was the Party of Allah able to gain control of mainstream Islamic movements. In the Philippines, Indonesia, Malaysia and Thailand it remained a pressure group, forcing mainstream organizations such as PAS, the MLF and the various Jimaats (societies) into adopting more radical positions. It advertised its active presence through attacks on wine shops, restaurants, girls' schools, cinemas, libraries and other 'places of sin' (*sic*). But once again the dramatic fall in the oil revenues of the Islamic Republic prevented the network of Holy Terror from expanding as fast as its leaders in Tehran had hoped.

From 1985 onwards, hampered by shortage of funds and its relative ignorance of social and political conditions in Southeast Asia, the Party of Allah had to treat its activities in the region as a long-term investment. Instead, it began devoting more resources to the Middle East, the 'heartland of Islam'. One key country in this heartland remained off limits until 1986 as far as the Party of Allah was concerned. Syria, having concluded an alliance with the Islamic Republic, had acted as a full and enterprising partner in most of the activities of the network of Holy Terror in Lebanon, Iraq and the Gulf States. Some analysts have even argued that President Assad opted for an alliance with Khomeini partly at least because he wanted to secure his 'Islamic' flank while continuing his duel with Iraq's Saddam Hussein. Syria, however, was not immune to Islamic fundamentalist agitation. Between 1979 and 1986 an estimated twenty-five thousand people were killed in more than a hundred different operations that pitched Assad's forces against those of Islamic insurgents.

Syria was probably the only Muslim country in which the Muslim Brotherhood remained a revolutionary force throughout the 1980s. Unlike the situation in Egypt and Jordan, where the Brotherhood had become part of the system, the Syrian Brothers remained true to the teachings of Shaikh Hassan al-Banna. This was partly because Syria was ruled by men belonging to the small quasi-Shi'ite minority known as the Alawites.[66] Assad's avowal of socialism and his alliance with the USSR made his regime doubly suspect in the eyes of the fundamentalists.[67]

The Syrian Brothers were divided into three groups. The most active, known as 'the fighting advanced guards', was led by Adnan Oqla and claimed to have more than three thousand highly trained guerrillas. The original training of the Brothers was provided by the PLO in its Jordanian camps in the late 1960s, but later the Brothers were able to set up their own secret camps inside Syria as well as in northern Lebanon, where they shared facilities with the guerrillas of the Lebanese Sunni fundamentalist leader Shaikh Saeed Shaaban.

The moderate faction of the Syrian Brothers came into being in 1965 and was led by Issam al-Attar who, from exile in Aachen in West Germany, preached the destruction of the Alawite 'usurper regime'. The third faction, led by Adnan Sadr-Eddin, established close links with Baghdad and specialized in car bomb attacks in Syrian cities. In November 1981 the group claimed responsibility for a car bombing in Damascus which cost more than 160 lives, and in January and April 1986 the group carried out a number of other similar attacks in Damascus, Homs, Hama, Aleppo and Antioch in which some three hundred people were reported killed. It is possible that Iraqi Ba'athist agents were closely involved in all the activities of the Sadr-Eddin faction, which remained devoted to indiscriminate terrorist attacks clearly designed to cause panic among ordinary people.

Oqla's faction, on the other hand, opted for selective attacks on targets closely associated with the Assad regime. Members of the Alawite minority were favourite victims of the Brothers, who also made a point of murdering as many members of the ruling Ba'ath party as they could. In June 1979 a commando force of sixty Brothers, led by a man named Omar Junnad, launched a surprise attack on an officers' training school in Aleppo. More than 260 cadets were killed, most of them Alawites, as were Junnad himself together with nineteen of his companions. The rest of his group were later captured and shot.

The most spectacular operation launched by the 'advance guard', however, occurred in February 1981 in Hama, when thousands of Brothers went on the rampage, killing members of the Ba'ath party, government officials, Alawite mullahs and army officers and burning their homes on the way. They slit the throats of scores of women and young children, mostly surprised in their sleep.[68] The government retaliated with even greater brutality: thousands of Brothers and their families were put to death in a house-to-house 'search and kill' operation led by the President's brother Rifa'at al-Assad and his special forces.[69] The Syrian authorities blamed the United States and Israel as purse-masters of the Brothers, and there was circumstantial evidence to support that claim.[70] The Brothers in turn describe the Assad regime as 'an instrument for murdering Muslims' in the hands of Moscow.[71]

During his term as Islamic Ambassador to Damascus, Ayatollah Muhtashami had on a number of occasions advised the Party of Allah leaders in Tehran to accede to some form of dialogue with the Syrian Brothers. After all, Assad's 'atheistic regime' remained a long-term enemy – even though it was currently a tactical ally in Iran's war against Iraq – and the Brothers, representing the main force of opposition in Syria, could not be forgotten by the party. But this advice was ignored until 1986 when, as already noted, contact between Tehran and the Syrian Brothers was established through Lebanese Sunni groups opposed to Assad.[72]

The deterioration of relations between Tehran and Damascus in 1986 was seen by the Attar group as an opportunity for starting discussions with the Party of Allah. The Syrian Brothers had always claimed that Khomeini and Assad were dreaming of creating a Shi'ite axis from Lebanon to the Persian Gulf. Imam Mussa Sadr's close links with Syria in the 1970s, followed by Khomeini's alliance with the Syrian

Ba'ath party in the 1980s, were cited as indications of a pan-Shi'ite plot to dominate the Muslim world. The Sadr-Eddin faction had tried in vain to seek support from Khomeini for the Syrian Brothers, and had concluded that the Party of Allah was nothing but an instrument of Shi'ite hegemony in the region and beyond.[73] But in May 1986 a Party of Allah delegation, led by Ayatollah Mahdi Karrubi, reportedly had a meeting with three representatives of the Syrian Brothers in Hamburg.[74] What was certain was that both the Party of Allah and the Syrian Ba'ath party attached at least as much importance to strictly political considerations as to any idealistic talk about pan-Shi'ism and the triumph of the House of Ali.[75]

One major Muslim country where the Party of Allah had not succeeded in gaining control of the fundamentalist movement was Egypt, the birthplace of modern revolutionary Islam and in many ways the trendsetter in the Arab world. The re-emergence of militant fundamentalism in Egypt preceded Khomeini's revolution in Iran and could be directly traced to the Muslim Brotherhood movement. Egypt's original brand of fundamentalism is, however, no less violent than that preached by the Party of Allah. It is often referred to as Qutbism, after Sayyed Muhammad Qutb, and its message could be summed up in Khomeini's celebrated formula: 'To kill and to die in the service of Allah is the highest duty of every true Muslim.' The Qutbists returned to the scene of violent politics in 1977, after nearly a decade of vengeful silence during which they abandoned every last illusion of peaceful progress towards an Islamic society, the ideal that they had inherited from the Muslim Brotherhood under Banna's successors. To mark their return they kidnapped and murdered Shaikh Muhammad al-Dhahabi, a leading doctor of theology and a former Minister of Religious Endowments.

The group responsible for the murder called itself al-Takfir wal-Hegira (Anathema and Withdrawal) and was led by an agronomist named Shukri Mustafa. It had developed into a secret society with a strong following among university students in Cairo and other major cities, and declared the existing Egyptian way of life to be a manifestation of *jahiliyah* (barbarity) as opposed to the ideal Islamic society. True Muslims had to liberate their thoughts from 'the stranglehold of barbarous ideas' before being able to reject the existing society and prepare for its violent overthrow.[76]

The fact that Qutbism bases its view of the world on a cut and dried Manichean division of all phenomena into good and evil, and Islamic and anti-Islamic, made it more easily understood by students prepared to accept a dualistic interpretation of existence after years of Marxist propaganda based on a mechanical version of dialectics.

A study completed in April 1986 listed more than thirty different clandestine associations that could be described as Qutbist.[77] President Sadat's assassins, the organizers of bloody riots in the cities of Asyut and Ismailia between 1981 and 1985, and the instigators of a revolt by police cadets near Cairo in 1986 were all members of one or other of these Qutbist groups. The Qutbists had a total membership of more than half a million, while the official Muslim Brotherhood claimed 3 million supporters. Islamic fundamentalism which, as has been shown, inevitably leads to violence, was in 1986 the only credible alternative to the existing socio-political system in the country. Many of the groups on the list could be described as sects not unlike the Moonies, with the important difference that they trained their members to kill and to die.

Between 1981 and 1986 there were more than seven hundred incidents involving revolutionary fundamentalists in Egypt. They included the murder of local officials, armed robberies, the throwing of acid at unveiled women, the beheading of 'enemies of Islam' in villages, the burning of houses belonging to infidels, the sacking of wine shops, restaurants, girls' schools and libraries, and the desecration of churches belonging to the Coptic minority – in other words, all the classic tactics of the Party of Allah.[78] In the same period more than three thousand fundamentalists were put on trial charged with anti-state activities, and more than a hundred were sentenced to death. No fewer than ten thousand militant fundamentalists served prison sentences during the period.

The Qutbist organizations used a variety of sobriquets – often to create confusion and protect themselves against police action – such as Islamic Jihad, Hezb al-Tahrir al-Islami (Islamic Liberation Party), ad-Da'awah (The Call), Nahdhah (Awakening) and Forqan (Distinction between Good and

Evil). The Egyptian authorities, however, were convinced that all the groups in question followed a single strategy and probably a single leadership based in a 'foreign country'.[79]

Some leaders of the Qutbist movement became household names in the 1980s, thanks partly to official propaganda against them. Shaikh Omar Abdul-Rahman, Abdul-Salam al-Faraj, Abbud az-Zemur and Karam Zuhdi were some of the heroes of the movement. But the hero of heroes remained Lieutenant Khalid Ahmad Showqi al-Islambouli, the man who shot Sadat. Cassettes relating his life story and including recitations of poems and songs written in his honour were smuggled into Egypt by the regime's opponents, together with full-colour portraits of him, printed on self-adhesive paper. The Party of Allah headquarters in Tehran was reported to be responsible for financing the promotion of Islambouli into a martyr-hero cult figure – 'the man who killed the Pharaoh'.[80]

The production and sale of cassettes of sermons delivered by militant fundamentalists, especially the blind Shaikh Kashk, became a prosperous industry. Between 1980 and 1986 more than 3 million cassettes and over a million copies of books and pamphlets were sold by Egyptian fundamentalists in Egypt, other parts of North Africa, western Europe and the Gulf States.[81] Fundamentalist preachers were outselling even Um Kulsum.[82]

Without securing a direct share in power, the Qutbists, who are often described as Egyptian Khomeinists, succeeded in dictating many of their policies to the government. Laws aimed at establishing some measure of equality between men and women were repealed in 1983, and a series of bans on 'un-Islamic practices', including the sale of alcohol, gambling and mixed bathing at public beaches, were imposed. The opposition parties in Parliament, including the alliance of the Wafd and the Muslim Brotherhood, planned their every move with one eye on the revolutionary Qutbists. The tactic of leading from behind – or pushing others to do part of your job without giving them the slightest credit – worked well for the Egyptian Khomeinists. Every concession granted by the Egyptian government, and every Qutbist slogan adopted by the official parties and the press, was seen as an additional sign of the system's weakness and further encouraged the more militant members of the fundamentalist groups.

Conscious that the armed forces provided the backbone of the 'barbarous' regime, the Qutbists made a special effort to convert the military to their cause and to infiltrate the army, the police and even the security services (Mukahbarat).

Like their counterparts in the Party of Allah, the Qutbists of Egypt represent a range of moods. One could find them living in fraternal communes on the margin of society, devoting themselves to the study of the Qur'an and the Hadiths in an atmosphere of inner peace and serenity. But they could also be seen organized in what Elias Canetti has described as 'the hunting crowd',[83] armed with cudgels, hatchets, Molotov cocktails and bottles of sulphuric acid, ready to unleash their boundless rage against 'the enemies of Allah' and all who 'deviate from His path'. The Qutbist appeared both as a pious shaikh sitting on the floor in a bare room, content with such frugal fare as *foull*,[84] and as a wealthy import-export baron riding about in a bullet-proof limousine and dining at the most expensive restaurants of Cairo. The Qutbist appeal, like that of Khomeini, was not limited to any particular class or age group, but terrorized and attracted large numbers from every kind of socio-economic background.[85]

Egypt's southern neighbour, Sudan, also experienced fundamentalism. There were two major groups: the Ansars (Companions), led by Sadeq al-Mahdi, a descendant of the nineteenth-century Mahdi, and the Muslim Brotherhood, with the lawyer Hassan al-Turabi at their head. Both groups have used violence against their opponents on various occasions throughout the 1970s and up to 1986, but neither developed any specifically terrorist arm, despite encouragement from Libya's Colonel Gaddafi, who subsidized both movements at different times.

Although politically less developed than Egypt, Sudan proved surprisingly immune to the influence of both the Party of Allah and the Egyptian Qutbists. The domination of Sudanese politics by the Ansars and the Brothers limited the appeal of more radical fundamentalist groups to small numbers of intellectuals in the larger cities.[86] But here too radical Islam of the type preached by Sayyed Qutb and Khomeini has a powerful rival in the shape of the semi-clandestine Hezb al-Tahrir al-Islami (Islamic Liberation Party),[87] which, rather than calling on Muslims to use force individually, bases its strategy on a conversion of the army to 'true Islam' so that the rule of Muhammad can be established through a military coup d'état. However, President Ja'afar Muhammad al-Numeiri's disastrous experiment in applying the *shari'ah*, assisted by Turabi, dealt a serious blow to the popularity of all Islamic fundamentalist groups in Sudan between 1984 and the dictator's overthrow in a coup d'état in 1985.[88]

The phenomenal progress of Islam in black Africa during the period 1960–86, when the followers of the 'Only True Faith' increased their numbers by an estimated 25 million,[89] brought with it unforeseen opportunities for the growth of radical fundamentalism. From 1980 radical fundamentalist groups linked with either the Party of Allah or the various Qutbist groups in Egypt were active in several East African countries. In Eritrea, the radical fundamentalist groups fought against the Ethiopian occupation of their territory under a leadership consisting mostly of Marxist guerrillas. In tiny Djibouti, the Islamic Jihad organization was active among schoolchildren and port workers until it was discreetly suppressed in 1984. Radical Muslim associations, using the Arabic term *Jama'ah*[90] to describe themselves, were also active in Kenya, Tanzania and Uganda.[91] Many of these groups were jointly financed by Saudi Arabia, Libya and the Islamic Republic which, despite their undisguised hatred for one another, cooperated in spreading Islam.

West Africa, where Muslims form a majority of the population in every country except Ghana, the Ivory Coast, Cameroon and Togo, attracted the special attention of fundamentalist groups from the end of 1979. In 1986 the Party of Allah financed and 'inspired' more than two hundred Qur'anic schools, half of them in Nigeria,[92] and several hundred *talabehs* from Senegal, Nigeria, Niger, Sierra Leone, Guinea and Mali were attending theological courses in Qom, Tehran and Mashhad.[93]

Senegal had its own native version of radical fundamentalism long before Khomeini's Islamic Revolution and certainly without any direct inspiration from the Qutbist movement either.[94] These radicals, led by people like El-Haj Muhammad Mahmud Niang, succeeded in creating their own breakaway miniature 'Islamic Republic' in the city of Touba in 1980. The apparatus of the Senegalese state, described as 'a creature of freemasons and colonialists',[95] was excluded from the city of some sixty thousand people and from its environs. The 'Islamic Republic' of Touba repealed all non-Islamic laws and applied the rules of the *shari'ah* to the letter. Touba was, nevertheless, not a base for revolutionary activity against the central government in Dakar; it merely offered an opportunity to those who saw it as their duty to perform *hegira* or withdrawal from the corrupt society around them.[96]

Those who wanted to go a step further in their quest for revolutionary Islam found some of their needs satisfied in Kaolak, where militants of the Party of Allah, openly asserting their allegiance to Khomeini, preached and prepared for 'the day of emancipation' under the leadership of the charismatic Ahmad Niasse, referred to as 'the ayatollah' by his followers, and his brother Shaikh Lamine. Lamine was a graduate of Tehran's school for combatant clergy[97] and a frequent visitor to the Islamic Republic. The Khomeinist movement led by the Niasse brothers published a weekly called *Wal Fajr* (*Dawn*), named after the codeword used for one of Iran's major military operations against Iraq in 1983. The magazine claimed a growing audience not only inside Senegal but also among Senegalese students and workers in France. It made no secret of its hatred for 'Jews, the Great Satan America, freemasons, communists, atheists and sodomites',[98] and advocated the forcible conversion to Islam of the country's Christians and Animists.

One of the first countries to lend support to the 1978–79 revolution in Iran was Algeria, despite the fact that it had described itself as a socialist state for more than two decades. Until 1980 Algerian leaders were able to claim with some justice that Islam played no major role in Algerian politics. Six years later, the country's constitution had to be amended to take into account the growing pressure of Muslim fundamentalism.

The appeal of Algerian socialism, which remained a matter mostly of form symbolized by a one-party system and a state-dominated economy, never went beyond party and government functionaries and certain city-dwellers who were able to share its privileges. Rural communities and the centres of urban poverty remained almost totally dominated by Islam. The Algerian war of independence of 1954–62 had in fact begun as just one sequence in the long struggle to preserve the country's Islamic character. The Society of Ulama,[99] founded by Ben Badis in the 1930s, and the various *jama'ah* (associations) that mushroomed everywhere in the 1950s, served as breeding grounds for a popular Islamic anti-colonial movement. During the war itself the mosques provided the network of popular support needed for confronting the might of the French army and the well-organized colonial settlers who were determined to fight to the bitter end. The advent of independence, however, left the Islamic societies without any significant share of power. The new state was dominated by intellectuals and army officers professing Third World-style socialism and trying to compete with the mosques through the local branches of their exclusive political organization, the Front pour la Libération Nationale (FLN).

In 1972 the government of President Houari Boumédienne ordered a crackdown on the Islamic societies and imprisoned a number of Muslim militants. Later, however, he was forced to recognize the power of his adversaries and opted for a policy of reconciliation. The Qiyam (Values) Society was allowed to keep a number of branches in Algiers and other major cities. A few months later some members of the society, co-opted by the FLN, created the Ahl ad-Da'awah (People of the Call) organization as the Islamic arm of the state. Subsequent events, however, showed that the Ahl ad-Da'awah were more interested in pushing the government into what they saw as 'the correct Islamic direction' than in defending the state against radical fundamentalists. They not only succeeded in preventing all legislation aimed at legal equality between men and women, but also 'encouraged' the government to repeal several un-Islamic laws.[100]

The inevitable limits of Ahl ad-Da'awah were dramatically illustrated in the summer of 1985 when a Muslim fundamentalist commando attacked the police academy in Soumaa, near Blida. The attackers met with little resistance because most of the cadets and instructors were away celebrating the Feast of Sacrifice, Islam's most important 'day of joy'. The attackers made away with more than a hundred hand guns and a number of Mas 36 rifles, plus quantities of ammunition. They left their signature' on the gate of the academy: 'Allah the Avenger is with us!'[101] The operation, carried out so close to the capital, came as a shock to the government, which decided to strike back in force.

A nationwide search for the attackers eventually led to the identification of a base they had set up in Larbaa, thirty kilometres southeast of Algiers. It was from here that the commando, calling itself Jund Allah (The Army of Allah), had in the meantime organized a series of bank robberies and attacks on military convoys. On 21 October 1985 a task force of elite troops backed by tanks and rocket launchers attacked the rebels' base and captured it after nine hours of fighting. The government forces lost fifteen men, with more than forty injured. They killed one rebel and captured three others, but the leader, identified as Mustafa Bou-Ali, succeeded in escaping together with nine companions.

Born in 1940, Bou-Ali had fought in the war of independence as an active member of the FLN, but broke with it after he found it 'dominated by men committed to the destruction of Islam'.[102] Choosing the codename Yassin, Bou-Ali disappeared in 1983 and, according to the Algerian authorities, spent some time in the Islamic Republic and Libya. He returned to Algeria at the end of 1984 and organized a number of small clandestine groups dedicated to the overthrow of the state. Early in 1985, however, most of these groups were discovered by the police and 135 activists were arrested. Bou-Ali was not among them, but he was subsequently sentenced to death *in absentia*.

Bou-Ali's commandos remained active in 1985 and 1986. In November 1985 they attacked a military convoy near Birtouna and later fought two battles against gendarmerie units at Attaba and Oued al-Alenge, south of Algiers. In 1986 the group carried out a number of bank robberies and attacks on typically 'un-Islamic' buildings such as girls' schools, libraries, restaurants and cinemas.

In the spring of 1986 the group led by Bou-Ali announced

its merger with several other fundamentalist organizations within a new movement called Islamic Jihad. The statement announcing the merger described the new movement as an arm of the Party of Allah – for the first time underlining its links with Khomeini's Islamic Republic.[103]

That radical Islam provided the main challenge to the stability of the Algerian state was further illustrated by the dramatic 'conversion' of Ahmad Ben Bella to the ideas of the Party of Allah in 1981–82.[104] The former guerrilla leader and President of the Algerian Republic had begun his career as a socialist with distinctly Leninist sympathies.[105] Starting a second political career, however, he presented himself as Khomeini's chief supporter in North Africa. In 1984 he launched the weekly *al-Badil* in Switzerland – where he had taken up residence after being forced to leave France – to propagate Khomeini's ideas concerning the state and revolution. *Al-Badil*, widely distributed among North African immigrants in France and also smuggled into Algeria, did not, however, propel Ben Bella into a position of leadership. In the eyes of the Party of Allah he remained suspect as an 'unrepentant socialist'.[106]

The Algerian government tried to stem the tide of Khomeinism by mobilizing the traditional clergy and toning down its own secular position. From 1985 onwards the Egyptian preacher Shaikh Muhammad al-Ghazzali was given maximum exposure by the official media in his campaign against both Khomeini and Gaddafi.[107] He presented Islam as a religion of 'humanism and progress', using almost exactly the same words as in the new Algerian constitution, which was approved in a referendum in January 1986. The immediate effect of Ghazzali's state-sponsored Islamism, however, was to legitimize the debate on Algeria's 'Islamic' future, thus giving the Khomeinist groups, especially in the universities, reason to claim that even the 'atheistic' state now recognized its error.[108]

In neighbouring Morocco, the emergence in the 1980s of the Party of Allah as a challenge to the established order did not take the form of an armed struggle, as it did in Algeria. Radical Islamic groups, which played a vital role in the independence struggle, were associated with the emerging state structure in Morocco right from the start. The Istiqlal (Independence) party, founded by the Islamic scholar and propagandist Allal al-Fassi, was a senior partner in many government coalitions between the 1950s and 1970s. The Moroccan royal family, which claimed descent from the Prophet Muhammad, presented itself as the natural custodian of the country's Islamic identity. The King assumed the title of Emir al-Momen'een (Commander of the Faithful) and claimed the position of the country's number one cleric.

Nevertheless Morocco too was faced with a growing Khomeinist movement long before the term was even invented. In 1970 and 1971 the first of many Islamic associations began to operate in Casablanca, Rabat, Tangier, Fez and Marrakesh. All of them called for 'the identification of the state and the society under Islam',[109] and all preached Holy War against 'the infidel threatening the very existence of the Only True Faith'.[110] In 1972 Abdul-Karim Mot'ee who was to win fame as Morocco's most charismatic exponent of radical Islam, founded the Jamiyat al-Shabab al-Islamiyah (Society of Muslim Youth). Mot'ee had come to radical Islam after spells as a socialist militant and a middle-ranking official at the Ministry of Education.

In addition to the standard themes of Muslim fundamentalists everywhere, Mot'ee developed the idea of 'fighting the enemy within'. He argued that to defend Islam against its external enemies it was essential first to eliminate those who 'wore an Islamic mask but acted as apostates' within Muslim countries. In other words, the existing governments in Muslim countries had to be overthrown, by force if necessary. Mot'ee's ideas were to have a decisive influence on the group of Saudi Arabian militants who seized the Mecca shrine in 1979. The Shabab movement, however, suffered from serious internecine feuds after 1979, mostly because of differing evaluations of Khomeini's Islamic Revolution.

In 1980 a number of Shabab militants created the Islamic Thinking Club with a view to concentrating their activities on the theoretical work needed to prepare Islam for the 'problems of today'. The club was close to but independent of the Jami'ah (Group) movement led by Abd Assalam Yassine, who is generally considered the most original of Moroccan radical Muslim theorists.[111] Like Mot'ee, Yassine came to Islam from socialism, which is reflected in the Marxist phraseology used in his writings.

Another group, al-Mujahed (The Holy Warrior), openly advocated the overthrow of the Moroccan monarchy and its replacement by an Islamic republic modelled on that of Khomeini.[112] Members of this group made no secret of their links with the Party of Allah's headquarters in Tehran, but claimed that the visits which they paid to the Islamic Republic were intended only as 'educational missions'.[113] The Mujahed group worked in close cooperation with the Moroccan branch of the Islamic Liberation (Tahrir) party which played a key role in fomenting riots in the kingdom's major cities in 1983 and 1984. An important function of the Tahrir party was the distribution inside Morocco of Khomeini's portraits and Arabic translations of his works. Some members of the group were also active in what one of their spokesmen described as 'cleansing' operations, such as forcing women to wear the veil by threatening them with acid or stabbing youths in jeans.[114]

The spread of radical Islamic thought, with its quest for universal revolution, was mainly confined to students, urban workers and the urban lower middle classes. It was met with determined hostility on the part of the traditional clergy, which with a few notable exceptions remained more interested in preserving their own privileges than in upsetting the apple cart in the name of religious idealism. One of the exceptions was Shaikh Muhammad al-Zemzami, an octogenarian preacher in Tangier, who from 1984 was referred to as Morocco's Khomeini. Although frequently imprisoned after his incendiary sermons, the shaikh did not cease to refer to the King as the Emir al-Khaen'een or Commander of the Traitors.[115] Tapes of his sermons commanded a ready market throughout North Africa.

In 1986 the Moroccan fundamentalist movement began to seek support among the armed forces. Publications smuggled into the kingdom by exiles stopped attacking the army, the King and his ministers, and instead invited 'brother officers' to join 'the struggle of the people'. Militants belonging to the Moroccan groups inspired by the Party of Allah also spoke of 'special efforts to persuade the army to abandon the traitor king and to move to the side of the dispossessed and the downtrodden'.[116] This represented a deviation from the classical Khomeinist revolutionary course, which insists that the 'Satanic rulers' are overthrown not through military coups d'état but as a result of popular revolts and 'the blood of the martyrs'. However the meeting between King Hassan and the Israeli Prime Minister Shimon Peres in France in July 1986 provoked a violent reaction from the fundamentalist opposition to the monarchy. In a declaration made in Paris on 30 July the Shabab (Youth) group even sentenced the King to death by hanging.

The third, and smallest, of the traditional Maghreb countries, Tunisia, saw the rise of militant fundamentalism later than Algeria or Morocco. In the early 1980s it was even conceivable that Tunisia would be spared the experience. The country's less oppressive political system and the tradition of social reform and secularization established by President Bourguiba were seen as ramparts against the rising tide of Khomeinism. By 1986, however, most experts agreed that it was in Tunisia that the Party of Allah had the strongest chance of establishing the first Islamic republic of the Maghreb. Between 1983 and 1986 Tunisian citizens had been arrested in several European countries and charged with a number of terrorist acts. Some confessed to having received terrorist training in the PLO and Party of Allah camps in Lebanon and the Islamic Republic.[117]

The first of a series of militant Islamic organizations dedicated to 'saving Tunisia from secularization' came into being in 1976 with the aim of acting as a peaceful pressure group. Called L'Action Islamique, it consisted of around two hundred intellectuals and university students under the leadership of Rached al-Ghannoushi. In 1981 the group changed its name to Harakat al-Ershad al-Islamiyah, or the Islamic Orientation Movement. It organized Qur'anic classes and offered seminars on the thoughts of Banna, Mawdoodi, Qutb and Khomeini. Through his brisk, concise papers, written in an emphatic style and distributed in secondary schools, universities and factories, Ghannoushi himself played a key role in popularizing many concepts of the Islamic Revolution. The Orientation Movement eventually became a school for far more radical militants, who broke with Ghannoushi and went on to create their own clandestine revolutionary cells. These cells, believed to number over 700, each with up to twelve members, had as their spiritual guide the theologian Abdul-Fattah Mocnor, often described as 'the Tunisian Khomeini'. From 1984 onwards the cells used the signature 'Islamic Jihad' whenever they took violent action against the government.

In November 1981 the government tried to regain control of some of the mosques seized by militant students and used as revolutionary safe houses. Eighty-seven militants were subsequently tried and imprisoned, but many of their leaders fled to France. Less than eight months later, the Khomeinists, as President Bourguiba himself called his radical Muslim adversaries, launched a nationwide campaign aimed at enforcing the wearing of the veil. Acid was thrown at three women undergraduates at the University of Tunis as a 'punishment for their immodest style of dress'.[118] This angered communist students, and a number of pitched battles ensued, leading to massive police intervention. By 1984, however, the communists had ceased to exist as an effective political force on Tunisian campuses. The bread riots that followed were nominally led by the Ghannoushi group, but the actual leadership at street level was provided by groups claiming affinity with the Party of Allah. The riots shook the Bourguiba regime to its foundations and forced the veteran leader to back down from his government's decision to raise a number of prices in accordance with the wishes of the International Monetary Fund. Bourguiba also ordered a cabinet reshuffle, in which the Interior Minister, Driss Guigea, served as scapegoat.

In February 1985 the Tunisian section of the Islamic Jihad announced its presence with a statement calling for the overthrow of Bourguiba and his 'punishment for crimes against Islam'.[119] These crimes included the abolition of polygamy, the passing of a law that made fasting during Ramadan optional, and 'failure to prevent the violation of Muslim rules on dress for men and women'.[120] It promised 'armed struggle' and invited all other fundamentalist groups to join its ranks in the 'Holy War ahead'. The first phase of the Holy War that followed consisted of acid attacks on unveiled women and the petrol bombing of business premises used by

American and French companies in Tunis.

The Jihad's 'armed struggle' continued with a series of attacks on banks, government offices and a gendarmerie station. Twenty-six people were arrested and tried by a military tribunal in July 1986. Four of the accused, including an army lieutenant, were sentenced to death. The leader of the group, Habib Dahoui, defended their action with reference to 'the duty of every Muslim to fight the infidel'. He said that he and his companions had begun preparing for an armed uprising in 1982, and that they had attacked banks and robbed a postal van to obtain money to fund the struggle. 'We wanted arms to fight against a regime that has sold itself to American and French imperialism,' Dahoui said. 'We wanted to create anarchy and a climate suitable for Islamic Revolution.'[121]

In their analysis of the current situation in the Muslim world, the strategists of the Party of Allah constantly refer to Tunisia as a country ripe for an Islamic Revolution. Three main reasons are given. First, by over-extending his personal power Bourguiba has prevented the emergence of a strong state machinery, complete with army and police, capable of putting up effective resistance. Second, Tunisians have had direct experience of secularization and know that Islam has been seriously and immediately threatened in their country. Finally, the Tunisian regime has neither the support of tribal groups, as in Morocco, nor can it rely on a powerful party structure, as in Algeria, to face up to the fundamentalist challenge.

Until 1982 Turkey was the only country with a Muslim majority to boast a secular state. Mustafa Kemal, known as Atatürk (the Father of the Turks), had identified Islam as the principal reason for his people's backwardness and their defeat at the hands of the Allies in World War I. To the founder of the Turkish Republic, Islam was 'the absurd theology of an immoral Bedouin'. It was to distance Turkey from the Arabs and Islam in particular that Atatürk adopted the Latin alphabet, abolished the Qur'anic system of education and declared religion to be an individual concern only. He dreamed of turning Turkey into 'a part of the European world', and it was to help him realize that dream that official historians in Ankara developed the theory that the Turkish people were descendants of Celtic tribes from western Europe.

Atatürk's reforms, however, failed to de-Islamicize Turkey, and the Democrat party of Celal Bayar and Adnan Menderes, which dominated Turkish politics in the 1940s and 1950s, owed much of its electoral appeal to its thinly disguised advocacy of Islamic values and traditions. The party, disbanded after a military coup d'état in 1960, did not disappear altogether; it was replaced by two new parties: Suleiman Demirel's Adalat (Justice) party and Necmettin Erbacan's party of Islamic Salvation. But it was not until 1980 that groups of Islamic militants began openly to insult the memory of Atatürk and to call for a return to Islam.[122] Mass demonstrations that year by Islamic fundamentalists proved a decisive factor in persuading the Turkish generals, who have always considered themselves the custodians of Kemalist values, to stage a coup d'état at a time when the country was also faced with a serious problem of urban guerrilla attacks by communist groups.

The generals were quick to realize the advantages of allowing the fundamentalists more freedom as a means of fighting the Marxist Left. The 1982 constitution drafted by the generals declared Qur'anic studies mandatory at primary and secondary schools, a measure greeted with jubilation in fundamentalist circles. 'The bones of the filthy Jew[123] are shaking in the hole that is his grave,' declared a statement issued by the Turkish Muslim Students' Association in Frankfurt. 'This is only one step, and a thousand more steps must be taken until the legacy of the Dönme animal[124] is fully shaken off.'[125]

From 1980 the number of Islamic associations, especially in universities, multiplied, as did the number of young men growing beards and young women adopting the veil. At some universities, notably in Istanbul, Kemalists tried to put up some resistance by banning both beards and the veil. The generals were split, with one group advocating a return to Kemalism while another encouraged the return-to-Islam movement as part of its campaign against both communist and Kurdish secessionist movements.

The 1983 general election marked a further step away from Kemalism. All parties contesting the election made a point of advertising the Islamic piety of their leaders. Candidates went out of their way to please peasant voters by sacrificing lambs at the shrines of saints, which once again became popular places of pilgrimage. The Anavatani Partisi (Motherland party), which was to win the election, began most of its electoral meetings with recitations from the Qur'an and in the name of Allah.

In 1984 General Kenan Evren, the President of the Republic, attended the Islamic summit conference in Casablanca, becoming the first Turkish head of state to do so.[126] Later, he broke another Kemalist tradition by becoming the first Turkish leader in more than sixty years to perform the Haj pilgrimage in Mecca. At the same time the Ankara government promulgated a series of laws regulating the advertising and sale of alcoholic beverages and the screening of films containing 'scenes that might hurt moral feelings'. The number of bearded men and veiled women increased dramatically, especially in the eastern provinces. All the fundamentalist militants who had been imprisoned after the coup d'état were set free, while the anti-Left campaign continued unabated.

The government's policy of offering concessions to fundamentalists was invariably construed as a sign of weakness by the Partisans of Allah, who continued to press for the 'full Islamicization' of Turkey. In the first half of 1986 alone more than fifty incidents involving fundamentalist groups were reported in the Turkish press. They ranged from the traditional throwing of acid at unveiled women to the burning of houses belonging to infidels. Most of the incidents took place in the eastern provinces, which were at the same time suffering from frequent armed clashes between the army and communist-Kurdish guerrilla groups.

The Party of Allah spent considerable energy and financial resources on propagating its ideas among Turkish workers and students in West Germany, France and Switzerland, but maintained a low profile inside Turkey itself because the Islamic Republic was heavily dependent on Turkish transit routes for its massive imports of food and arms needed for the war against Iraq. Party of Allah leaders were content with pushing the Turkish government further in the right direction without, however, abandoning their long-term hope of turning Turkey into an Islamic republic.[127] Premier Turgut Ozal, himself a practising Muslim, gave the Partisans of Allah comfort by repealing a number of Kemalist laws and passing new legislation aimed at protecting Islam. In 1986 new laws making 'blasphemy' punishable by imprisonment, and regulations preventing Christian missionaries from seeking converts among Muslims, were passed – to the delight of the Party of Allah, which nevertheless demanded more. A law making apostasy punishable by lengthy imprisonment was also being drafted in the autumn of 1986.

For the Party of Allah, Turkey represented an investment in the future. Turkish militants were trained in both the Islamic Republic and Lebanon and indoctrination classes were held for Turkish immigrants in Europe. The Iranian Embassy in Ankara and its consulates in Istanbul and other Turkish cities distributed millions of copies of Khomeini's works translated into Turkish, together with tapes of fundamentalist sermons by Turkish mullahs being trained in Qom.[128] The Islamic Republic also beamed two Turkish-language radio programmes to Turkey, hammering in the main themes of the Party of Allah's doctrine of revolt.

The Islamic fundamentalist movement of the 1980s spared none of the Muslim countries. It struck roots in societies as widely different as Indonesia and Algeria. And in every instance it led to violence as a means of furthering its political objectives.

12

Neither East, Nor West

> Take the news to the Jews: the army of Muhammad has returned! We are on our way to Jerusalem!
>
> Muhammad Abdul-Salaam Faraj[1]

In its different forms, from Banna's Brothers to Khomeini's Party of Allah, Islamic fundamentalism has always viewed itself as a force capable of conquering the contemporary world from without. It cannot conceive of either coexistence or political compromise. To the exponents of Holy Terror, Islam must either dominate or be dominated. Their Manichean analysis of existence allows an area in between only in the sense of *hegira* or withdrawal, which is to be used as preparation for the next battle. The vision of a world based on religious and political pluralism is repugnant to the supporters of Holy Terror. To the Muslim fundamentalist pluralism is another word for *sherk*, which means pantheism, a sin punishable by death in *shari'ah*.

Human history, as seen by the fundamentalists, consists of a series of wars between Islam and 'the rest, which is not Islam'.[2] All that was good was Islamic, and all those who were good and close to God were Muslims even before the advent of Islam. According to Dr Aziz Pasha, President of the Union of Islamic Associations in Britain and Eire, even 'Adam, Moses and Jesus' were Muslims. For Islam means 'surrender to the wishes of Allah'.[3] Since Muhammad was the last Prophet dispatched by Allah there is no need for other religions, including revealed ones. So those who adamantly refuse to convert to Islam are, to all intents and purposes, enemies of Allah Himself.

What is 'un-Islamic' in the contemporary world is, according to the theorists of Holy Terror, 'a monster with four heads'.[4] The first and principal head and 'the most dangerous' is that of 'the Jew, the eternal schemer against God'.[5] The creation of Israel and its wars against the Arabs have only aggravated a deep-rooted hatred and suspicion that preceded the re-emergence of the Jewish state.[6]

The second head of the monster is symbolized by the Cross. The fundamentalists sincerely believe that the Crusades have never ended and that the 'Christian powers' of the West remain determined to try to eliminate Islam from the face of the earth.[7] Unlike Jews, who are all 'bad and corrupt', some Christians are 'in-between', that is to say deserving of tolerance. These 'harmless' Christians are those who, like monks and nuns, keep to themselves and do not try to convert others to their faith. The majority, however, consist of the 'Crusaders'. Western writers and poets, businessmen, film-makers, diplomats, politicians, musicians, artists and so on are all 'Crusaders', as are the cursed Orientalists whose sole mission consists of 'spreading falsehood against Islam'.[8]

According to the theorists of Holy Terror it is possible to convert Christians to Islam, whereas Jews will never abandon their faith. Jews who pretend to have converted to Islam are 'agents, on secret missions'.[9] All those who tried to Westernize Muslim countries are said to have been Jews, starting with the Khedive Mehmet Ali Pasha and including Kemal Atatürk, Reza Shah Pahlavi, his son Muhammad Reza Shah and even Gamal Abdul-Nasser.[10] Anwar Sadat was 'a Jew who lived like a Jew and died like a Jew'.[11] Yasser Arafat, leader of the Palestine Liberation Organization, is also a Jew and a 'secret agent of world Jewry'.[12] The principle is that it is impossible for anyone born into a genuine Muslim family to act against the fundamentalist interpretation of Islam; those who do not see Islam as the exponents of Holy Terror see it must by definition be Jews.[13]

The third head of the monster belongs to atheism, whose chief contemporary manifestation is communism of all varieties. Both atheism and communism, although now independent from Judaism, are claimed to have been originally devised by Jews. Both Marx and Lenin were Jews, as are 'most leaders of communist parties throughout the world'.[14] In theory at least, the supporters of Holy Terror must combat the USSR with the same ardour with which they fight the American Great Satan, which according to Khomeini symbolizes the principal threat to Islam in the modern world.

Finally, the monster's fourth head represents secularism, which the theorists of Holy Terror take to mean many different things. Those who advocate the separation of the mosque and the state are quite obviously 'secular sinners'. But even the idea that Islam should be propagated and enforced by example rather than terror tactics is often described as 'secularism'. It is not enough to be a fully practising Muslim on one's own; one must keep one's eyes and ears open to spot any deviation from Islam and stamp it out, either by individual initiative or through collective action with other believers. All those who advocate modernization, progress, pluralism and other eminently Western political concepts are classed among 'them' – the enemies of Islam – and rejected by 'us' – the *jama'ah* at group level and the *ummah* at the level of the universal community of Muslims. If they are on the Left they are agents of world communism, and if advocating liberalism they represent the Crusading West. The slogan 'Neither East nor West' was originally coined by Banna, but gained wide popularity after Khomeini's revolution.

Throughout the past 150 years both the East, in the shape of the Tsarist Empire and then the USSR, and the West, represented first by the British Raj and the French Empire and later by the United States, have tried to enlist for their own side Islam's undoubted power of mobilizing the masses. In the nineteenth century and up until the 1950s both Britain and Russia bribed the mullahs in Iran and Afghanistan. In India, the British used Muslims as junior partners in running the Raj. And in Egypt the Muslim Brotherhood was supported by, and in part even financed by, the British as a means of counterbalancing the influence of both the nationalists and the communists. Napoleon won the hearts of the Egyptians partly by spreading the rumour that he had secretly converted to Islam. And some of the two thousand or so German agents active in Iran between 1936 and 1941 claimed to have become Muslims, and occasionally even benefited from the tradition of taking temporary wives. Hitler himself was reputed to be a secret convert, as were both Mussolini and Franco.

The conversion of Christians to Islam, especially if they are well-known people, is celebrated as a triumph for Islam. A booklet written by Nurul Dhoha in 1982 to introduce some of 'the greatest men and women of Christianity who have converted to Islam' has been translated into almost every Muslim language and sold millions of copies.[15] It informs readers that Islam is 'conquering the hearts and minds of the best, the purest and the most aware in the Christian West'. Among those named are Jacques Cousteau, the marine explorer, and the choreographer Maurice Béjart.[16]

The West is depicted as either 'a universe of violence and barbarity',[17] or at best a civilization in decline. It certainly cannot be regarded as a model for Muslims to follow. In sentencing Ahmad Ksarvai, an advocate of European-style secularization, to death in 1942, Khomeini wrote of the West in uncompromising terms:

> Have the Europeans discovered the ideal society? Can one consider the European nation so civilized as to wish to take it as a model, as do some lunatics? Europe's ideology consists of nothing but blood-sucking, man-eating and the burning of countries. Its only aim is to live a depraved life of anarchy in which lust rules supreme. What is there in common between [Europe] and Islam, which is the religion of mercy and justice?[18]

Hatred for Europe was succeeded in the 1970s by hatred for the United States. It is significant that anti-Americanism was first propagated as a major theme of Muslim fundamentalism by young men and women from Islamic countries who had spent time in the United States as students or workers. As remarked earlier, the group of 'students' which took the US diplomats hostage in Tehran in 1979 was led by graduates of American universities. In Lebanon many of the hostage-holding units of the Party of Allah operate under commanders who have studied in the United States. A large number of party militants in Lebanon, the Islamic Republic, Egypt, the Gulf States and Iraq were directly recruited in the United States from Muslim students and workers, many of whom were married to Americans before joining the party. In most cases their American wives were repudiated on orders from their religious guides, but sometimes the militants were allowed to keep them after 'proving' their wives' true conversion to fundamentalist Islam.

The West in general and the United States in particular are castigated not only for their 'unfairness' to the Islamic world but because of their 'defiance of the rules of Allah'.[19] The West is seen as a civilization of lazy people obsessed with longevity, physical beauty, financial success and material possessions. It is also 'colonialist, aggressive, self-assured, barbarous and racist'.[20] Western democracy is 'the greatest confidence trick ever carried off by man',[21] and will inevitably lead to 'prostitution as a community's way of life'.[22]

Islam must beware of Western technology, whose principal result is the 'dehumanization of social relations'.[23] Majid Anaraki, a Party of Allah writer who spent several years in southern California, sees the West as 'a collection of casinos, supermarkets and whore-houses linked together by endless highways passing through nowhere'.[24] He continues:

> All that money, all that effort, all those resources that are wasted so that idiotic women and shallow men can prolong their lives. . . . You see ancient women who refuse to die at a normal time and who continue to paint themselves and crave youthful lovers right to the edge of the grave. . . . The Western man kills without mercy but is scared of death. . . . A civilization whose men are not prepared to die for its ideals is bound to die, and that is the inevitable fate of the West, which has no ideals worth dying for. . . . To eat tons of hamburgers and popcorn, to imbibe oceans of Coca-Cola and whisky, to watch hundreds of hours of stupid television, to copulate mechanically a few hundred times, to be on guard every minute against being robbed, raped or murdered. That is the American way of life.[25]

The fundamentalist recognizes the immense attraction that the West and the 'American way of life' have for the average city-dwelling Muslim. The West has a great deal to offer them, especially in the scientific, economic and technological fields; the Party of Allah therefore has to paint as black a picture as possible.

What the party fears most, however, is the contagion of such 'Satanic ideas' as Western-style democracy. It has not forgotten that it was a democratically elected government in Iran which sentenced the leading ayatollah of the day to death and hanged him in public in 1911. The basic concept of democracy – giving mortal man the right to legislate his own affairs and ignore the rules of religion, if and when necessary – is the exact opposite of Islam's message of 'total and unconditional surrender' to the will of God in all domains. And since that 'will' is defined and applied by the mullahs, the muftis, the shaikhs and the mawlavis, the most immediate effect of the introduction of a Western-style democratic system would be to put an end to the Party of Allah and its clerical leaders.

Since at least 1979 the West, and in particular the United States, has appeared to the Party of Allah weak, confused and indecisive. The handling of the US Embassy crisis in Tehran by the Carter administration convinced the Partisans of Allah that Khomeini was right in his claim that 'America cannot do a damn thing'. The US government continued to base its policies on a number of illusions and misunderstandings.

It also did not recognize the true nature of Islamic fundamentalism, which is quite different from its Christian counterpart. Even before the Embassy drama, Tehran knew that some members of the Carter team were fascinated by Khomeini and his revolution.[26] The USA was fully expected to react in strength to the plight of its diplomats. Carter, however, decided to enter into a diplomatic game which the Partisans of Allah neither accepted nor understood. The rescue operation eventually organized on Carter's orders ended in disaster. The Partisans were jubilant, but at the same time did not understand how a single small failure could put a superpower on the defensive for a very long time. Carter did not see Khomeini as a political leader, which he certainly was, but as a 'holy man'. When the head of the French Secret Service suggested to Carter in 1980 that Khomeini be kidnapped and then released in exchange for the hostages, the President was indignant. 'One cannot do that to a holy man,' he told the French 'super spy', the Count of Maranche.

It was with great astonishment that the Partisans of Allah discovered the value of holding Western hostages. Hostage-taking has for centuries been an integral part of political and diplomatic life in the Muslim East, but the Western powers traditionally involved in the region had never allowed it to be practised against their own nationals with impunity. What surprised the Partisans of Allah above everything else was the impression given by the United States that it was prepared to sacrifice its major national interests to secure the release of its diplomats. Nasser Zamani, a Muslim sociologist who has studied the hostage crisis, explained the unexpected prolongation of the drama by 'the fact that the two sides did not attach the same importance to the lives of individuals'.[27] He wrote:

> The group commanded by the Ayatollah [in the crisis] was puzzled as to why a big power could not accept a small sacrifice of people in its service. . . . It was probably those militants who had been educated in the United States itself who told the Ayatollah that, like the serials they had seen on American TV, a hostage was a sure guarantee of power for the hostage-holder.[28]

In sharp contrast to the American attitude towards hostages, the Party of Allah would never dream of offering the slightest concession to secure the release of its own members being held hostage or prisoner by its enemies. A dramatic illustration of this point is the case of Muhammad-Javad Tondguyan, who was Khomeini's Oil Minister and the cabinet's strong man in 1981 when he was captured, together with two of his deputies, by the Iraqis near the Khuzestan war front. On countless occasions the Iraqis offered to negotiate the release of the minister, a civilian and therefore not a prisoner of war, provided the mullahs agreed to ask the International Red Cross to arrange a deal. The Party of Allah, however, has refused even to respond to Iraqi demands put through the Red Cross and the late Swedish Premier, Olof Palme. Tondguyan, a favourite of Khomeini's, is considered to be 'a soldier of Islam' who is 'performing his Holy War in an Iraqi prison camp'.[29] Maronite Christians and Druzes, who began seizing hostages from the ranks of the Party of Allah in Lebanon in 1983, were by 1986 convinced that the tactic did not have the usual effect on Khomeini's Holy Terror militants.

Another major misunderstanding of Holy Terror by the West results from the assumption that the Partisans of Allah, being ferociously anti-communist, could become allies of the western powers in a struggle against the USSR. As early as 1956 the then Secretary of State, John Foster Dulles, had toyed with the idea of creating an 'Islamic alliance' consisting of Turkey, Iran, Iraq, Pakistan and probably Saudi Arabia. The scheme did not get off the ground for several reasons. Turkey was still determined to remain a secular state and shunned any suggestion of being described as Islamic. In 1958 the Iraqi monarchy was overthrown in a bloody coup d'état that brought to power a coalition of nationalist and pro-Moscow officers. Saudi Arabia for its part did not wish to be associated with countries which it did not recognize as fully Islamic; while the Shah of Iran, remembering his father's campaign against the mullahs, was less than enthusiastic about joining a holy Islamic alliance. But the main hitch was that Britain insisted on being a member of whatever alliance emerged in a region that formed part of its traditional sphere of influence.[30] Visiting Tehran in 1958, President Eisenhower put some emphasis on the incompatibility of Islam and communism and tried to portray the United States as a power prepared to protect Muslim nations against the 'atheist' Soviet Union. The fact that a pro-Western but at the same time militant Islam is a contradiction in terms was conveniently ignored. The dream of a 'green belt of Islamic forces' hemming in the USSR continued to live.

Ignorance of the psychology of the members of Holy Terror has not been a prerogative of the United States, however. In 1984 the West Germans sent their Foreign Minister, Hans-Dietrich Genscher, to the Islamic Republic to lecture the mullahs on human rights. All he received in exchange was a diplomatic slap in the face, while his visit was presented by the official media as a sign that 'Satanic forces' were bowing to the power of Islam.

The French perpetrated a rich collection of faux pas in their dealings with Holy Terror. To ensure the release of French hostages in Beirut, as well as in the Islamic Republic itself, successive French governments enlisted the services of a variety of intermediaries ranging from bogus businessmen through a paediatrician from Normandy to an ex-journalist turned diplomat. They did not realize that by acting outside the established channels of diplomacy they were putting France on the same footing as the Party of Allah in a complicated game of dark intrigue and blackmail.

Known leaders and militants of the Holy Terror network visited France between 1980 and 1986 on a number of occasions and received the red carpet treatment. One such visitor was Imad Mugniyeh, one of the leaders of the TWA hijack drama in Beirut in June 1985. The CIA monitored Mugniyeh's movements and even gave his address and telephone number in Paris to the French authorities. But the government preferred to turn a blind eye, even though Mugniyeh's visit to Paris in March 1986 was heavily publicized in the French media.[31] Another Party of Allah militant to visit Paris with official pomp and ceremony was Ali-Reza Moayeri, one of the leaders of the 'students' who seized the US Embassy in Tehran in 1979. In April 1986 Moayeri was received by all the top French leaders, including the Prime Minister and the President.[32]

Despite the hospitality extended to Party of Allah representatives by the French government, France remained 'number two enemy', after the United States. A dozen terrorist attacks were carried out against the French contingent in the UNIFIL, an international force created to supervise a cease-fire in southern Lebanon. Twenty French soldiers were killed and many more injured in these attacks between 1984 and October 1986. All attacks were carried out by the Party of Allah, which also played a supportive role in the wave of terrorist operations that hit Paris in September 1986. Blamed by the French police on the relatives of Georges Ibrahim Abdullah, who was serving a prison term in France for alleged involvement in the murder of an American and an Israeli diplomat in Paris in 1982, the operations were almost certainly jointly planned and carried out by several Lebanese-based groups, including the Islamic Jihad and ASALA, the Armenian terror organization. Messages sent after each operation demanded the release not only of Abdallah, but also of Arnice Naqqache, a condemned terrorist who worked for Khomeini, and of Varoujan Garbidjian, an ASALA member. The terror campaign against France showed that the Party of Allah was prepared to form tactical alliances with other terrorist organizations in specific circumstances.

The rather crude stick-and-carrot policy used against Holy Terror by the West since 1980 failed because the Partisans of

Allah did not read the signals sent to them in the way expected. To them any concession given is a sign of weakness and automatically invites further aggression on their part. The wielding of the stick by the West, on the other hand, is considered to be perfectly normal and a temporary hardship which has to be endured.

The United States and some of its Western allies pursued a policy of sanctions against the Islamic Republic between 1980 and 1986, but no serious attempt was ever made to impose them. On the contrary, US exports to the Islamic Republic rose to some 1800 million dollars in 1984 from less than 300 million in 1980.[33] Commenting on the Western policy of sanctions, Behzad Nabavi, Khomeini's Minister for Heavy Industries, said in 1985: 'What embargo? Those people in the West will put their own mothers on auction for profit.'[34]

It is often automatically assumed that the West is hated by the Partisans of Allah principally because of US support for Israel. In fact it is Israel which is hated partly because of its association with the West, rather than the other way round, and the Jewish state is constantly referred to as 'an outpost of the West'. Some analysts have persuaded themselves that the key to stamping out the menace of Holy Terror is the solution of the Arab–Israeli conflict. But Holy Terror is only indirectly related to the presence of Israel in the Middle East. The Partisans of Allah have killed many more Palestinians than Israel ever did. And the dead in the Iran–Iraq war, who numbered around 700,000 by 1986, could hardly be described as victims of Israel.

Holy Terror has a history that goes back over a thousand years, long before Israel was put on the map of the Middle East. It is enough to attend some of the *jama'ah* meetings in Cairo, or some of the gatherings of the Party of Allah in Beirut, Tehran or Tunis, to realize that Holy Terror dreams of liberating many more countries than Israel. To most theoreticians the destruction of Islam's 'internal enemies' appears far more urgent a task than the elimination of Israel.

The Party of Allah's seizure of power in Iran in 1979 was welcomed by all those Western intellectuals who have – at least since World War II – developed their own Manichean view of existence. To them it is sufficient for a political movement to be anti-Western – especially if it is anti-American – to merit sympathy and support. The idea that two wrongs may at a given moment face one another seldom occurs to these champions of the Third World. Michel Foucault, an idol of the French liberal Left in the 1970s, spoke of his fascination with the 'explosion of spiritual energy' on the streets of Tehran in the context of 'a spontaneous explosion of political awareness'.[35] He conveniently chose to ignore the terror tactics used by the Party of Allah to bring about that 'spiritual energy'. He was not interested in unveiled women who had had acid thrown at them and in factory workers who had had their homes burned down by the Party of Allah simply because they refused to take part in anti-government strikes. Nor would he take into account the fact that what appeared to him, and to many other Western observers, as a spontaneous outburst was in reality a carefully planned revolution – the fruit of nearly twenty years of hard, often violent, work by hundreds of highly trained revolutionaries and guerrillas led by the mullahs in the name of Khomeini.

Other Western commentators have used equally astonishing arguments in their bid to understand Holy Terror. In their case, understanding often leads to automatic justification of the most heinous crimes. They say that Khomeini, for example, is popular and thus imply that he has every right to send schoolchildren into minefields. They speak of 'the simplicity of his life – a few rugs to sit on, lentil soup and prayers five times a day',[36] forgetting that Hitler too was popular in his time and observed a frugal diet. Since the United States is an 'imperialist power', so the standard argument runs, it is perfectly understandable, and by implication justifiable, that its innocent citizens should be taken hostage and murdered.

One Western commentator, the American 'Iranologist' Marvin Zonis, has seen in the rise of Holy Terror what he calls 'the single most impressive political ideology which has been proposed in the twentieth century since the Bolshevik Revolution'.[37] The fact that Holy Terror represents little more than a hotch-potch of medieval thought and methods directly borrowed from both fascism and communism, especially as far as mob manipulation is concerned, is swept under the carpet. The truth is that Holy Terror is a form of government and not an ideology. Its main theorists claim legitimacy on the basis of the Qur'an, which, as any student of Islam knows, lends itself to many different and even conflicting interpretations when it comes to practical politics.

The fascination of some Western intellectuals and political leaders with Holy Terror, at times not unlike the sentiments provoked by Nazism and Stalinism in the 1930s, is counterbalanced by an equally illogical hatred of Islamic militancy which seems to be replacing the myth of the Yellow Peril as the obsession of certain circles in the West. Dozens of books with such titles as *How the West Can Win* and *How Can It Be Won?* have been published on the theme of Islamic terrorism. Unlike those intellectuals whose attitude towards Holy Terror is inspired by an idealism that can only lead to terror, the 'winning' lobby start from a level of ignorance that can only lead to war. Both groups forget the essential truth that a major objective of all terrorist movements is to cajole or force their adversaries into acting in violation of their own principles. The real or imagined sufferings of a group or an entire nation could not justify the infliction of the same on others. Grievances, even when truly legitimate, do not provide a licence to kill in the name of the cause. At the same time, the fact that an adversary recognizes no laws but his own is no excuse for ignoring the rule of law altogether. The West should neither agree to play the role of the victim, as atonement for real or imagined wrongs done to Islam, nor condone the new, computerized version of the Crusades recommended by Rambo-style 'winners'. The wisest policy for the West would be to defend itself within its own system of values and be constantly aware that the worst damage one's adversary can do is to make one resemble him.

The 'winners' have offered a variety of solutions ranging from enlisting the support of the Mafia and hired killers to dropping nuclear bombs on Tripoli, Damascus, Baalbek and Tehran. But that is no more and no less than playing the deadly game of terror according to the rules set by the Party of Allah. With the exception – so far – of the nuclear option, all the other proposed solutions have been tried by the West in its confrontation with Holy Terror – with few or no positive results.

The West should defend its values and ideals on a global basis and must therefore not allow itself to be seen as the protector of regimes whose politics and practices are incompatible with the values espoused by the West. Without making a value judgement on the system of government in the United States and, say, that in Saudi Arabia, clearly they are entirely different worlds. Leaving aside short- and medium-term economic and strategic advantages, there is no reason why the USA should defend the existing Saudi system against the wishes of its own people. The natural allies of the United States in Saudi Arabia are neither the princes who oppose constitutional government nor the protagonists of Holy Terror such as Johaiman and Muhammad al-Qahtani. These allies must be looked for among the urban middle class, the educated elite and all those who value such concepts as the rule of law, the intrinsic worth of the individual, and freedom of expression. By practising the opposite of what it preaches the West acts as an unwitting source of support for the Party of Allah.

In countries where the potential choice is limited to a corrupt and medievalist ruling clique friendly to the West, and the forces of Holy Terror, it is both prudent and just to continue supporting the former on a short-term basis. But in many Muslim countries the choice is not so limited. In Pakistan, for example, the removal of General Zia's Islamic dictatorship would not lead to the emergence of the Party of Allah as the country's future government. In Indonesia, Malaysia and Bangladesh the overthrow, or at least the restructuring, of largely corrupt and unpopular ruling elites would not mean the automatic exclusion of the West's legitimate interests. There can be no general recipe for dealing with the current crisis in the Islamic world.

Qutb, Khomeini, Shukri Mustafa and other theorists of Holy Terror have always been aware that the main threat to their aim of the ideal Islamic society is the propagation of Western ideas. Mustafa put it succinctly: 'The West cannot destroy Islam by its bombs or its economic might and technology. . . . But its deadliest weapons are its pagan ideas –

ideas such as legislation by mortal men in defiance of divine laws. . . . The West has killed God and buried him and is teaching the rest of the world to do so.'[38] Khomeini adds: 'We must break those pens that teach people there is something other than divine law. We must smash those mouths that tell the people they are free to say whatever they please, regardless of right and wrong in accordance with the commands of the Almighty.'[39]

Also facing the challenge of fundamentalist Islam, the USSR has – despite its longer and more direct experience of the subject – shown an almost equally surprising inability to develop a coherent strategy. The Bolshevik Revolution owed some of its initial success in asserting its domination over the vast Tsarist Empire to the support it attracted from the Muslims of the Caucasus and Central Asia. Lenin's promise of autonomy and independence for all those ethnic minorities who asked for it, together with the Bolsheviks' constant preaching of justice and equality – two values with special appeal to Muslims – secured for the new Leninist state a force strong enough to counter-balance the challenge of 'the remnants of the reactionary ruling cliques'.

It did not take long, however, before the Muslims, including those who had become communists largely because of their anti-colonial sentiments, realized that the empire Lenin and his successor Stalin wanted to build was to be even more determined in hanging onto the fruits of past conquests than was that of the tsars. In September 1920 a revolt led by Shaikh Najm al-Din, who claimed the title of Imam, spread from the mountains of Daghestan to practically the whole of the Muslim Caucasus. Imam Najm, as the leader of the insurgents came to be known, was assisted by another early 'Khomeinist', Uzun Haji, who only a year earlier had fought alongside the Red Army against the White Russian forces of Denikin in the civil war. The Muslim revolt in Daghestan quickly spread to Azerbaijan and led to the Red Army's first urban guerrilla experience. The insurgents wanted to create an Islamic republic based on the theocratic model established by Imam Shamel, but the revolt was ruthlessly crushed and the last of the rebels escaped into Turkey in the winter of 1921.

The Islamic challenge to the Soviets did not, however, end

there. Muslim militants who had joined the Bolsheviks in the hope of helping to create a society of justice and equality[40] soon found their champion and spokesman in Mir Sayyed Sultan Galiev, a Tatar who claimed to be a descendant of the Prophet Muhammad. Sayyed Sultan had joined the Bolshevik party in 1916 after having attended a Qur'anic school and flirting with a career as a mullah. He gave his name to what came to be known under Stalin as an anti-party conspiracy and was executed for his 'Galievism'.[41] Galiev and some of his close associates, such as Borhan Mansurov, Adel Shah Kutuy and Fateh Karimi, never completely abandoned their own brand of Marxism while propagating Islamic values. In a sense they were the precursors of what was to become the Islamic Marxism of the 1960s, best represented by people like Ali Shariati and the People's Mujahedin Organization of Iran.

In 1927 no more than 11.5 per cent of the total population of the USSR were Muslims; in 1986 Muslims were estimated to represent nearly 18 per cent of the population, or a total of 53 million. This made the USSR the sixth largest 'Muslim' country in the world after Indonesia, Nigeria, Bangladesh, India and Pakistan. Population trends established in the 1980s showed that by the year 2000 Muslims could well number more than 80 million or some 26 per cent of the total population of the USSR, while true Russians would represent no more than 22 per cent. The Soviet Union is therefore faced with a Muslim problem both within and beyond its frontiers.

Khomeini's Islamic Revolution in Iran was at first regarded with great suspicion by Moscow. Andrei Gromyko, then Foreign Minister, did not conceal his belief that Khomeini's movement was a 'reactionary enterprise' which ran against 'the course of progress'.[42] It was, in the end, the Azerbaijan party which succeeded in persuading the Politburo that Khomeini should be supported. The idea was that the 'central contradiction' in Muslim countries was that which pitched 'the masses' against 'imperialism led by the United States' and that any movement that opposed 'American hegemony' ought to be supported regardless of its reactionary policies in other domains. This argument, defended by Geidar Aliyev, a Politburo member, and others in the Azerbaijan party, is also supported by some of the USSR's staunchest allies in the

Muslim world, such as Syria, Libya and South Yemen.

It is in Central Asian communist parties, notably those in the Tadzhikistan and Turkmenistan republics, that Islamic fundamentalism is seen not as a tactical ally of the USSR in its global fight against the United States but as an 'objective partner of imperialism'. The Uzbek communist chief, Din-Muhammad Kunayev, has been an outspoken critic of much of what the Party of Allah stands for. The fact that it is the Central Asian republics which feel the burden of the Afghanistan war most directly is perhaps one reason for the aversion which local communists, most of Muslim origin, display to Islamic fundamentalism.

The Soviet Union is well aware that the problem it is facing in Afghanistan is not limited to most Aghans' understandable desire to rid their country of foreign troops. The Afghan resistance movement has not confined itself to a minimum programme of securing the nation's independence and territorial integrity, but openly advocates the creation of an Islamic society.[43] It is in the name of Allah, and not of nationalism in the Western meaning of the term, that Soviet troops are gunned down in the mountains of Afghanistan. In some of the liberated zones the resistance movement has already brought into existence its ideal Islamic society. Here, women have been pushed back into the veil, polygamy has been legalized, girls are kept out of school and the mullahs and mawlavis exercise their tyrannical power in all spheres of life.[44]

The debate concerning the role of Islamic fundamentalism in international affairs is not limited to the communist party of the Soviet Union and its branches in the Central Asian republics of the USSR. It interests many other communist parties, including some of those already in power, in all countries where Islam is present. The Bulgarian communist party, for example, is a firm advocate of the idea that Islamic fundamentalism must be ruthlessly suppressed as the embodiment of reactionary feudal forces in society. The Bulgarian government itself showed the way by launching a de-Islamicization campaign aimed at 'liberating' the country's estimated 1.2 million Muslims from 'the tyranny of a decadent ideology'.

Between 1979, when the campaign was started, and 1986 every Bulgarian citizen of Muslim origin was forced to change his or her 'Islamic' name for a Slav one. Numerous Muslim villages were occupied for weeks by the party militia while government agents carried out their programme of Slavicization. All Qur'anic schools were closed, and tens of thousands of copies of the Muslim Holy Book were burned in public.[45] Ramadan fasting, public prayers, the call of the muezzin and all other manifestations of the Faith were banned, and the ban rigorously enforced.[46] In some cases, ancient mosques and shrines of Muslim saints were turned into museums, car parks or even casinos and hotels.[47] Dozens of Muslim graveyards were levelled so that the land they occupied could be used for new housing estates.[48] Many Muslims reacted by crossing the border into Turkey, where they became political refugees; others decided to fight back and created the Alliance of Monotheists.[49] The Alliance claims that between 1983 and 1986 at least forty of its members were either executed or killed 'resisting the agents of the hammer and sickle'.[50] In 1984 the Alliance made contact with the Party of Allah in Qom, Tehran, Baalbek and Beirut, and sent full delegations to three international conferences of Muslim militants held in Tehran in 1985 and 1986.

The fact that most Bulgarian Muslims are of Turkish origin split their resistance movement into two camps: those who espouse pan-Turkism and look to Ankara for support, and those who openly identify with Khomeini's network of Holy Terror in the name of Islamic internationalism. In a statement published in several Muslim and European capitals in June 1986, the main organization of militant Bulgarian Muslims, the Alliance of Monotheists, warned that it was preparing 'the first phase of a defensive Holy War against the government of Slavic Crusaders'.[51] It warned foreign tourists to stay away from Bulgaria and threatened to 'blow to bits all those who try to cover our land with the filth of alcohol, gambling and prostitution'.[52] The Alliance was by no means the only militant Islamic group advocating the use of terror in Bulgaria: in 1986 a number of smaller groups were already involved in attacks against official buildings and tourist facilities. These attacks, described in the official media as 'incidents provoked by foreign criminals', followed the almost classical pattern set by the Party of Allah in other countries: setting fire to shops selling alcohol, breaking the windows of girls' schools, and in one case planting a home-made bomb in a small tourist hotel in Stara Zagora.

By 1986 the Party of Allah was not yet strong enough seriously to threaten Bulgaria's stability, but its activities were menacing enough to persuade the Bulgarian communist party to undertake an extensive study of the rise of Islamic fundamentalism in the 1970s and 1980s. The findings of the study, presumably completed in February 1986, were not made public, but echoes found their way to the Bulgarian press and to some Turkish newspapers.[53] Those findings based themselves on one central assumption: Islam cannot remain a movement for justice and progress for long, and is bound to end up on the side of 'feudal groups and imperialism'. It is possible to speculate that the Bulgarian communist party may have played a key role in persuading the Soviet communist party and other 'sister' parties to tone down their original enthusiasm for Islamic revival as a means of excluding the West from important regions of Asia and Africa.

The Soviets and their allies had smiled with satisfaction when the Party of Allah massacred American and French soldiers in their sleep in Lebanon. But things began to look different when the network of Holy Terror extended the same tactics to Soviet-occupied Afghanistan, with the further threat of taking its original brand of terrorism into the heart of the socialist camp itself. Islamic fundamentalism originally looked like a stick with which the two superpowers could hit one another in different countries: for example the United States could use it against the pro-Moscow regime of Hafez al-Assad in Syria or the Soviet-sponsored government in Kabul, while the USSR returned the compliment in such countries as Iran, Pakistan and Saudi Arabia. Both sides, however, realized before long that the Islamic stick was able and willing to hit the hand that tried to use it.

The temptation to use a violent new movement against one's adversaries is almost as old as diplomatic rivalry itself. Quite a few Western capitalists fell for it in the case of Hitler's Nazi movement, while Stalin toyed with the idea of turning the Third Reich into the gravedigger of Western capitalism. More recently, on a much smaller scale and in a totally different context, both Israel and Syria – mortal enemies in all other respects – have tried in turn to use the Party of Allah against one another. By October 1986, however, both sides seemed to be moving in the direction of an unpublicized alliance against the network of Holy Terror.

In the potentially much more important case of Afghanistan it is possible to argue that CIA investment in Holy Terror groups – ironically enough supported also by Khomeini – has had the immediate effect of hardening Soviet policy. The appointment in the spring of 1986 of General Muhammad Najib-Allah as the new secretary-general of the Afghan communist party, to replace President Babrak Karmal, was a sure sign of Soviet resolve not to seek a diplomatic solution to the problem but to fight its Afghan War to the finish. Washington's inability to understand the simple fact that Moscow cannot accept a military setback combined with an ideological defeat in Afghanistan prevented a revision of the policy of support for the Partisans of Allah in the Afghan War. The Soviet communist party leader Mikhail Gorbachov's offer to reopen negotiations on Afghanistan in the summer of 1986 did not mean that he was prepared to abandon Moscow's basic aims in that country. Faithful to Lenin's diction of 'One step backwards, two steps forwards', he was offering minor concessions in the hope of securing the USSR's long-term position in Afghanistan.

The fact was, however, that the United States, the Afghan communist party and its secular opponents were, in a broader historical perspective, all on the same side in the social theatre of the war in Afghanistan. What prevented all those concerned from recognizing this fact were considerations of military strategy on the part of the two superpowers and more than a generation of jealousy and hatred between Afghanistan's secular nationalist and liberal forces on the one hand and the different Marxist-Leninist groups on the other. Despite Iran's experience, which showed that the Party of Allah hangs liberals and Marxists from the same tree, the possibility of a united secular front dedicated to protecting Afghanistan from suffering a similar fate seemed remote in 1986. And both Moscow and Washington seemed determined to prevent their respective client forces from even considering an alliance of forces opposed to Holy Terror as a means of ending the country's ordeal.

13

The Future of Islam: A Conclusion

> A Third Spiritual Way. . . . We all believed in it. But it was only an illusion.
>
> Dariush Shayegan[1]

At the beginning of 1985 Field Marshal Ja'afar Muhammad al-Numeiri looked like a man convinced of a long and tranquil reign ahead of him in the Sudan, where he had just completed the building of a 'truly Islamic state'. Numeiri had come to his own version of 'hard and pure Islam' after years of flirtation with socialism, Arab Ba'athism, Nasserism, nationalism and pro-American liberalism. His decision to impose the *shari'ah* as the law of the land, and to use his army for enforcing the veil, had been taken under the influence of Hassan Turabi's Muslim Brotherhood. The majority of the Sudan's 20 million inhabitants were Muslims and were therefore expected to welcome the prospect of life under Islamic law.

In March 1985, however, a series of anti-Numeiri demonstrations organized in the University of Khartoum brought together students, lawyers, schoolchildren, office workers and even housewives. The movement quickly spread into the streets of the capital and its twin city of Omdurman. All the demonstrators were shouting the same slogan: 'Down with the *shari'ah*!' For the first time in Islam's contemporary history tens of thousands of Muslims openly rejected life under the law of the Qur'an, preferring Sudan's traditional legal system, largely put together by the British in the nineteenth and early twentieth centuries. The people who marched against Qur'anic law were not members of the Westernized economic or social elites, nor could they all be members of the Sudanese communist party, which had never represented a serious force in the country's politics. The vast majority of the demonstrators were poor workers, peasants come to town, students from modest families, and above all women determined not to be forced into purdah and all that it represented in loss of social status and legal rights.

The Sudanese had put up with Numeiri's many experiments for nearly twenty years but were in no mood to accept the rigid Islamic republic he wanted to create in the hope of depriving his own Party of Allah adversaries of their central theme. Numeiri was eventually deposed on 6 April while on a state visit to Washington. By August 1986, after a general election, a civilian coalition government was in power in Khartoum and already committed to making the application of the *shari'ah* optional. In practice, Qur'anic law was no longer enforced beyond a ban on the sale of pork and on the serving of alcohol in most restaurants.

The anti-*shari'ah* backlash in the Sudan was by no means the only one, although it deserves special attention because of its roots at the humblest levels of society. In Egypt, where the various groups and parties that constitute the Holy Terror movement were the strongest in the whole of Islam, a counter-movement began to assert itself in 1986. A number of intellectuals who had learned by experience that they could not pretend to represent 'true Islam' against the mullahs and militants, as Sadat had once tried to do, decided to risk their careers and their lives and called on 'all those who believe in the future' to take on the Party of Allah at an ideological level. Early in 1986 a Cairo lawyer, Nur Farwaj, pronounced a sentence no one had had the courage to utter in the land of Islam for nearly a decade: 'The *shari'ah* is a collection of reactionary tribal rules unsuited to contemporary societies.'[2] Another lawyer, Faraj Fada, a persuasive speaker as well as a passionate essayist, went even further and published a pamphlet under the provocative title of *No to Shari'ah*. He put his argument directly: Islam has no policy suitable for modern society and should not be mixed with politics. Instead of entering into lengthy discussions all we have to do as thinking people is to cry out together: 'No to *shari'ah*'.[3]

Fada's pamphlet, which he liked to refer to as 'the book',

became an unexpected success and certainly sold as many copies as the most popular writings of Shaikh Kashk, Egypt's version of Khomeini. *No to Shari'ah* was also quickly translated into other Islamic languages and found a considerable echo in Turkey, Iran and Pakistan. Banned in the Islamic Republic, it joined another far more provocative work, Ali Dashti's *Twenty-three Years*, on the bestseller list of 'illegal and anti-Islamic books'.[4]

The record of the Party of Allah in government, both in the Islamic Republic and in the areas of Lebanon under its control, was subjected to closer public scrutiny in many Muslim countries and condemned even by some of the most influential figures in traditional-style fundamentalism.[5] By 1984 Shaikh Omar al-Talmassani had concluded that the network of Holy Terror would only lead Islam to 'spiritual suicide'.[6] And Zaynab al-Ghazzali, another 'saint' of the Muslim Brotherhood in Egypt, spoke of her conviction that the movement symbolized by Khomeini would take the 'same path to perdition' that took the Kharejites of the seventh century into oblivion. She saw as the main weakness of the Partisans of Allah the fact that 'they divide Muslims into good and bad and thus reject some. . . . Theirs is a suicidal policy which will lead them to self-destruction.'[7]

Right from the beginning, Nasserites and other Arab nationalist groups figured among the principal targets of the revived fundamentalist movement. In 1981 attempts to organize nationwide gatherings to mark the tenth anniversary of the death of the first *raïs* in Egypt were abandoned under direct pressure from militant fundamentalist groups. Bookshops selling Nasser's pamphlets or books on him were set on fire in Cairo, Alexandria, Asyut and Port Said. Students suspected of Nasserite tendencies were savagely beaten up by Partisans of Allah on the campus of the Ain al-Shams University. By 1986, however, Nasserite and other nationalist groups were very much back in evidence. Nationalism, attacked by the Partisans of Allah as a Western plot aimed at dividing the Muslims, showed signs of regaining some of its lost prestige in Egypt.

The experience of Iran, at first enthusiastically welcomed but not properly analyzed, began to force the political elite in

Egypt and other Muslim countries to rethink some of their earlier assumptions. Nationalists, liberals, socialists, communists and social democrats began to realize that the tremendous force of Khomeini's revolution had been partly due to the Ayatollah's success in harnessing under his command the whole of the nation's political energies. Once it was clear that the Party of Allah in government would in no way consent to any form of power-sharing, the reassertion of one's true political identity became a matter of life and death in many Muslim countries. Westernized intellectuals who – whether out of ignoble opportunism or because they misunderstood the situation – had agreed to conceal their true political identities in order to help the Party of Allah win power paid dearly for their mistake. The tragic fate of Iran's Westernized elites, who did not appreciate the bitter fact that the Shah was closer to them than the Ayatollah could ever be, was by 1986 recognized in many Muslim countries as an example to avoid. The Iraqi government, at war against the Party of Allah since 1980, used the Iranian tragedy as a central theme in its own propaganda aimed at preventing the creation of a vast coalition of opposition forces under the leadership of Khomeinist mullahs.[8]

Another factor that contributed to the slow but steady build-up of a new form of intellectual resistance to Holy Terror groups throughout the Muslim world was the revelation that Islamic fundamentalism almost inevitably led to violence against both individuals and communities. Under the iron rule of Assad-Allah Lajevardi, one of Khomeini's closest friends and associates, Tehran's Evin Prison was seen as a model of the Party of Allah's rule in practice. Between 1981 and 1985 an average of five people a day were executed at Evin; the majority of those put to death were students and intellectuals, mostly from left-wing parties, who had concealed their true political colours in order to help the mullahs overthrow the Shah.

From 1986 the term *ebraz howyaat* or 'announcing one's [ideological] identity' represented an important concept among Muslim intellectuals, once they realized that the future tyranny implicit in the programme of the Party of Allah could be far more violent and degrading than that of any current dictatorship. The idea was that Westernized intellectuals opposing dictatorships in Muslim countries should fight them openly and remain constantly on guard against the domination of any popular movement by the Partisans of Allah.

In Egypt, revelations in the media by the widow of Major Abboud al-Zammor, a member of the commando that murdered Sadat, sent tremors through the country. She related how Zammor, 'originally a man like any other, one who smoked and even allowed me to attend university unveiled', suddenly changed into 'a different creature' after joining the Islamic Holy War organization. 'First he told me and his mother that we ought not to eat cucumbers, as this could awaken in us instincts that are hard to control,' she went on. 'Then he forced both of us to wear the veil and forbade us to watch television. He also ordered us not to serve stuffed vine leaves any more as this would – according to his organization – heat our blood and lead to deviations.'[9] Zammor's widow, a simple, straightforward woman from a peasant background, was not the only one to share her experience with the public. Other women, including nurses who had had acid thrown at them because of their 'immodest behaviour', began to talk from 1985. They spoke of the incredible pressure put on them by Party of Allah militants, including many Western-educated doctors, to end their careers, wear the veil and become 'good wives'.

The Party of Allah's attitude to women, founded on a mixture of fascination, fear and hatred, had at the start of the 1980s been kept as well guarded as a family secret. Some sections of the party even tried to pretend that the full emancipation of women could not be achieved except through their version of Islam. In Tunisia in 1984, the disciples of Rached al-Ghannoushi were surprised when, in one of his typical 'manifestos', he declared women to have 'every right to be present at all levels of decision-making in the movement'. Women militants seized upon the edict to demand equal voting rights as well as the chairmanship of some of the revolutionary cells. The male reaction came quickly and Ghannoushi was openly threatened with rebellion. He agreed to issue a new 'manifesto' cancelling the previous one and urging women to return to their 'original place in Islam'. The move silenced many male militants but led to the resignation of scores of women, mostly university students, from the movement.

This slowly mounting challenge against the Party of Allah appeared by the summer of 1986 to have become an irreversible trend in many countries. In the Islamic Republic itself, doctors of medicine organized a series of general strikes against a government decision preventing male physicians, surgeons and dentists from treating female patients. More importantly, Ayatollah Khomeini agreed to postpone indefinitely his dream of bringing the country under the exclusive rule of the *shari'ah*. Seven years after his Islamic Revolution almost all the laws inherited from the *ancien régime* remained in force, including the Family Protection Act, which had horrified him in the early 1970s by giving women the right to seek a divorce. The build-up of resistance to Holy Terror as a system of government was described by one member of the Islamic Majlis in July 1986: 'The old society and its Western roots is proving to be far stronger than any of us imagined. . . . People prefer ordinary comforts to lofty ideals. . . . Our mosques are emptier than ever. Islamic rule has proved incapable of removing injustice or eliminating poverty. I am deeply pessimistic. Government as Allah intended it is not for tomorrow.'[10]

Very few fundamentalist leaders and activists, however, would share that view. Most would see in it little more than a sign of faint-heartedness on the part of a disillusioned revolutionary. It might take the slow build-up of resistance against the Party of Allah years to stem the tide of fundamentalism in many Muslim countries. In some countries – Egypt, for example – the Holy Terror movement and the secular forces trying to stand up to it are growing simultaneously; in October 1986 there were signs that Holy Terror was winning the race.

In mid-1986 the Holy Terror movement was losing its grip on the intellectual elites in many Muslim countries, but many of its clerical leaders saw this as a positive development. They were content with their control of the dispossessed masses – the muscle that can storm public buildings and control the sprawling slum streets of Muslim capitals. In his message to the Mecca pilgrims on 10 August 1986 Khomeini said that the Islamic Revolution was only just beginning and that many Muslim countries would go Iran's way before 'the Satanic world' could stop 'this inevitable movement of history'.

The Muslim world, with its deep social wounds and almost traditional penchant for violence, remained a fertile ground for the seeds of revolution sown by the heirs of Hassan Sabbah and Hassan al-Banna. 'Satanic forces', represented by the rich, the Westernized middle class, religious minorities and any foreigners working in the realm of Islam remained to be fought and destroyed at local and national levels in many Muslim countries. And the global fight against 'the enemies of Allah' continued to capture the imagination of the poor and the downtrodden, who compensated for their sufferings in this world by dreaming of the promised Paradise of Muhammad. Nothing would shake their determination to 'cleanse' the world with faith, fire and blood.

In Egypt, militant Muslim students often put themselves at the head of gangs of paupers from the Cairo slums to eject Coptic Christians from the universities. In Iran the campaign for the forcible conversion of the Baha'is to Islam became popular at the lowest levels of society in the early 1980s. But in both instances a deep sense of disappointment replaced early enthusiasm as the poor and downtrodden began to show more compassion for their fellow humans than did their educated and better-off leaders. Mullahs in the province of Yazd complained bitterly about poor Muslim peasants who refused to identify Baha'i families or to participate in shedding their blood in accordance with the rules of the Party of Allah.

The idea that poor peasants in the Muslim world provided fertile ground for the Party of Allah was by 1986 more open to question in the wake of experiences in many countries. In the Islamic Republic itself, in 1984 and 1985 more than 80 per cent of the electorate in the rural areas refused to take part in either presidential or parliamentary elections, despite pronouncements by Khomeini that voting was 'a divine duty'. In Turkey, attempts by fundamentalist groups to brand Turgot Ozal's synthesis of Islam and modernization a 'new trick by the West' failed, and his Motherland party scored unexpected victories in local elections throughout the country in 1985. Ozal's biggest successes were registered in the poorest and most deeply religious regions. Malaysia's Prime Minister, Mahatir Muhammad, achieved an even more impressive victory when his National Front coalition won more than two-thirds of the votes in the general election of 1986. The fundamentalist coalition, PAS, secured only one parliamentary seat and collected less than 4 per cent of the popular vote. In Senegal, mullahs dispatched to make sure that African Muslim women covered their breasts and adopted the *chador* were driven out of many villages with derision, despite the fact that they had come with suitcases full of cash and promises of more to come.

In 1986, for the first time in six years, hardly any members of the Party of Allah were successful in elections held among student bodies in the occupied West Bank or in Jordanian universities. The party suffered similar setbacks in Muslim student unions in France, Belgium, the United Kingdom and Italy. To be sure, Islam in general remained an important part of the electoral discourse and secular student unions, such as had existed in the 1960s, were nowhere in evidence. But the Islam being talked about was clearly not the same as that propagated by Holy Terror.[11]

The failure of the Islamic Republic to improve the lives of the people, its endless war with Iraq, the all but clear refusal of Iraqi Shi'ites to rise against their government, the inability of Holy Terror economists to offer a credible alternative to either capitalism or communism – in spite of various farcical experiments with interest-free banks and 'Islamic planning' – and an increasing perception of the Party of Allah as little more than an instrument of violence, are facts that can no longer be ignored in an overall assessment of the world of Islam in the 1980s.

During the 1950s and 1960s many Western observers saw the political future of Muslim countries as the outcome of a three-way fight involving European-style nationalism, best symbolized by Mossadeq and Nasser; communism, represented by powerful parties in Iran, Iraq and Syria; and traditionalism of the kind that ruled Saudi Arabia, North Yemen (before the Egyptian-inspired coup d'état) and Libya (before Gaddafi's seizure of power). The Muslim Brotherhood and the Fedayeen of Islam were dismissed as marginal forces incapable of affecting the central course of events in Islam.

The imperfections of this analysis were best illustrated by Khomeini's successful revolution and the emergence of Holy Terror as a force to reckon with in many Muslim countries. But this in turn promoted an equally inadequate understanding of the political life of Islam in the 1980s. It was automatically assumed that the vast majority of Muslims wanted to be ruled in Khomeini's style, and that more than 150 years of exposure to Western ideas, as well as Western domination and injustice, had left behind nothing but a deep and gaping wound. The fact, however, is that such eminently Western ideas as democracy, socialism, the worth of the individual and national sovereignty still enjoy an important measure of support in most of the socially more advanced Muslim countries – Egypt, Turkey, Iran, Lebanon, Tunisia, Algeria and Pakistan. Some Western observers expressed surprise when women politicians emerged as national opposition leaders in both Pakistan and Bangladesh in 1986, despite much grumbling from the local mullahs and Partisans of Allah.

It is often forgotten that during the past three decades millions of Muslims have been educated in the West or in Western schools in their own countries, and that no fewer than 15 million workers, mostly from Turkey, the Muslim regions of Yugoslavia and North Africa, have gained direct experience of the West in the same period. Such first-hand contacts did not always lead to hatred of the West, as happened with some militant students who attended American universities in the 1960s and 1970s. In many cases, Muslims who came into direct contact with the West resented it not because of the freedom and prosperity in Europe and America, but because the Western powers were seen as the protectors of corrupt and dictatorial regimes in many Islamic countries.

The Party of Allah presented a programme for 're-becoming ourselves' at a time when Western ideologies were suffering a tactical retreat, mainly as a result of a universal trend towards pragmatism but also because their local representatives in the world of Islam did not practise what they preached. But those who tried to 're-become' themselves through the recipe offered by Holy Terror became 'someone quite different'.[12]

The central political problem in the Muslim world is that of every other contemporary society: the distinction between people's private lives and their public ones. The Party of Allah proposes to solve the problem simply by allowing public life totally and irrevocably to annexe the area set aside for private life.[13] The attempt to do so has led to violence and failed wherever it has been made – most dramatically in the Islamic Republic. The question of democracy and the separation of the mosque from the state is very much alive in every Islamic society today. Even the Party of Allah is obliged to pay lip service to democratic values by organizing elections – something totally alien to Islam.

Islamic fundamentalism had lingered in the background of Muslim political life for generations, making occasional bloody irruptions. It resembled Count Dracula, the prince of the 'undead', who rejected the past while haunting the present. Because it was believed to belong to the realm of the 'undead', fundamentalist Islam did not cause much alarm among Westernized Muslim elites until the mid-1980s. Khomeini showed that the 'undead' was in fact very much alive and capable of killing in order to prolong its own life. From the mid-1980s the Party of Allah and its network of Holy Terror could not be dismissed. They had to be faced and fought, and must eventually be defeated by 'forces of life' in the Muslim world itself before Islamic societies can tackle the inescapable problem of modernization.[14]

Maxime Rodinson, the distinguished French Islamicist, prophesied in the 1950s that the global duel between socialism and capitalism would one day have to be fought in the realm of Islam as well. In 1979 Rodinson appeared like a false prophet, but in 1986 one could no longer be so sure. Islam as a civilization has proved rich, resilient and sufficiently receptive to change not to fear its current political upheavals. It is the background of all culture in every Muslim country, and the intellectual home even of those of its children who have the courage to reject its claim to possess divine authority. The reduction of Islam to the level of a political ideology can only lead to its rejection as a religion also – especially by the masses in the long run. Every attempt at turning Islam into a doctrine of political power inevitably leads to terrorism: the Kharejites, the Qarmathians, the Assassins, the Muslim Brotherhood and the Fedayeen of Islam all attempted what Khomeini's movement of Holy Terror offered in the 1980s. The path charted by the Party of Allah is an impasse that would leave Islam with the problem of terrorism for many years to come.[15]

From a strategic point of view the current movement of Holy Terror is at once stronger and weaker than its predecessors. It is stronger because neither the state structures inside the Muslim countries nor the foreign powers threatened by Holy Terror are capable, for obvious reasons, of meeting its violence with a corresponding measure of counter-violence.[16] It is weaker, on the other hand, because it has to compete with many other ideologies from a position of weakness. Holy Terror has no answers to the political, economic and social problems of today. It does not even know how to ask the pertinent questions. Unable to offer a life worth living, it advocates death as Man's highest and noblest goal. Despite attempts by some Western professors (of the type who enjoys other people's revolutions from a suitable distance) to bestow on the political and economic writings of Holy Terror theoreticians some semblance of rationality and consistency, what we are offered is nothing but half-understood quotations from the Qur'an and dubious Hadiths or sayings of the Prophet sprinkled with pseudo-Marxist jargon. The attempt to elevate protest into a theory of state cannot be dignified merely by its presentation as 'Islamic philosophy'. The fact is that the very expression 'Islamic philosophy', as applied to the writings of Khomeini, Baqer Sadr, Ragheb Harb, Qutb, Mawdoodi, Lajevardi and Khalkhali, is a contradiction in terms. The Party of Allah admits of no doubt and no speculation. It does not recommend thinking, but 'repeating' the 'Truth as revealed once and for all' in the Holy Book.

The claim by some Western admirers of Holy Terror that the government of the Party of Allah is precisely the type of rule desired by a majority of Muslims had by 1986 been exposed as an exaggeration. It must nevertheless be emphasized that Muslims have never rejected the choice of a pluralist, democratic society based on the Universal Declaration of Human Rights and 'other such Satanic Western values'.

Muslims have never freely chosen death over life, war over peace, and terror over the rule of law. Those who claim that Islam, being 'the religion of the sword', can lead only to violence and war forget that less than a third of Muslims live in countries converted to Islam by conquest.[17]

The idea that the Muslim world could or should cut itself off from the contemporary world in order to live in accordance with its traditional spiritual values seems to some Muslim intellectuals an invention of Western Islamicists. The precursors of the Islamicists of the 1980s in the West, known as the Orientalists, were largely responsible for the invention of various brands of nationalism in Muslim countries. Persians in the 1930s, for instance, were invited to push Islam into the background in order to claim the heritage of Cyrus the Great, of whom they had not heard before the arrival on the scene of European archaeologists and Orientalists. Arab nationalism, traced back to the *Epic of Gilgamesh*, was also invented for the most part by Western romantics. As for Turkey, Mustafa Kemal imported large numbers of European scholars in order to help him invent the myth of a Turkish nation related to the Celts. In every case the Orientalists achieved some success, and Western-style nationalism did become part of the overall political tradition of the larger Islamic states.

Islamic fundamentalism of the 1980s, referred to by some writers as Islamism in order to indicate the essentially Western mode of expression it has adopted, is certainly not an invention of Islamicists. But it remains a result of the original clash and subsequent fusion of Western-style 'Third-Worldism' of the type best symbolized by people like Franz Fanon and the tradition of terror within Islam itself. Also present within it are strong Marxist and fascist influences that have nothing to do with Islam either as a religion or as a political doctrine. Some Muslim scholars see the Holy Terror movement as a twisted version of 'secularization in the name of Islam'.[18] In their view it is the totalitarian state that turns religion into an appendix of itself, while claiming to aim at the exact opposite. In the Islamic Republic, for example, the day-to-day political needs of the state are invariably given precedence over the exigencies of the Faith. The argument is ingenious in its simplicity as put by Khomeini himself: the

Islamic Republic must be preserved, otherwise Islam will be destroyed, while our republic cannot exist if Islam vanishes.

In a sense, therefore, what we are witnessing is not a religious revival in the Muslim world but the inclusion of religion in political life after decades of separation. The future of Islam will not be decided by theological debate concerning Qur'anic principles and the finer shades of meaning in the sayings of the Prophet. It will be decided by Islam's ability to adapt itself to the hopes, needs, aspirations and realities of the contemporary world. It may be the only 'Divine Truth', but it still has to cope with the facts of life concerning nearly a billion human beings from many different, and often even irreconcilable, historical backgrounds. The idea that the Senegalese, the Persians, the Malaysians and the Arabs can shape a single and unique future within Islam is as absurd as tying together the political future of the Poles and the Filipinos simply because both are Christian nations. And in both Poland and the Philippines Christianity was as alive and active as Islam was in any Muslim country in the 1980s.

Islam cannot ignore the fact that the Renaissance, the French Revolution, the Industrial Revolution, the dramatic technological progress of the past three centuries and its own violent contact with Western colonialism have led to the creation of a global system in which it is virtually impossible for a single nation or group of nations to wall themselves in with the hope of shaping a separate destiny. Until even 150 years ago 'the perfect harmony of form and content' enabled Islam to live in relative tranquillity and be content with its own ghetto in a changing world. That harmony was destroyed by colonialism, war, the infiltration of Western ideas among Muslim elites and the growing economic interdependence of all countries. As Shayegan put it:

> While the West entered into history through the dramatic changes of the nineteenth and twentieth centuries, the other part of humanity [Islam] remained untouched by all that movement. It was to receive its effects much later in the form of fully made pa ckages: fully made machines as well as ideologies and ideas – positivism, and later Marxism also. . . . Third World revolutions in the twentieth century, like the one in Iran, made of the rejection of the West a symbol of their quest for authenticity. But the West

> has, paradoxically, avenged itself thanks to its ideologies, and [Third World] revolutions have fallen into what is called 'the ruses of reason'. By trying to deny history they have historicized themselves, and by wanting to spiritualize the world they have secularized themselves. And in wishing to reject the West they have become Westernized.[19]

In other words, in wanting to distance Islam from a world that it considers 'Satanic' because it is created and dominated by the West, the Party of Allah has done more to push Islam into that world than any other movement in Muslim countries during the past 150 years. Ever since its divine revelation more than fourteen centuries ago, Islam's central 'slogan' has been the celebrated formula known to every Muslim: 'There is no God but Allah, and Muhammad is the Prophet of Allah.' The movement of Holy Terror has added to it other slogans, including 'Death to America', 'Death to Russia' and 'Death to Israel'. They have made millions of Muslims aware for the first time of the existence and reality of these 'enemies of Islam'. By wishing them dead, Khomeini brought them to life even in the remotest villages of the Islamic world. Another effect of Khomeini's revolution was the redefinition of Islam as a faith concerned not with the broader and permanent issues of human existence but with the existing balance of political and military power in the Middle East.

The discovery of 'the other', even when it comes in the violent and twisted form offered by Holy Terror, is the first step towards eventual self-doubt. In hating 'the other' one is bound to end up seeking the reasons for this 'otherness'. Neither the generals nor the rank and file of Holy Terror could escape the inevitable questions: Why do we desire the death of those whom we wish to see destroyed? What makes them different from us? Why can we not defeat them in the existing context of our relationship with them? Do they really deserve to be so hated? Would it not be wiser for us to become like them, at least in some respects? Is a return to Medina both desirable and feasible, or do we have to look to a future we may be able to shape rather than to a past which now belongs more to history than it does to us?

Epilogue

The Cake, the Bible and the Colts

Early in September 1986 five men, all holding Irish passports and wearing the uniform of an air cargo company, checked in at Tehran's Independence Hotel (formerly the Royal Hilton) with a number of gifts for 'Iranian friends'. These included a copy of the Bible autographed by President Reagan, a cake shaped in the form of a key, and eight brand-new Colt revolvers. The man heading this strange group was soon discovered by the hotel staff to be an American. He was, in fact, Robert McFarlane, Reagan's former Director for National Security and still a key administration adviser. He had with him Lieutenant-Colonel North, a member of Reagan's National Security Council, and three other army officers as well as an interpreter.

The autographed copy of the Bible was destined for Ayatollah Khomeini, the 'supreme guide' of the Party of Allah. The cake, bought in Wiesbaden in West Germany, was meant to symbolise the 'opening of locked doors' between the United States and the Islamic Republic. The Colts were meant as gifts for the eight highest-ranking leaders of the Party of Allah, whose love of guns is widely known.

Reports of McFarlane's secret visit were first leaked through leaflets distributed by the Hadafiyoun (idealists) branch of the Party of Allah in the holy city of Qom in October 1986. These were later taken up by a Syrian-financed newspaper in Lebanon, whose published account of the Irano-American deals prompted Tehran and Washington to offer their own marginally differing accounts of the events. Information pieced together from a variety of Iranian, American, Lebanese and other Arab sources showed that the Reagan administration initiated the contacts with Iran through more than a dozen intermediaries from February 1985 onwards. Elliot Richardson, a former Attorney General in the Nixon administration, established one of the most important links with Iran through Cyrus Hashemi, a cousin of the speaker of the Islamic Majlis (parliament), Ali-Akbar Hashemi Rafsanjani. McFarlane visited Tehran at least three times to conduct negotiations that led to the shipment of arms and military spare parts to the Islamic Republic in exchange for the liberation of three American hostages: the Reverend Benjamin Weir, the Reverend Lawrence Jenco and David Jacobsen. In all three cases, Tehran and Washington used Terry Waite, the special envoy of the Archbishop of Canterbury, as a suitable cover so that the real reasons for the release of the hostages could remain secret.

These dealings with the 'Great Satan' were strongly opposed by some factions within the Party of Allah. The Hadafiyoun even organised the kidnapping of a Syrian diplomat in Tehran in October 1986 as a warning to the Majlis speaker that the Party of Allah could organise the seizure of hostages in the Islamic capital itself. Hashemi-Rafsanjani, the Majlis speaker, retaliated by organizing the arrest of Mehdi Hashemi, the father-figure of the Hadafiyoun and for long the nominal head of the organization for the export of the Islamic Revolution. The fact that the United States had agreed to make a deal over the hostages was seen in the Middle East as a major victory for the Party of Allah and its policy of 'pressurizing the enemies of Islam into capitulation'. The U.S. did not only give arms to Iran but also agreed to 'de-freeze' some 500 million dollars of Iranian money held in a New York bank since 1979. In addition Washington promised to stop passing on to Iraq military intelligence gathered by its 'flying radars', AWACS, operating from Saudi Arabia.

The United States was not the only power trying to make a deal with the Party of Allah in order to secure for itself some measure of protection against the network of Islamic Holy Terror. The French government of premier Jacques Chirac also began negotiating with the Party of Allah as early as April

1986, a few weeks after coming into power. France agreed to reduce its support for Iraq in the Gulf war and to return to Iran a loan of over 1,000 million dollars granted by the Shah in 1974. In addition, the French government ordered the expulsion of Massoud Rajavi, the leader of an Iraqi-financed anti-Khomeini guerrilla group that had been in exile near Paris since 1981. In exchange, the Party of Allah released two French hostages – the 84-year old Caville Sontag and Marcel Coudary, in November 1986.

Western hostages still held by the Party of Allah in Lebanon and in the Islamic Republic numbered 25 at the end of November 1986. These included seven Frenchmen, five Britons, five Americans and lone captives from other countries such as Italy and the Irish Republic.

The British government has continued its efforts to reach an accommodation with the network of Holy Terror. According to an *Observer* report on November 9, these efforts included the resumption of activities in Iran by British Petroleum, and facilities for Iranian arms purchases in London. These concessions were expected to strengthen the hand of Terry Waite in his secret talks with the kidnappers in Lebanon. Waite would serve as 'the cellophane wrapping' of a package, the content of which is worked out through secret deals between the states directly involved in the drama.

Revelations concerning concessions made by the United States and France in secret deals with Holy Terror came as a great morale-booster to the Party of Allah in the autumn of 1986, at a time it was facing mounting political difficulties in several Muslim countries. Rafsanjani, who was emerging as the most powerful figure within the Party of Allah, said on November 4, 1986: 'our policy has succeeded, and the enemies of Islam are crawling towards us, begging to be noticed'.

Appendix

A *Islam Is Not a Religion of Pacifists*

There are two kinds of war in Islam: one is called Jihad [Holy War], which means the conquest of [other] countries in accordance with certain conditions. The other [type] is war to preserve the independence of the [Muslim] country and the repulsion of foreigners. Jihad or Holy War, which is for the conquest of [other] countries and kingdoms, becomes incumbent after the formation of the Islamic state in the presence of the Imam or in accordance with his command. Then Islam makes it incumbent on all adult males, provided they are not disabled and incapacitated, to prepare themselves for the conquest of [other] countries so that the writ of Islam is obeyed in every country in the world.

But world public opinion should know that Islamic conquest is not the same as conquests made by other rulers of the world. The latter want to conquer the world for their own personal profit, whereas Islam's conquest is aimed at serving the interests of the inhabitants of the globe as a whole. [Non-Islamic] conquerors want to rule the world so that they can spread through it every injustice and sexual indecency, whereas Islam wants to conquer the world in order to promote spiritual values, and to prepare mankind for justice and divine rule.

[Non-Islamic] conquerors sacrifice the lives and possessions of the people to their own leisure and pleasure. But Islam does not allow its leaders and generals to enjoy themselves or to have a moment's leisure; in this way the lives and property of people can be protected and the bases of injustice destroyed in the world.

Islam's Holy War is a struggle against idolatry, sexual deviation, plunder, repression and cruelty. The war waged by [non-Islamic] conquerors, however, aims at promoting lust and animal pleasures. They care not if whole countries are wiped out and many families left homeless. But those who study Islamic Holy War will understand why Islam wants to conquer the whole world. All the countries conquered by Islam or to be conquered in the future will be marked for everlasting salvation. For they shall live under Light Celestial Law. . . .

Those who know nothing of Islam pretend that Islam counsels against war. Those [who say this] are witless. Islam says: Kill all the unbelievers just as they would kill you all! Does this mean that Muslims should sit back until they are devoured by [the unbelievers]? Islam says: Kill them [the non-Muslims], put them to the sword and scatter [their armies]. Does this mean sitting back until [non-Muslims] overcome us? Islam says: Kill in the service of Allah those who may want to kill you! Does this mean that we should surrender [to the enemy]? Islam says: Whatever good there is exists thanks to the sword and in the shadow of the sword! People cannot be made obedient except with the sword! The sword is the key to Paradise, which can be opened only for Holy Warriors!

There are hundreds of other [Qur'anic] psalms and Hadiths [sayings of the Prophet] urging Muslims to value war and to fight. Does all that mean that Islam is a religion that prevents men from waging war? I spit upon those foolish souls who make such a claim.

Ayatollah Ruhollah Khomeini in *Kashf al-Asrar* (*Key to the Secrets*), Qom, 1986. (Originally published in Qom in 1942 and reprinted in Teheran in 1980 and 1983.)

B *Death Is Not an End but a Continuation*

Unlike those [other religions] which consider death to be the end of man's life, in the vision of the Qur'an death is not the end of life but its continuation in another form. Man's evolutionary movement towards infinity, towards the full accomplishment of life, continues after death. Thus death is no more than a hyphen between two parts of man's existence. . . .

In the Qur'an's vision chaos and sedition are but two instruments, two means of measurement for the individual as well as for society as a whole. . . . Through chaos, sedition and other forms of hardship, the individual is tested; his purity, the depth of his faith and his commitment [to the cause] are measured so that he can have his just reward. . . .

The Qur'an rejects the [Marxist] idea of many classes in society. Basing itself on true historical realities, the Qur'an recognizes only two classes in society: the rulers, who are tyrants, exploiters and members of the party of Satan, form one of the two classes. They are always in a minority. The other class, according to the Qur'an, is that of the ruled, the vast majority of people who are dispossessed, exploited and subjected to injustice – the members of the Party of Allah. The whole history of mankind consists of the struggle between these two mutually exclusive classes. The rulers, with Satan in their command, have always fought those who have upheld mankind's objectives: Abel against Cain, Nimrod against Abraham, the Pharaoh against Moses, Abu-Sufyan, Abu-Jahl and Abu-Lahab against Muhammad, Muawyyah against Ali, Yazid against Hussein and the present-day heirs to the government of Satan against us – members of the Party of Allah. . . .

The ideal society of Islam and the Qur'an is one [that is] for justice and against tyranny. In it all signs of idolatry and whatever else is considered by the Qur'an to be invalid have disappeared. As far as Islam is concerned, there are no basic differences between the slave-owning society, the feudal society, capitalism and communism. All 'isms' – fascism, Marxism, liberalism, racism, socialism, existentialism, capitalism etc. are against Islam. Why? Simply because all of them have one thing in common: they are not based on the vision of the Qur'an. . . .

One [social] group that is the enemy of the Qur'an by definition is known under the name of *muturaffin* or those who want to have a good time in this world. Their presence is deadly both before and after the establishment of the Qur'anic rule under the Party of Allah. They usually stay out of politics, but even when they participate in political life their basic aim does not change. That aim is to satisfy their animal lust, to enjoy themselves and indulge their base desires. Their opposition to the new Islamic revolutionary system is motivated by the fact that [the new government] is opposed to their levity and debauchery. These [elements] know how to make a lot of money and get rich, so that they can finance the good time they constantly seek. . . . These [elements] will never reconcile themselves to the idea of an [austere] life in accordance with the strictures of the Faith. . . .

Struggle and Holy War are essential characteristics of an Islamic community that has attained self-awareness and is dynamic. The Islamic community, in accordance with the laws of creation that stipulate movement as the sole guarantee for survival, cannot stand still. It knows that a single moment of inaction might spell its perdition. . . . Peace and quiet have no meaning for the members of the party of God. They do not waste a single second and constantly fight to uproot the rule of tyranny and crime. . . . The divine society does not allow its members to sit back and enjoy themselves in the belief that everything is now properly arranged. We cannot and must not think that we can go on holiday, enjoy ourselves, or even devote ourselves entirely to prayer. . . . The Islamic man must be constantly on the watch to prevent the commission of sin and to rectify every wrong. . . .

Tyrants and members of the party of Satan often use armed violence in order to suppress the movement of the Partisans of Allah. Thus war becomes inevitable. It is the duty of Muslims to take up arms in support of the oppressed, especially if the oppressed in question have converted to Islam. Islam does not recognize earthly frontiers [between countries]; what matters to Islam are the frontiers of Faith. . . . Islamic wars have always been the continuation of Islamic ideological struggle. . . . The Qur'an teaches that those who suffer from tyranny possess every right to have recourse to war. It also teaches us to kill the idolaters and the unbelievers who reject Islam and wage war on us. Islam's objective from war is the establishment of the government of Allah and thus the culmination of the process of evolution. . . .

The Qur'an teaches us to kill those who make trouble, but it also insists that we should not overdo it. The Qur'an forbids excess in killing and emphasizes the fact that the aim of the duty of *qital* [killing] is not to kill everyone but to eliminate only the ringleaders and some of their agents. . . . Islam recognizes revenge as an authorized value, but insists that we should not go too far. . . . The Qur'an invites us to kill until troublemakers are eliminated. What is meant by trouble is the oppression imposed on Muslims by non-Muslim governments or governments that are Islamic in appearance only. To end that we are allowed to take up arms and to kill. . . . War and bloody revolution are necessary to preserve the Faith, otherwise Muslims suffering oppression may give up their beliefs. . . . But it is equally important to wage an ideological struggle, to take the message of Islam everywhere and to show the whole of mankind that only Islam can save it from annihilation. . . . Revolution is like a match put to the harvest of tyranny so that a huge fire can be lit. But to keep this fire alive and ever glowing one needs the fuel of doctrine that must be propagated with true zeal. . . .

Only Islam can offer the possibility of [making] a genuine revolution. We have all seen what has happened to the Chinese revolution which once made so much noise about its defence of Marxism but is now moving in the opposite ideological direction, so as to resemble an imperialist [society]. As for the Soviet Union, which claims to be the cradle of communism, nothing has really changed and exploitation continues as before. . . .

Gholam-Reza Fada'i Araqi, *Hezb-Allah va Hezb-Shaytan* (*The Party of Allah and the Party of Satan*), Qom, 1986

C *The Day Divine Light Opened My Eyes*

In the Name of Allah the Avenger!
Respected Mother, Exulted Imam,[1]
I address this, my last will, to both of you for a simple reason: it was my mother who brought me into this world so that the Imam can show me the path to a better world – the path of martyrdom. To my mother I owe my earthly life, a most humble offering to the cause of the Imam. For what am I? A mere speck of dust in a whirlwind, shoved this way and that and never knowing why. This was my state as long as my eyes were closed with the leaden weight of dark ignorance. I thought life meant only growing up, going through an education, finding a mate and founding a family – a life of work and of repose. I knew not that my foolish concept of life had been inculcated in me by the vicious propaganda of those enemies of Islam whose corrupt culture of Cross-worship has dominated and polluted our land for too long. They want us [i.e. the Muslims] to throw off our guard, to relax, to begin to love life above everything else, to believe that happiness in this world is all that man requires. They try to seduce us with schools and houses so that we abandon our Faith and become like them, so that our womenfolk can become prostitutes and our youth corrupted by sexual pleasure. Once our never-forgotten Guide Imam Mussa Sadr had opened our eyes in this land of darkness, they [the Christians?] made him stay away from us in the hope that the fire he had lit would soon be put out by the passage of time as well as by the intrigues of the enemies of Islam. But the Almighty was vigilant. For He had noticed our keen desire to be saved, our disdain for a restful life and our hatred of corrup-

tion of all kinds, whether of money or of a sexual nature. It was thus that the light of Imam Khomeini – may Allah never allow his enemies to have peace – began to shine on this lost and forgotten country. The youth of Lebanon discovered the Party of Allah and learned the sweet name of Khomeini – a name whose sweetness burns the tongue and warms the heart of every true believer. We learned to cry out: 'Allah is the One, Khomeini is the Guide!' And from then on Lebanon was ours, the world was ours so that we could spit on it with disdain – we who seek another world. We saw the Light. We learned that Allah will always reserve His triumph for the downtrodden. We saw how He took our trembling hands and commanded us: 'Shi'ites of the south, of Sur and of Sidon and of the Jabal, stand up and fight!' I stood up and began to walk for the first time. Only then did I realize that throughout the previous twenty years of my life I had only crawled. I had crawled in the filth of humiliation. I had claimed to be a Shi'ite, that is to say a follower of Ali, the everlasting symbol of manly courage. And yet I had been a coward. I had watched as the party of Satan conquered my land to make our boys wear indecent clothes and behave like girls and to teach our womenfolk to lust after superficial things and carnal joy. They [the unbelievers?] taught us to drink wine so that we would forget the blood of Hussein, the Master of Martyrs. We were turned into walking piles of filth and did not deserve a second look. And yet, Khomeini showed us the path. He spoke the will of Allah, and those who had the good fortune to hear his voice first were taken away from the dirt of this world and led to the gate of the garden whose key is martyrdom. I am at the door now, and praise and thank the Almighty for my good fortune. I am seeking the key to the gate of the garden. And I pray day and night to be allowed to feel the key in my hand, to be allowed to hear the key turn in the lock of the garden gate. And then to enter the garden, to see its wonders. The Imam has commanded me to kill. I shall kill for him. The Imam has commanded me to die. I shall die for him. I may be taken away at any moment. I pray constantly to be taken away at any moment – fighting sword in hand in the service of Allah, as were the companions of Hussein in the Karbala desert.[2] All I ask for is that my little Safwan[3] be brought up in the tradition of martyrdom from the earliest age, so that he does not waste as many years as I wasted. This trust I bequeath to my mother and friends and all others who have had the good fortune to become members of the Party of Allah. . . .

The full text of this will by Rada Muhammad N'eman was published in Lebanon by *Payam Shahid* (*Message of the Martyr*) in a special issue, October 1985

[1]Meaning Ayatollah Khomeini, who has assumed the title of Imam.

[2]The desert of Karbala in southern Iraq is where Hussein, the third Imam of duodecimal Shi'ism, was killed in battle against the troops of the Umayyid Caliph Yazid ben Muawyyah in the seventh century.

[3]Presumably the name of the writer's son.

D *The Infidel Who Cherish Life*

The miscreant fears death as the absolute evil. The civilization of the infidel makes of life – of its preservation, its standards – a supreme value. For them [i.e. the infidels] happiness begins and ends with life, while death is [considered to be] the trouble-maker, the undesirable intruder. Speaking of death is taboo for them [the infidels]. The undertaker's business must have, as its first necessity, discretion. Hurry up! The corpse must be removed with speed! Quick, forget it all! For the faithful who are still at the beginning of their waking [process], death continues to appear as an enemy – so great is the attraction of immediate life. But little by little, as he draws closer to Allah and strengthens his links with Him, death changes its significance and becomes the long-awaited moment for an encounter so ardently desired. The ego attaches itself to the nest of its habits. But the spirit, aroused and whipped up by nostalgia, wants to fly back to its origins. When the ego is silenced, the death of this temporary and burdensome body will be [considered] a welcome deliverance.

Our Prophet says: 'He who likes to encounter Allah will find out that Allah likes to encounter him. And he who detests an encounter with Allah will find out that He, too, detests meeting him!' Our mother Aicha,[1] who heard these words, asked the Prophet: 'O Messenger of Allah! Does this mean that we ought not to dislike death?'

The Prophet replied: 'It is not so simple. The faithful [man] who is aware of Allah's love and knows all there is in His Paradise welcomes death. The infidel, on the other hand, knows of the just punishment that awaits the likes of him, and therefore does not wish to die. He hates meeting Allah, and therefore Allah hates meeting him.

Loving Allah for His generosity and His Paradise is the degree of faith that the Prophet describes in the Hadith above. Ihsan[2] consists of wanting Allah for Himself, regardless of His generosity, the bounties He can bestow on us and His Paradise. In both cases death is the necessary and desired passage, regardless of the fact that the ego steps back in the face of the unknown.

The faithful are recommended to prepare the

mortal remains of their brothers themselves at the time of burial. This is meant as an exercise of self-detachment from this base life. The faithful must personally lay their brethren into their last abode. Islam does not recognize professional undertakers. Funeral ceremonies presided over by professionals are bound to lead to a misuse of death as a social convention. . . . The Prophet, speaking to one of his companions, Abu-Dharr, had this to say: 'Visit the graveyards. That will remind you of the Last Life. Clean and prepare the corpse [for burial]. For the company of the dead will leave on you a profound impression. . . .

Abd Assalam Yassine, *La Révolution à l'heure de l'Islam*, Marseilles, 1981

[1]Aicha was the Prophet's favourite wife. Sunni Muslims refer to her as Umm ul-Momeneen (Mother of the Faithful).

[2]Literally: beatitude.

E *The Emancipation of Man from His Attachment to This World*

The establishment of the rule of justice and the ability to face the difficult task of constructing [it], requires motives that spring from consciousness and a sense of responsibility and of attachment to duty. These motives are constantly struggling against an obstacle that prevents their birth and growth. This obstacle is [our] attachment to this world and its seductions – to life on this Earth, no matter what form it assumes. This attachment often petrifies Man and prevents him from taking part in the constructive task. For taking part in any major task of construction necessitates much effort and suffering and many sacrifices. It also requires courageous endurance and abnegation for the welfare and happiness of human society.

It is therefore not within the possibilities of him who is attached to the seductions of this world and earthly life to abandon these worthless objectives and break out of the closed circle of petty daily problems in order to take part in the great task of construction. . . .

Attachment to this world is the base of all deviation. He who devotes himself to this world abandons the role of God's vice-regent on Earth. He who plunges himself into the delights of this world and [enjoys] its distractions forgets the memory of Allah and thus loses all that this unique and mighty divinity offers Man in order to link him with the heavens.

Islam [unlike alien doctrines now dominating Muslim countries through the state apparatus] has on numerous occasions proved its ability to assemble, in the name of Holy War, important numbers of believers. This is in contrast with the failure of the [non-Islamic] state to implement its policy of conscription despite systematic use of coercion. And now imagine what would happen if Islam assumed the government of the *Ummah* [Community of Believers]. Imagine the massive mobilization we would be able to accomplish [for Holy War].

Muhammad-Baqer al-Sadr, *Sources of Power in the Islamic State*, Tehran, 1983

F Hegira: *An Effective Means of Struggle*

One of the most effective and fruitful forms of struggle towards [the creation] of a divine human society, as [dreamed of] by the Party of Allah, is *hegira*. *Hegira* means going away, leaving, emigrating, cutting oneself off, withdrawal. In its Islamic meaning *hegira* signifies the withdrawal of Muslims from a society in which, because of tyranny and the domination of corrupt thoughts, true believers cannot continue to live in accordance with their beliefs. In such a society, conditions of life [for true believers] are so harsh that they have no choice but to die or to renounce their Faith. It is then that a third choice is suggested: that of cutting oneself off, even to the point of going into exile. But this way can be chosen only with the understanding that the period of *hegira* will not be too long, and that it will be used for the purpose of gathering forces in order to return and destroy the enemy. This choice of exile is not meant to ensure [for those who make it] a life of joy and happiness. The idea is to go away to preserve one's Faith and then return to put the agents of Satan to the sword. Thus those who leave [the country] to escape their duty of fighting the agents of Satan cannot claim to have accomplished the duty of *hegira*. They have merely fled their homes and have no merit. . . .

No excuse will be accepted from those who submit to the rules of a Satanic society and who do not accomplish *hegira*. Those who can withdraw but refuse to do so for whatever reason will be held responsible. As they lie dying, they will see angels appearing to them to ask: 'Why did you accept all that? Was not Allah's land vast enough to offer you a corner of peace?' . . .

Those who take the path of *hegira* in the name of Allah, if they die or are killed on the way will be rewarded by the Almighty. They will lose nothing that they deserve. . . . The fact that most of the 124,000 prophets sent to mankind by the Almighty have been forced at one time or another to perform *hegira* – either to go into exile or to withdraw into the desert – shows that travellers on the Path of Justice are often forced to withdraw from Satan-dominated societies: Abraham, Moses, Jesus and our own Prophet were all forced into exile. . . .

The *hegira* is a means of struggle for those who have no links with this world, those who cannot be enslaved by earthly possessions and interests. . . .

Gholam-Reza Fada'i-Araqi, *Hezb-Allah va Hezb-Shaytan (The Party of Allah and the Party of Satan)*, Qom, 1986

G *He Who Puts the Gun in Our Hand*

God Almighty is always on the side of the dispossessed. He is a revolutionary and sides with all true revolutionaries. The Almighty cannot be a conservative; He cannot sit back and watch while members of the party of Satan rule the world, plunder the wealth of the planet and commit other forms of heinous sin. . . . The Holy Book shows how God sided with Moses, who was a true revolutionary leading the dispossessed to freedom against the Pharaoh. Moses was ready to kill, and if necessary to be killed, in the pursuit of his goals. He was ready to cheat, to lie, to sow dissension [among the enemy] and to steal in order to gain his noble ends. . . . Jesus was no revolutionary, although he used the vocabulary of a revolutionary. Some say he never took hold of a sword, or else he too would have created a sea of blood by cutting down the heathen. Others say he was a reformist by temperament and that is why he did not succeed in founding a state. But Allah knows best in all matters. . . . Our own Prophet – blessed be his soul – was even more of a revolutionary than was Moses. He was a general, a statesman, an administrator, an economist, a jurist and a first-class manager all in one. . . . Would he hesitate to put the guilty to the sword? Never, three times never! No one would dare step out of line while he was in charge. . . . In the Qur'an's historic vision Allah's support and the revolutionary struggle of the people must come together, so that Satanic rulers are brought down and put to death. A people that is not prepared to kill and to die in order to create a just society cannot expect any support from Allah. The Almighty has promised us that the day will come when the whole of mankind will live united under the banner of Islam, when the sign of the Crescent, the symbol of Muhammad, will be supreme everywhere. . . . But that day must be hastened through our Jihad, through our readiness to offer our lives and to shed the unclean blood of those who do not see the light brought from the Heavens by Muhammad in his *mi'raj*.[1] . . . It is Allah who puts the gun in our hand. But we cannot expect Him to pull the trigger as well simply because we are faint-hearted. . . .

Muhammad Taqi Partovi Sabzevari, *Ayandeh Nehzat Islami* (*The Future of the Islamic Movement*), Qom, 1986

[1]Nocturnal voyages to the 'court' of Allah.

H The Heroes of the Imam

They were all volunteers. They were all aged fourteen, fifteen and sixteen to twenty. They were there to turn the minefield into a rose garden. They were blossoms in half bloom. They would rise before dawn, which is the time for roses to open up their petals. They would then run over the mines, creating a duststorm which roared like thunder. Eyes would then see nothing. Ears would then hear nothing.

And then the duststorm would settle and a blessed silence would cover the field. We could then see fragments of broken young bodies covering the plain: scraps of flesh and bones, some stuck to thorn bushes or pebbles. It was as if the sky had rained flesh and blood and pieces of broken bone on that field. . . .

Some of the children, however, had found a way of keeping their bodies more or less intact at the time of their heroic end. They covered themselves with blankets before walking over the mines. Thus the bits and pieces that were left could be gathered together more easily for dispatch to their proud parents back home. They did this partly to facilitate the task of our orientation officials, who needed bodies to show to other young ones, to incite them to take the same path to Paradise. . . .

Ettelaat daily, Tehran, 30 January 1982

Notes

Introduction

1. In the monthly *al-Badil* (*Alternative*), which Ahmad Ben-Bella, the former Algerian President now in exile, publishes in Switzerland, he castigates the West for accusing Islam of terrorism. A television debate on the subject was held in Paris in May 1986, during which several Muslim intellectuals, including the Tunisian Muhammad Arkoun, spoke of 'an international conspiracy' to equate Islam with terrorism.
2. Delta Force was the name of a commando group set up by President Carter in 1980 for the purpose of freeing the American hostages in Tehran. Their mission failed when one of the helicopters they were using broke down. The group was nevertheless retained as the nucleus of a future anti-terrorist unit.
3. See Appendices B and F for excerpts from the Manifesto of the Party of Allah. The idea of forcible conversion of non-Muslims has been at the centre of religious debate since the beginning of Islamic history. The Prophet said there must be no constraints in the Faith; but violence has often been used for the purpose of forcing minorities to accept Islam. A current example is provided in the Islamic Republic today by the Baha'is, an offshoot of duodecimal Shi'ism, which later developed into an independent faith.
4. Abu-Nidal transferred most of his 'fighters' to Damascus from Tripoli shortly before the American raid on Libya on 15 April 1986. In a recent (1986) interview the 'most wanted man in the world' claimed that he was Syrian by birth and was therefore back home in Syria.
5. The Hadiths are the sayings of the Prophet and, in the case of Shi'ites, of the twelve Imams. To some Muslim theologians the

Hadiths enjoy as much authority as the text of the Qur'an itself.

6. Leon Klinghoeffer, a disabled man in his seventies, was 'chosen' to be murdered on the order of Abu-Abbas, the commando leader, because he admitted to being Jewish. Abbas later claimed that Klinghoeffer had been pushed into the sea by his own wife, who accompanied him on the luxury cruise.
7. Jamahiriyah – literally, the republics – is a name given to the Libyan state by Gaddafi in order to emphasize its uniqueness.
8. The Zimbabwe African People's Union (ZAPU), led by Robert Mugabe, and the Zimbabwe African National Union (ZANU), with Joshua Nkomo at its head.
9. Including Israel.
10. Meaning 'The Land of the Pure', this is the name which Sikh separatists use for the Punjab, which they want to see become independent of India. The Sikh faith is a distinct and well-established religion in India; but the Sikh political movement in the Punjab is largely concerned with political independence for the province rather than the righting of any specific wrongs perpetrated against the Sikhs as a religious community.
11. Since 1979 the MLF has emphasized its Islamic background in order to obtain financial support as well as arms from Saudi Arabia, Egypt, Libya, Iran and other Muslim countries. But it is essentially concerned with securing autonomy and, eventually, independence for the province of Mindanao, and is not a religious-*cum*-political movement. This is why some of its leaders are accused of deviation from the Faith by more militant Islamic elements linked with Iran.
12. Union Nacional por la Independence Totale do Angola. Savimbi visited the United States in 1986 and was received as a head of state by President Reagan.
13. Cellules Communistes Combattantes. This group was responsible for a series of bloody attacks, notably against NATO targets, in Belgium during 1985 and 1986.
14. Aldo Moro, the Italian statesman, was abducted and murdered after being accused of being a CIA agent. The kidnappers of the American General James Dozier in Italy also claimed that he was linked with US 'imperialist activities in Europe'. US military installations in West Germany provide a favourite target for the type of terrorist in question. The hostility of these groups towards the United States stands in sharp contrast to efforts by the IRA and, to a lesser extent, ETA to win sympathy and support from the American public.
15. The term '*publicitaire*' is suggested by Gérard Chaliand, who in

fact makes more limited use of it in his own analysis, *Terrorismes et guerrillas* (Paris, 1985).

16. For coverage of the Soviet link with various terrorist organizations, especially in the West, see Edouard Sablier's *Le Fil rouge*.
17. The Islamic–Marxist group Mujahedeen Khalq (People's Combatants), which was active in Iran in the early 1980s, carried out a series of terror attacks in Tehran with the specific aim of proving its fighting presence inside the Islamic Republic. The Iraqi government, which had asked for such proof, was convinced and began financing the organization from 1983 onwards.
18. On Friday, 25 December 1985 two groups of terrorists launched simultaneous attacks on Vienna and Rome airports, killing fourteen passengers and injuring a further 120. Four of the terrorists were killed, and four others wounded and captured. The attacks, quickly claimed by Abu-Nidal, were ordered by Syria and Libya and carried out by al-Fatah dissidents as a means of undermining a series of diplomatic moves then being made for the purpose of drawing Jordan into the Camp David peace talks. These attacks, and other smaller-scale ones that followed it, produced the desired result and persuaded King Hussein of Jordan to abandon the indirect dialogue he had begun with the Israelis on the one hand and Yasser Arafat on the other. By the beginning of 1986 he was moving in the opposite direction and drawing closer to Syria's President Assad.
19. Abu-Abbas, who masterminded and led the operation, later moved to Yugoslavia before visiting Baghdad and then Tripoli. In 1986 he began promoting himself as a successor to Arafat on the strength of his role in the *Achille Lauro* episode.
20. These roots are looked at in subsequent chapters.
21. Hezb-Allah manifesto.
22. *Sarcheshmeh Qodrat dar Hokumat Eslami* (*The Source of Power in the Islamic State*), Tehran, 1980, p. 37.
23. *Yadnameh* (*Memoriam*), Tehran, 1985, pp. 8 and 9.
24. *Khajparastan* and *salibiyoun* (Crusaders) are terms used by Muslim fundamentalists to describe the Christian minority in Lebanon and beyond. In Iran the term *Issawi* or 'followers of Jesus' is preferred.
25. Ambassador Robert Oakley, director of the US State Department's anti-terrorism unit, said in a private interview in February 1986: 'We recognize terrorism as a form of warfare – low-intensity war, that is. We know it is not easy to fight, and requires a long-term approach.'

26. The term 'path of shame' is used in fundamentalist political literature for the purpose of describing any negotiated settlement with the enemy. More specifically, it refers to the PLO's policy of seeking a place at a negotiating table with Israel.
27. The Arabic word used is *zaval*, which means 'wiping out' or 'effacing'.
28. Syria suffered further humiliation when it failed to secure the release of French hostages in March 1986.
29. *Dar Rah e Haq* (*On the Path of Justice*), Tehran, 1980, pp. 70 and 71.
30. This is how Ayatollah Ehsan Bakhsh, Friday Prayer Leader in Rasht on the Caspian Sea, commented on relations with Nicaragua:

    > We know that those people [i.e. the Nicaraguan government] have come a long way in serving the objectives of Islam by putting the [American] Great Satan to shame. But we must not forget that they, too, remain tied to a filthy ideology. We must persuade them to come the whole way and accept Islam as the only solution before we can offer assistance.

    The ayatollah's comments were reported in the weekly *Bazaar*, 30 March 1985.

Chapter 1

1. Founder and leader of the Ikhwan al-Moslemeen (The Muslim Brotherhood).
2. A fictitious name.
3. Only Shi'ite Muslims recognize temporary marriages as legal.
4. 'Ashura, the tenth day of the month of Muharram on the Arabic lunar calendar, marks the martyrdom of Hussein, the third Imam of duodecimal Shi'ism, in southern Mesopotamia in the seventh century.
5. Literally: The House of Faith.
6. Literally: The House of War. The land of the infidels is also referred to as Dar al-Kufr or the House of the Heathen.
7. The phrase is Ayatollah Morteza Motahari's, and he used it to describe Westernized intellectuals.
8. This phrase refers basically to homosexuals, who are punishable by death in the Islamic Republic.
9. In a Friday prayer speech on 13 June 1986, broadcast by Tehran Radio.

10. Ibid.
11. Speech to members of the Revolutionary Guard in Ahvaz on 5 June 1984, broadcast by Tehran Radio.
12. *Les Sources du pouvoir dans l'état Islamique*, Bibliothèque AHL-ELBEIT, Paris, 1981.
13. The phrase was one of Amir Abbas Hoveyda's favourite ways of describing the social reform programme that, as the Shah's longest-serving Prime Minister, he put into effect between 1965 and 1977.
14. Interview, May 1986.
15. The exact number of Muslims remains a subject of controversy. Western sources prefer the figure of 800 million, while Muslims themselves seem convinced that their numbers exceed the 1000 million mark.
16. The People's Republican party, led by Ismet Inönü, enjoyed Atatürk's special favour, while the much smaller Democrat party was not allowed to grow into a party of government until after the founder of the republic had departed.
17. Al-Mujahid al-Kabir. Bourguiba makes a point of either directly choosing or at least approving every appointment at the top and middle levels of the state machine.
18. Mirza Malkam Khan, a nineteenth-century intellectual and diplomat and a founder of freemasonry in Iran, was an example. While publishing a newspaper called *Kanoon* (*The Law*), which promoted the idea of a constitution, he let slip no opportunity for illegal self-enrichment. His greed led to a major scandal while he was serving as Nassereddin Shah's Ambassador to the Court of St James in London.
19. An important example is Algeria, but there too revolutionary legitimacy was quickly lost as a one-party system led by a group of colonels was established.
20. Until the Constitutional Revolution of 1906 the grand ayatollahs gave the Shah signed and sealed certificates authorizing him to rule in the name of the Hidden Imam, the last of the twelve Imams who disappeared in Samara, Mesopotamia in the tenth century.
21. The Constitutional Revolution created a unique alliance between modernizing intellectuals and 'progressive' mullahs against royal despotism as well as religious fanaticism.
22. See note 20 above.
23. The army is involved in running the government in the following countries: Indonesia, Bangladesh, Pakistan, Aghanistan, Turkey, South Yemen, North Yemen, Iraq, Syria, Egypt, Libya,

Algeria, Sudan, Somalia, Mauritania, Guinea and Nigeria. More than two hundred military coups d'état have taken place in Muslim countries since World War II.

24. Malaysian Muslim Students' Association leaflet, Washington DC, March 1984.
25. *Khums*, the payment of one-fifth of all income to the religious authorities, is specific to Shi'ite Islam. Sunni Muslims use the *zakat* system, which amounts to a fixed wealth tax.
26. Throwing stones at a person is the supreme insult in Islamic custom. It is Satan who must suffer the throwing of stones, and bears the title of Rajeem or 'He Who Has Been Subjected to the Throwing of Stones'. The punishment is reserved for adulteresses under *shari'ah* (Islamic law), but is rarely used in practice.
27. The doings of the Prophet are known under the title of *Sirrat al-Nabi* or *The Messenger's Vademecum* and enjoy almost as much authority as Qur'anic rules.
28. The Arabic term for the identification of infidelity is *takfir*, which is used as a codename for numerous secret societies of Muslim militants in the Middle East.
29. A Pakistani Sunni mullah (d. 1971), whose work on the principles of an Islamic state has gained wide popularity in fundamentalist circles. Mawdoodi's ideas have also been used by General Muhammad Zia ul-Haq to justify his military coup d'état in 1977 against the elected government of Zulfiqar Ali Bhutto. General Zia describes himself as a 'soldier of Islam' and says he is dedicated to the creation of an Islamic state based on Mawdoodi's ideas. Supporters of Mawdoodi, however, consider Zia a usurper and deny that any part of their master's project has been implemented by the military-dominated government in Islamabad.
30. Takfir wal-Hegira leaflet, n.d. Circulating in Cairo in October 1981, but probably written several months before that. On *hegira*, see Appendix F.
31. Ayatollah Hussein-Ali Montazeri, *Towzih al-Masayel* (*Explanation of Problems*), Tehran, 1985, p. 11.
32. Ibid, p. 77.
33. Ibid, p. 78.
34. Ayatollah Ehsan-Bakhsh, speech broadcast by Tehran Radio, 30 June 1983.
35. At a press conference in Tehran, 20 July 1983.
36. The restitution of *dhimma* figures in almost all lists of demands put forward by fundamentalist groups in Egypt. It was

mentioned as 'a sacred necessity' in an open letter sent by fundamentalist *ulema* (clergy) to President Muhammad Honsi-Mubarak in May 1984.

37. Shaikh Muhammad-Ali al-Jouzou, Lebanese Sunni leader, quoted in *Sobh Azadehgan*, Tehran, 4 February 1983.
38. Quoted in *L'Orient le jour*, Beirut, 19 October 1983.
39. Abdul-Karim Biazar-Shirazi, *Ebadat va Khodsazi* (*Prayer and Self-improvement*), Mashhad, 1986, pp. 118 and 119. Henceforth *Ebadat*.
40. Ibid, p. 97.
41. Very strict rules surround the wearing of the Islamic *hejab* or cover; they apply to both men and women, although they are more elaborate and more rigorously enforced for women. Men should not shave their beards – although they may trim them and dye them with henna – for the beard is considered to be 'a partial veil' bestowed on the human male by Allah. Men must also avoid wearing short-sleeved shirts and shun 'sensational colours such as green, red and blue'. Women should cover themselves from head to toe, leaving only their faces and hands exposed. They must restrict themselves to 'decent colours' – white, black, grey, navy blue and dark brown. Women should not wear make-up or 'remove hair from their eyebrows'. They are allowed to use perfume only when asked by their husbands to 'become pleasant'. The rules of *hejab* are spelt out in detail in a booklet prepared by the Islamic Majlis and published in Tehran in 1985. All the above quotations are taken from the booklet.
42. After the Islamic Revolution, it was claimed that Sharif-Vaqefi had in fact been a pious Muslim and had been assassinated by Marxists!
43. Quoted in M. Dehnavi, *Imam Khomeini*, Tehran, 1980, p. 371.
44. See Introduction, note 24.
45. *Nahayat e Amr* (*The Finite of the Infinite*), Tehran, 1986, p. 91. Henceforth *Nahayat*.
46. The phrase is that of Muhammad Navab-Safavi, founder of the Fedayeen of Islam. Quoted in *Ebadat*, p. 175.
47. Muhammad-Taqi Partovi, *Ayandeh Nehzat Islami* (The Future of the Islamic Movement), Qom, 1986, p. 63. Henceforth *Ayandeh*.
48. Ibid., p. 116.
49. In Arabic: *Oqtul al-mudhi, qabl an al-udhi.*
50. *Collected Letters, Speeches, Messages and Edicts*, Tehran, 1983, p. 51.

51. *Ayandeh*, p. 137. See also Appendix G.
52. *Jame'eh va Hokumat Islami* (*Islamic Society and Government*), Tehran, 1985 (second edition), p. 59. The book originally came out in 1946 and was widely distributed in hand-written form. Navab-Safavi, a key figure in the fundamentalist movement, will be introduced in later chapters.
53. See note 50 above.
54. The People of the Shawl are the Prophet himself, his daughter Fatimah, her husband Ali and their two sons Hassan and Hussein. The expression refers to a tradition according to which the Prophet covered those with his own shawl who were nearest and dearest to him.
55. In Arabic: *Allah al-Muntaqim!* The choice of this particular title for Allah by Sadat's assassin has been lavishly praised by fundamentalist writers in Beirut, Tehran, Kuala Lumpur and many other major centres of Islam.
56. 'Shaikh' is an Arabic title which can be given to any man of authority.

Chapter 2

1. *Ayandeh dar Qalamrow Islam* (*The Future of Islam*), Tehran, 1979, p. 33. Qutb was the Supreme Guide of the Muslim Brotherhood in Egypt until his execution on President Nasser's orders in 1966.
2. He must be *aqil* (sane), *baligh* (adult), *jayez at-tassarruf* (authorized to intervene) and *mukhtar* (autonomous).
3. The first four Caliphs are known as Khulfa er-Rashedeen, or 'properly guided Caliphs', because they had known the Prophet personally and had presumably benefited from his teachings directly.
4. Firuz was a freed slave of Persian origin. According to some historians he assassinated Omar as an enemy of Persia, for it was under Omar that the Arabs invaded the Persian Empire. To Shi'ites Firuz is a saint and his tomb, near Kashan in central Iran, is a place of pilgrimage. Shi'ites celebrate the anniversary of Omar's murder with great pomp and joy.
5. Relatives of Othman claimed that Ali had inspired the plot to kill the Caliph. It was in the name of avenging Othman that Muawwyyah raised the banner of revolt against Ali.
6. Abdul-Rahman was one of three conspirators who had sworn to murder Ali and his two rivals Muawwyyah and Amr Ibn-As on

the same day. But only Abdul-Rahman managed to remain true to his oath.

7. The word 'Shi'ite' means 'partisan' in Arabic, and applies to partisans of Ali, the son-in-law of the Prophet. According to Shi'ites Ali, and not Abu-Bakr, should have succeeded the Prophet as Caliph. But contrary to the common description of Shi'ites as supporters of Ali in what might appear to the uninitiated as no more than a political struggle for power, the differences between the Shi'ites and the Sunnis, who form some 90 per cent of all Muslims, go much deeper than that. The Shi'ites have added two principles of their own to the three principles of Islam. These are *Adl*, the belief that divine justice must be meted out in this world, and *Imamah*, which means the government of the *Ummah* (community of the faithful) by an Imam, who must be *ma'asum* or chaste in the sense of being totally incapable of committing any sin. The idea of *'ismah* or chastity lies at the heart of the doctrinal schism between Sunni and Shi'ite Islam. (The three basic principles of Islam, shared by both Sunnis and Shi'ites, are: the one-ness of God; the recognition of the function of God's messenger, the last of whom is Muhammad; and the Day of Reckoning.)

   Militant fundamentalism, however, wastes little or no time on such doctrinal questions. In practice, Sunni fundamentalists come extremely close to Shi'ites in obeying their guides as religious or revolutionary leaders and accepting the principle of *Adl* as the basis for their political action. Sunni fundamentalists also share the essentially Shi'ite idea that all existing governments in all Muslim countries are illegitimate because they are not founded on the *shari'ah*, the religious law, and do not carry out the rules of the Faith to the letter.
8. Qur'anic school.
9. Muwaffiq had two other pupils who were to distinguish themselves. One was Omar Khayyam, the great Persian mathematician and inventor of algebra, who is better known in the West for the poems known as the *Rubaiyat*. The other was Nizam al-Mulk, who was to become Grand Vizir of the Seljuk sultans. According to one legend the three became close friends; the truth, however, is that Hassan Sabbah ordered the assassination of Nizam al-Mulk, and referred to the Grand Vizir as 'the peasant'.
10. Then a caravan halt between Rey, south of present-day Tehran, and the rich province of Azerbaijan.
11. The fact that Hassan Sabbah regarded the Seljuk Turks as aliens,

despite their conversion to Islam, is cited by some historians as an argument for the widespread belief that Hassan was a Persian nationalist and a secret Zoroastrian. This theory even claims that the entire Shi'ite movement was started by Persian nationalists who wished to de-Islamicize Iran while keeping an appearance of Qur'anic belief. Many of Iran's prehistoric religious beliefs continue to live on not only in mainstream Shi'ism but in the theories and practices of other much smaller sects such as the Alawites (Nosairis) in Turkey, Syria and Lebanon, the Druzes in Syria, Lebanon and Israel, the Ali-Allahis in Iraq and Iran, and the Yazidis in Iran, Iraq and Syria. All these sects have secret rites to which only the initiated have access. At least some of them might have retained the pretence of an Islamic identity throughout history in order to avoid persecution and massacre. The present leader of the Yazidis, Emir Muawwyyah, has had the courage to admit openly that his people were, and have been ever since the advent of Islam, Zoroastrians 'in secret'. In 1982 he published in Paris a book entitled *To Us Spoke Zarathustra*, in which he wrote that fear of persecution and massacre had forced the Yazidis as well as the Alawites, the Druzes and numerous other sects in the Middle East to claim a Muslim identity. (For a further discussion of the Sunni–Shi'ite differences and the influence of Zoroastrianism on Shi'ism see my *The Spirit of Allah: Khomeini and the Islamic Revolution*, London, 1985 and Washington DC, 1986.)

12. A higher form of *maktab* where theology, philosophy and, in the period in question, a number of sciences were taught. Later, the *madrassah* consisted of a theological seminary only.
13. According to the Ismailites, the function of Imam was transferred to Muhammad, the son of Ismail and the grandson of Imam Jaafar Sadiq, the sixth Imam of duodecimal Shi'ism. Muhammad is referred to as Saheb az-Zaman or Lord of the Time. Over the past thousand years this quarrel about who should have succeeded the sixth Imam has led to the development of two very different versions of Shi'ism – one could almost say that duodecimal Shi'ism and Ismailism are two different, though not necessarily mutually exclusive, religions.
14. The term *fedayeen* is used by at least three different communist guerrilla organizations in Iran: one pro-Soviet, one Maoist and one allied to the pro-Iraqi People's Mujahedeen (Combatants) organization. The deep-rooted religious origin of the word has not prevented Marxist-Leninists from using it.
15. The most complete, though not necessarily unbiased, accounts

of Hassan Sabbah's life and the Alamut experience are given by three Muslim historians: Ata Malak Joweini, Ibn Athir and Ibn al-Hakim.

16. In his *Siasat-Nameh* (*Study of Politics*) Nizam al-Mulk offers a dispassionate account of the political realities of his time. This *magnum opus* is often compared to Machiavelli's *The Prince* as a 'zoological' study of the world of politics in societies afflicted by absolutism.
17. Houris are beauties charged with the task of responding to the carnal needs of the faithful in Paradise. The Qur'an does not specify their sex.
18. On 16 October 1092 the Grand Vizir met his death in the small town of Sahneh, near Nahavand in western Iran. He was returning from the audience hall at the head of his wives when a man disguised as a Sufi approached him and attacked him with a knife. The assassin shouted: 'The death of this Satan is the beginning of happiness!'
19. The phrase is Ibn Athir's.
20. Quoted in Philippe Aziz, *Les Sectes secrètes de l'Islam*, Paris, 1983. De Sacy's account goes on:

> A fact that supports this theory [of the use of hashish and other narcotic substances by the *fedayeen*] is that one of the most celebrated Arab writers attributes the introduction of a potion prepared from Indian plants to the Ismailites of Persia. . . . It is not impossible that the hashish or parts of that plant may have been used, together with other substances unknown to us, for the purpose of creating a state of frenzy and violent furore. It is known that opium, whose hallucinogenic effects are similar to those of the preparations made with hashish, is used by Amok [Malaysian tribesmen] in order to reach a state of wild excitement in which, no longer being masters of their own selves, they massacre whoever happens to be in their path, while they themselves advance blindly amid lances and swords. According to travellers, the preparation in question is made of a mixture of lemon juice and opium left to intermingle for a number of days.

21. A spirit distilled from the wine.
22. For example Farid Bonakdar in *Islam va Marxism* (*Islam and Marxism*), Tehran, 1979.
23. A theme used by Baghdad Radio since 1980.

24. The poetry and prose of Nasser Khosrow Qobadiani are an example: nowhere in his work is there any suggestion that the Ismailites in general or the Alamut community in particular used narcotics.
25. Literally: the Outsiders. The name was applied to Muslim wa rriors who decided to remain outside the power struggle between Ali Ibn Abi-Talib, the fourth Caliph, and Muawwyyah Ibn Abu-Sufyan, the ambitious governor of Syria. The Kharejites were forced out of Mesopotamia and sought sanctuary on the west shore of the Persian Gulf, where they set up ephemeral principalities.

Chapter 3

1. The six were Hafez Abdul-Hamid, Ahmad al-Hasari, Fu'ad Ibrahim, Abdul-Rahman Hassab-Allah, Ismail Izz and Zaki al-Maghrebi.
2. The Islamic community, believers throughout the world.
3. Hassan al-Banna, *Muzakirat ad-Daawah wa al-Da'iyah* (*Memoirs of the Call and of Preaching*), Cairo and Beirut, n.d., probably 1958, pp. 73 and 74.
4. The words of the oath were: 'We swear to Allah to be the soldiers of the message of Islam – a message that contains the life of the fatherland and the force of the Muslim *Ummah*.'
5. In Arabic: Ikhwan al-Moslemeen. The organization is often referred to simply as Ikhwan or 'The Brethren'.
6. *Zendegi Morshed* (*Life of the Guide*), Qom, n.d., probably 1960, pp. 30 and 31.
7. *Wafd* means 'delegation' in Arabic. The Wafd party, banned under President Nasser in the early 1950s, was allowed to resume a legal life under Sadat and is now represented in the Egyptian Parliament. Its leader, Fuad Seraggeddin, concluded a coalition pact with the then Supreme Guide of the Muslim Brotherhood, Shaikh Omar al-Talmassani, in the 1984 general election.
8. *Zendegi Morshed*, p. 22.
9. Often referred to as Afghani, he was born in Assadabad, west of Tehran, probably in 1828 and died in 1898. He presented himself as a Sunni from Afghanistan, although he was in fact a duodecimal Shi'ite, so that he would find a larger audience in the Islamic world. Admitted into a masonic lodge, he was an early founder of freemasonry in the Muslim East. A mullah wearing the black turban which denoted his claim of descent from the

Prophet, Sayyed Jamaleddin was a persuasive speaker but a superficial thinker. Today, he is revered in Ayatollah Khomeini's Islamic Republic as one of the saints of fundamentalism.

10. Mirza Reza Kermani is now venerated as a 'true soldier of Islam' by militant fundamentalists in Iran and elsewhere. Nassereddin Shah was assassinated in 1898, the same year that Sayyed Jamaleddin died in exile.
11. The expression is Shaikh Hassan's own.
12. Raza popularized the term *salafiyah*, which means fundamentalism.
13. *Muzakirat ad-Daawah wa al-Da'iyah*, p. 119.
14. Abdul-Wahhab founded the Wahhabi movement, which preaches a return to the strict application of Qur'anic rules together with an ascetic way of life.
15. Or: 'Prepare!' It refers, of course, to being ready and prepared for Holy War.
16. Shaikh Hassan was even interrogated on the subject by the Minister of Education, and was found 'not guilty of any impropriety'. But his response to critics within the organization was original: 'The money I received from the company is Egyptian money in any case. The company has no right to be here, and therefore has no money of its own! Our aim is to get everything back from the company. All I have done is to take a modest step in that direction.'
17. These and other anecdotes concerning the Brotherhood come from an unpublished monograph by Abdullah Ghomi, *Fundamentalism in Egypt*, 1986.
18. Ibid.
19. The Brothers' propaganda was partly responsible for securing popular support for the Axis in most Muslim countries, as well as among Indian Muslims, many of whom refused to join the British army to fight Hitler.
20. The Egyptian royal family was of Albanian origin and made a point of advertising its foreignness. Many high-ranking government officials also boasted about their Albanian or Turkish ancestry.
21. Among them were Gamal Abdul-Nasser and Muhammad Anwar Sadat.
22. According to Ghomi (see note 17 above), this often meant a mere declaration by the Supreme Guide that so-and-so had sinned against Islam and had to be 'removed'.
23. In Arabic: *Mufsid fel-Ardh*. The term is used to describe almost anyone whose living presence in this world might in any way cause harm to Islam.

24. The phrase is that of Salih al-Ashmawi, who founded the periodical *ad-Da'awah* (*The Call*).
25. Shaikh Hassan's phrase, quoted by Ghomi (see note 17 above).
26. According to Grand Ayatollah Mahmoud Qomi, who knew Shaikh Hassan personally, the Supreme Guide was a strong supporter of ending the theological disputes between Shi'ites and Sunnis. Shaikh Hassan, Qomi and Shaikh Shaltut, then Dean of the Al-Azhar theological school in Cairo, became founding members of Dar al-Taqreeb beyn al-Mazahib al-Islamiyal (Foundation for the Convergence of Islamic Ways), which had its headquarters in Cairo. The driving force behind the movement was Qomi, who wrote its first constitution in 1947.
27. Hodeibi went around making speeches against clandestine activity. One of his favourite phrases was 'There is nothing secret in Islam, as the Qur'an is so transparent.'
28. It was Ayatollah Khomeini who first discovered that the regular army, a Western-style institution, would not willingly side with an Islamic revolutionary movement. In Turkey, Iraq, Syria, Algeria, Morocco and some other Muslim countries the army is the chief adversary of fundamentalist movements.
29. The Pakistani military ruler President Zia ul-Haq made considerable use of fundamentalist groups in the campaign against his political rivals between 1978 and 1986. But he too was not prepared to share power with the fundamentalists.
30. The word is difficult to translate. It means the state of being an Arab, or 'Arabness', and has become a key concept in contemporary Arab political life. The fundamentalists consider *uruba* another name for *jahiliyah*, or the period of ignorance before Islam arrived in Arabia.
31. The pamphlet was eventually withdrawn in 1956 when Nasser decided that he was a nationalist after all. What is interesting is that the same ghost writer wrote both versions.
32. According to the report, no fewer than 33 per cent of air force officers, for example, were members of the Muslim Brotherhood's secret military branch. The movement enjoyed a similar position within the ground forces as well as in the police.
33. Nasser was at this time already recognized as the virtual ruler of Egypt.
34. Hassan al-Tuhami, a close adviser of Nasser and secret police chief for a number of years, indirectly confirms this theory in his memoirs, quoted by Olivier Carre and Gérard Michaud in *Les Frères Musulmans*, Paris, 1983. The book also quotes Miles

Copeland, a CIA operative specializing in Muslim countries, as confirming rumours that the CIA, having 'encouraged' Nasser's coup d'état, later advised him to arrange 'something spectacular' in order to build up his personal popularity.

35. In private conversation in Cairo in 1972. Sadat seemed to have forgotten his own role in persecuting the Brothers under Nasser.
36. This phrase, apparently borrowed from Leon Trotsky, was a favourite of Nasser's and has become, thanks to his speeches, part of the political vocabulary of the Muslim Middle East.
37. Mukhabarat means 'communications' in Arabic. The organization, and its more sinister wing, Mabahith, gradually extended their influence throughout the state apparatus.
38. The term has become a weapon in the fundamentalists' arsenal of abuse against their enemies. Khomeini uses it to describe the Mujahedeen Khalq guerrillas, who profess a mixture of Islam and Marxism.
39. I am indebted to A. Ghomi for his account of Sayyed Qutb's ideas.
40. In a conversation in Cairo in 1984, Shaikh Omar said he saw no reason why Islam could not adopt the parliamentary system of democracy. 'The only step Islam cannot accept is the dictatorship of theologians,' he said with reference to Khomeini's Islamic Republic.

Chapter 4

1. Founder of the Fedayeen of Islam. Quoted in *Navab va Yaranash* (*Nawab and His Companions*), Tehran, 1981. (See bibliography.)
2. In Arabic: Mowlay Motaqqian. This is one of Ali's numerous titles.
3. The life of the djin (spirits or ghosts) has always intrigued Shi'ite mullahs. Ayatollah Ali-Akbar Meshkini, President of the Assembly of Experts in the Islamic Republic, boasts of his 'thirty years of research' into the subject.
4. In 1968 graveyards covered a total area of more than 20 square kilometres, leaving virtually no land for the development of new suburbs. The Ba'athist government later ordered the destruction of many graveyards: some were turned into public parks, while the land 'recovered' from others was used for new housing projects. The import of corpses was formally banned in 1971.
5. *Navab va Yaranash*, p. 13.
6. The founder of the Fedayeen of Islam had not managed to

complete his theological studies, and preferred to describe himself as a man of action.

7. Quoted by Firuz Akbari in *Tariq Shohada* (*The Way of the Martyrs*), Tehran, 1979. Henceforth *Tariq*.
8. *Donyay Fedayeen Islam* (*The World of the Fedayeen of Islam*), Tehran, 1980, p. 69.
9. Navab va Yaranash, p. 113.
10. Muhammad Navab-Safavi, *Jame'eh va Hokumat Islami* (*Islamic Society and Government*), Qom, 1980, p. 71.
11. Ibid. p. 91.
12. For Khomeini's encounter and relations with Navab-Safavi, see my *The Spirit of Allah: Khomeini and the Islamic Revolution*, London, 1985 and Washington DC, 1986.
13. Gholam-Hossein Omrani, *Tarikhcheh Mobarezat Ruhaniyat dar Iran* (*Brief History of the Struggle of the Clergy in Iran*), Tehran, 1980.
14. A call by mullahs in 1942 for the closure of Tehran University and a return to Qur'anic schools provoked only derision even among the illiterate masses. Attempts by the mullahs at persuading the Allies to ban Muslims from frequenting cinemas were also ridiculed.
15. See Kasravi's *Shiagari* (*Shi'ism*), Tehran, 1943 and 1946, and West Germany, 1984.
16. Ibid.
17. Modern Persian contains a large number of Arabic words, but Kasravi and others have shown that it is possible to use an alternative vocabulary to create a 'purified' form of the language. Kasravi and his disciples also advocated discarding the Arabic alphabet in favour of Latin script, a suggestion seen as a deliberate step away from Islam.
18. Ruhollah Khomeini, *Kashf al-Asrar* (*Key to the Secrets*), Tehran, 1980, p. 232.
19. In Arabic: *Jond Allah*. The name was, however, not chosen for the group, but was to be used by an offshoot of the movement in the late 1970s.
20. See Ali Davani, *Nehzat Ruhaniyat dar Iran* (*The Clerical Movement in Iran*), vol. IV, Tehran, 1980–83, pp. 33 and 34.
21. *Tariq*, p. 94.
22. Shaikh Sadeq Khalkhali, interview in *Payam Shaheed* (*Message of the Martyr*), vol. XXIV, Qom, 1980.
23. Hazhir had been transferred to the Ministry of Justice at the time of his murder, but his 'sentence' had been passed during his premiership.

24. The truth had to wait until after the victory of Ayatollah Khomeini's Islamic Revolution, when Fakhr-Ara'i was introduced as a 'soldier of Islam' and a 'martyr of the Qur'an'.
25. Muhammad Navab-Safavi. See note 10 above, p. 65.
26. From personal notes by Haj Nasser Tahami, who was an active member of the Fedayeen though never involved in the terrorist part of its operations.
27. Ibid.
28. The oil refinery city near the Persian Gulf. Abadan, known as the 'Wimbledon of the Gulf', was in 1950 certainly as quiet and as Victorian as that London suburb.
29. *Haram* (what is not permitted) and *halal* (what is permitted) are spelled out in numerous theological treatises. The system divides between the two virtually the whole of the universe and every conceivable human activity, with a few borderline cases that are either *mustahab* (desirable) or *makruh* (undesirable).
30. *Parcham Islam* (*The Banner of Islam*), vol. XXIII, Qom, 1950.
31. According to Tahami's account. See note 26 above.
32. In Arabic: *tabakhtor*.
33. Muhammad Navab-Safavi. See note 10 above, p. 17.
34. Founded by Ayatollah Shaikh Mahmoud Halabi, it devoted its energies to the identification of members of the Baha'i faith so that they could be 'invited back to Islam'. The Hojatieh Society was disbanded on Khomeini's orders in 1984, but in 1985 reconstituted itself as a secret organization.

Chapter 5

1. Made on the fourth anniversary of the disappearance of Imam Mussa Sadr, Beirut, September 1982.
2. Related by Grand Ayatollah Mar'ashi-Najafi in a conversation in Qom, September 1978.
3. The other two are Iraq and Bahrain. North Yemen also has a Shi'ite majority. But the Yemeni Shi'ites belong to the Zaidi sect and differ on a number of key doctrinal points from the duodecimal Shi'ites in Iran, Iraq and Lebanon.
4. e.g. former President Camille Chamoun, in an interview in Tehran in 1969. Chamoun had been President when the Lebanese civil war of 1958 took place.
5. Israel and Saudi Arabia based their respective and widely different theories of state on religion. All the others advocated nationalism, whether Arab, Iranian or Turkish.
6. The families in question were Khalil, As'ad, Zayn, Hamadah,

Haydar and Osseiran. Despite the sharp decline in their power and influence, they still play a prominent role in Lebanese politics.

7. Especially the province of Khuzestan, which Nasser liked to refer to as Arabistan.
8. The Druzes form the third largest religious community in Lebanon, after Muslims and Christians. Their religion, sometimes considered to be a branch of Islam, is in fact an independent faith that includes elements of Hinduism.
9. A further 5 million Lebanese pounds was distributed by the Iranian Embassy among the owners of several Beirut newspapers, according to SAVAK documents published after the Islamic Revolution in 1979.
10. Even as late as 1978 the Shah spoke of his 'affection' for Sadr in a private conversation at the Niavaran Palace in Tehran. This came in reply to a question about His Majesty's decision to launch a campaign aimed at saving Sadr, who was at the time supposed to be a prisoner in Libya. The Shah assigned to one of his ambassadors the mission of 'saving Sadr who enjoys our affection'.
11. In *Asrar Faaliyat hay zed-Iran dar Kharej az Keshvar* (*Secrets of Anti-Iranian Activities Abroad*), Ministry of Information booklet, Tehran, 1975.
12. Iranian law does not recognize dual nationality. Sadr had to accept Lebanese nationality in order to become President of the High Council of Shi'ites.
13. Almost all Lebanese Shi'ites, and Sadr himself, considered Grand Ayatollah Muhsen Hakim-Tabataba'i as a 'source of imitation' until the latter's death in 1968, when the majority shifted their allegiance to Grand Ayatollah Abol-Qassem Mussavi Kho'i.
14. See note 11 above, pp. 48 and 49.
15. Nakhshab spent some time in the United States before his death in 1965.
16. *Yadnameh Shadid Chamran* (*In Memoriam: Chamran the Martyr*), third edition, Tehran, 1984, p. 89.
17. At that time there were more than 130,000 Iranian students in the United States.
18. One of them, Muhammad Safari-Lenegerudi, related his experience during his trial at a military tribunal in Tehran in 1976: 'My deep Islamic convictions soon became known at London University and it was at the invitation of a Pakistani [student] that I became a member of the Islamic Association.

There I came to know a man by the name of Baqerian who, after many sessions, asked me whether I would like to go to a Palestinian camp to train as a guerrilla. . . .' After a brief period of instruction in Baghdad Safari-Lenegerudi ended up in a PLO camp in Lebanon. His training consisted of 'shooting, the use of a machine gun, the preparation of explosives, the use of hand grenades, the art of clandestinity and surprise attacks. . . .' Safari-Lenegerudi was sentenced to death and executed. Quoted in *Manteq Zur* (*The Logic of Force*), Tehran, 1977, and in *Asrar* (see note 11 above), pp. 23 and 24.

19. Al-Hassan was a member of the PLO High Command. He made the claim in an interview with Tehran Radio on 20 February 1979. The claim is, no doubt, an exaggeration. Government estimates under the Shah put the number of Iranian 'guerrillas' trained by the PLO at 'around three hundred'.
20. The camp had been constructed by the United Nations Work and Relief Authority in 1948 to house refugees from Palestine.
21. According to Chamran, in an interview published by *Pasdar Islam*, Tehran, February 1980.
22. This is how Gaddafi sees 'the solution' for Lebanon's Christian minority:

> It is clear what they should do. They, or their descendants, must correct the historical error committed by their ancestors in refusing to convert to Islam. This is the only way to end confessional conflicts! In this way the Lebanese Christians will be truly reintegrated into the Arab nation. To finish with Lebanon's Christians, let me point out that religion is inseparable from nationality: they are two facets of the same phenomenon. Since the religion of the Arab nation is Islam, all Arabs should either be Muslims or become Muslims in the future.

Gaddafi: *Je suis un opposant à l'échelon mondial*, Lausanne, 1984, p. 31.

23 According to Asrar, p. 33. See note 11 above.

24. Assad also distrusted Sadr and maintained secret contacts with the traditionally influential Shi'ite families, who were dismayed by the revolutionary vocabulary of the Imam and his American-trained 'Young Turks'.
25. Philippe Aziz, *Les Sectes secrètes de l'Islam*, Paris, 1983, p. 118.
26. He had informed the three grand ayatollahs of Qom to that effect early in August 1978.
27. The tent was bombed during the American raid on Tripoli on 15

April 1986. Gaddafi was not in it at the time.

28. This account of the fateful meeting, based on information provided by a former high-ranking official in Libyan Intelligence, was given by Abdul-Aziz Dahmani in *Jeune Afrique*, 3 December 1980.
29. Ibid.
30. Berri, in an interview with *as-Siyassah*, Kuwait, quoted by *Ettelaat*, Tehran, 22 September 1984.

Chapter 6

1. In *Nehzat Islami dar Sadsal Akhir* (*Islamic Movements in the Last One Hundred Years*), Tehran, 1979, p. 83.
2. In Arabic: *Hojat al-Islam*. The title is the equivalent of a BA issued by a theological college.
3. In *Nehzat Ruhaniyat dar Iran* (*The Clerical Movement in Iran*), vol. IX, Tehran, 1980–83, p. 34.
4. *Rah e Ma* (*Our Path*), Party of Allah 'theoretical booklet', Tehran, 1982, p. 11.
5. In an interview in December 1982, quoted by Sobh Azadehgan.
6. Or *Jame'eh Towhidi*, which means literally the Unitarian Movement. The term was invented by the Iraqi Shi'ite leader Ayatollah Muhammad Baqer Sadr.
7. *Rah e Ma*, p. 22. See note 4 above.
8. Ibid., p. 23.
9. *Hezb-Allah va Hezb-Shaytan* (*The Party of Allah and the Party of Satan*), Tehran, 1984, p. 76.
10. Two thousand rials, or around £3 sterling.
11. Some of the groups that merged into the Party of Allah were Hadafiha (Isfahan), Fedayeen of Islam (led by Sadeq Khalkhali), Abazar, Mujahedeen of Islam (led by Behzad Nabavi and Muhammad Gharazi), Mahdavioun, Hayat Motalefeh Islami (Coalescing Islamic Missions), Fajr Enqelab (Dawn of the Revolution), Hezb Mellall Islami (Party of Islamic Nations), al-Ghad (Rendezvous), Jebhheh Towhidi Saf (The Unitary Front of the Line) and Hezb Azadi Islami (Islamic Freedom Party).
12. In Persian: '*Hezb faqat Hezb-Allah, Rahbar faqat Ruhollah!*'
13. In 1986 there were 253 mosques and 119 *takiyehs* in Tehran. The organization of the regular Friday prayer session at Tehran University is the responsibility of a special branch of the Party of Allah, reported to have an annual budget of around £10 million sterling.
14. These attacks are discussed in more detail in Chapter 5.

15. Supporters of this idea are known as the Eternal Martyr School. Their opponents, who believe that Hussein knew he would die and chose martyrdom on purpose, belong to the Conscious Martyr School.
16. *Gharb Gharib* (*The Exotic West*), Tehran, 1980, p. 87. Henceforth *Gharb*.
17. The wording of the oath was provided by Hissam, a former member of the Party of Allah, who left the movement after growing disillusioned with it. Later he escaped from Iran and was granted political asylum in Sweden. He talked to the author on condition that no details were published concerning his identity, for fear of assassination.
18. The decision to stop offering cash and other incentives to the families of the 'martyrs' was announced in an original way. Ayatollah Ali-Akbar Meshkini, the regime's number three after Khomeini and Ayatollah Hussein-Ali Montazeri, appeared on TV to inform the people of a dream he had had the night before. In it the martyred Imam Hussein had arrived at Meshkini's bedside on a white horse and woken the ayatollah, saying, 'One does not become a martyr for Allah in order to secure material benefits. So why does your government offer cash, washing machines and refrigerators to the families of those who have lost a dear one in the Holy War? I want this practice stopped instantly!'
19. Quarrels over strategy between regular army commanders and the Party of Allah military experts after the operations at the Fao peninsula in Iraq created a sense of disenchantment with the war. Also the Islamic regime as a whole was experiencing a crisis of confidence because of its economic difficulties and increasingly open factional feuds.
20. The Saudis tried to cope with the problem by reducing their budget by some 30 per cent and imposing a sharp reduction on the number of foreigners working in the kingdom.
21. This is an important religious duty of every practising Muslim.
22. The *komiteh* (from the French *comités*) were created to protect the Islamic Revolution in its first days, but managed to develop into a permanent feature of Islamic rule. They are all under the political control of the Party of Allah.
23. *Jomhuri Islami*, 9 January 1986.
24. Broadcast by Tehran Radio, 11 January 1986.
25. The black market itself is run by the Party of Allah as a means of 'milking the rich'. The government monopoly on imported goods enables the Islamic regime to hand over the distribution of

various commodities, notably foodstuffs, to branches of the Party of Allah, so that prices several times higher than those officially fixed can be charged to 'undeservedly rich' customers. Many middle-class families spend more than half their income buying food ration cards from families connected with the Party of Allah.

26. Quoted in the monthly *Baseej*, vol. XIII, Tehran, 1986. It is not clear what this 'special combat training' means, but various speeches by the commanders of the Revolutionary Guard, and *Baseej*, mention 'operations behind enemy lines'.
27. The list was later reduced to nineteen names. General Oveissi, who was on the list, was assassinated in Paris in June 1984. An attempt at killing Admiral Ahmad Madani, Khomeini's Defence Minister in the early days of the Islamic Republic, failed in Paris in March 1986.
28. Forqan wants an Islamic regime without mullahs and is now active in exile in Paris. It is inspired by the writings of Ali Shariati, a French-educated sociologist who died in Plymouth, England, in 1977.
29. Members of the imperial family who figured on Khalkhali's death list lived under heavy guard in Egypt and Morocco.
30. The attempt on Bakhtiar's life, in July 1980, failed. In the attack the hit squad killed a French policeman and one of Bakhtiar's French neighbours, and all the members of the squad were arrested and imprisoned. Their release has been one of the main conditions set by Khomeini for ordering an end to all Islamic terrorist activities against France.
31. At the time of his murder Tabataba'i was a representative of Bakhtiar's movement in the United States.
32. According to opposition sources in exile; but Davoud's presence in Iran was also signalled by the official Islamic media. In early January 1986 Davoud headed a three-man delegation of black Muslims from the United States at a meeting with Hojat al-Islam Khameneh'i, President of the Islamic Republic, at which Khameneh'i announced the formation of a special organization dedicated to the creation of an Islamic republic by black Muslims in the United States.
33. In a speech broadcast by Tehran Radio, 12 September 1980.
34. His official title was the Iranian's Representative in the High Command of the Revolutionary Guard.
35. He had been one of the few revolutionary mullahs who did not seek political office after the Shah was overthrown.
36. According to Khomeini, who spoke on the occasion of Mahalati's death in an air crash near the Iraq border in 1985.

Chapter 7

1. Muhammad Darwish is one of the most famous contemporary Palestinian poets. He lives in Paris.
2. Hissam (a pseudonym), one of the first students at the camp, recalled in an interview in February 1986 in Malmö, Sweden, that there were six Iraqis, three Tunisians, two Moroccans, one Saudi, one Bahraini and one Jordanian at Manzarieh in 1982.
3. Hissam, in the interview cited in note 2 above.
4. Ibid.
5. Kolhaduz, together with a dozen other military commanders, was killed in a mysterious air crash in 1983.
6. At the time Rifa'at al-Assad commanded Syria's special commando units.
7. Ba'athist Iraq was at odds with Iran between 1968 and 1975. During that period an estimated three hundred Iranians working with opposition parties were trained by the Iraqis in sabotage and guerrilla work.
8. He had previously helped to create the Revolutionary Guard, and later became Minister of Islamic Orientation.
9. This was perhaps due to the influence of Ayatollah Montazeri, a native of the province of Isfahan. He and his son, who was to die in an explosion later in 1982, used their positions in the regime to promote their own candidates. The idea at the time was that Manzarieh would create the elite of an international Islamic brigade.
10. According to Hissam. See note 2 above.
11. Ibid.
12. Ibid. From personal notes.
13. A biography of the Prophet Muhammad. Before the Islamic Revolution the Persian translation, prepared on the orders of Empress Farah, was denounced by the exiled Khomeini in a statement from Najaf as 'a Zionist plot to tarnish the image of our blessed Prophet'. After the revolution, however, hundreds of thousands of copies were printed and distributed throughout the country on Khomeini's orders.
14. Zaydan was a Christian Egyptian writer. His book was translated by Muhammad-Ali Shirazi in 1952, but became a best-seller only after the Islamic Revolution.
15. This refers to documents seized during the hostage crisis at the United States Embassy in Tehran by a group calling itself Students Following the Imam's Line. The group dubbed the Embassy 'a nest of spies'.

16. Translated by one of the Shah's generals, Mahmoud Kay.
17. Under the rules of the Islamic Republic executions must be performed by individuals and not by a group.
18. Hissam. See note 2 above.
19. He also supervised Iran's interests in Lebanon.
20. Hissam. See note 2 above.
21. An armband made of leather, on which is inscribed a *sura* from the Qur'an protecting the faithful from the evil eye. It must be worn under one's clothes and carefully concealed from public gaze.
22. Hissam. See note 2 above.
23. Pieces of the Imam's turbans are believed to be endowed with special qualities such as helping to cure certain illnesses and bringing luck to believers. Hojat al-Islam Ansari Kermani, one of Khomeini's secretaries, described the 'turban-sharing' ceremony in his book *Vizhegihayi az Zendegi Imam* (*Anecdotes from the Life of the Imam*), Tehran, 1983.
24. Quoted in *Le Figaro*, Paris, 11 January 1986.
25. The journalist Parviz Naqibi, who worked with the Islamic Radio and TV organization in Tehran for a while, came to know of two foreign women who had been trained at the camp: Rhonda Santiago, a US citizen, and Bernadette Durand, a citizen of the Irish Republic.
26. *Le Figaro*, 11 January 1986.
27. Visited by a Moroccan journalist, Muhammad Selhami. *Jeune Afrique*, 25 January 1984.
28. See Chapter 9 for information on pan-Islamic movements.
29. *Le Figaro*, 11 January 1986.
30. The camp may have been closed since then.
31. A squadron of MiG 17 fighters bought from the People's Republic of China are used for training purposes at the base.
32. *Le Figaro*, 11 January 1986.
33. Colonel Barmaki left Iran clandestinely via the Pakistan border 'some time around autumn 1985', convinced that the Islamic Revolution was being led astray. Granted political asylum in Denmark, he spoke in a private interview in Copenhagen in April 1986.
34. Ibid.
35. The booklet is entitled *Yom Eddin* (*The Day of the Faith*), and the priorities listed are:
    1. The elimination of Israel and the liberation of Jerusalem.
    2. The expulsion of the United States from the Muslim world.
    3. The ending of the Soviet occupation of Afghanistan.

4. The creation of Muslim self-determination movements in the USSR's Central Asian republics.

5. The creation of a Muslim state for Filipino Muslims.

6. Self-determination for Muslims in India.

7. The restoration of Muslim rule to Zanzibar.

8. One or more independent states for black Muslims in the United States.

9. The creation of an Islamic state in Eritrea.

10. The restoration of the Muslim character of Andalusia (Andolus) and islands(?).

11. The mobilization of Muslims in western Europe for securing rights.

12. The punishment of known and determined wrongdoers against Islam throughout the world.

36. Figures supplied by the High Council of Islamic Revolution in Iraq.
37. See, for example, *Libération*, Paris, 25 July 1985. The highly respected daily devoted four pages of that issue, including its front page, to 'secret documents' concerning the creation of an 'international Islamic Brigade'.
38. See, for example, Senator Jesse Helms (Republican, North Carolina), testimony to the United States Senate, Congressional Report, 7 February 1985.
39. See, for example, *Le Parisien*, Paris, 26 November 1985.
40. The university, which was supposed to bear the name of Jaafar Sadeq, the sixth Imam of Shi'ism, has not yet been set up owing to lack of funds and academic staff.
41. This estimate was supplied to me personally by Captain Zomorrodi, before the revolution one of Iran's leading experts in guerrilla warfare. He now lives and teaches in the United States.
42. Ibid.
43. Since then Montazeri has been spending more time in Tehran deputizing for Khomeini in an increasing number of fields. The Imam's serious illness in May 1986 was the reason for Montazeri's more direct involvement in the day-to-day affairs of the republic.
44. In a sermon broadcast by Tehran Radio, 11 June 1986.
45. In a speech broadcast by Tehran Radio, 10 February 1986.
46. In a speech broadcast by Tehran radio on 12 February 1986.
47. ASALA bases and offices were transferred to Lebanon in December 1984 after a rapprochement between the Islamic Republic and Turkey.

48. Renamed Ururumiah by the Ayatollah.
49. *Sobh Azadehgan*, Tehran, 27 December 1983.
50. The man who killed President Sadat in 1981.
51. An Egyptian policeman who opened fire on a group of Israeli tourists in the Sinai on 5 October 1985, killing two women and three children.
52. A young woman who drove a truck full of explosives into an Israeli position in southern Lebanon in March 1985.
53. A woman PLO guerrilla fighter, who specialized in the hijacking of civilian aircraft in the 1970s.
54. The man who assassinated Prime Minister Hassan-Ali Mansur in Tehran in 1965.
55. Islamic Ministry of Foreign Affairs annual report, section on Liberation Movements, Tehran, March 1984.

Chapter 8

1. He was a leader of the Lebanese branch of the Party of Allah until his murder in 1984.
2. The tradition is attributed to the sixth Imam, Jaafar Sadeq.
3. One of Khomeini's many titles.
4. In the weekly *Resalat Islam*, Qom, 28 February 1979.
5. See, for example, *Le Figaro*, 11 January 1986.
6. Ibid.
7. *Sunday Times*, London, 15 January 1984.
8. He changed his name to Khosrowshahi apparently to avoid being mistaken for an Armenian. He returned to Tehran in 1986 after the publication of documents showing that he had maintained links with the Shah's secret police, SAVAK, before the revolution. See Hussein Akhavan-Towhidi, *Dar Pas e Pardeh Tazvir* (*Behind the Mask of Hypocrisy*), Paris, 1986.
9. According to a former employee of the bank, interviewed in London in September 1985.
10. French anti-terrorist police sources, interviewed in Paris in August 1985 and January 1986.
11. Places of religious gathering. A *takiyeh* could be an ordinary house or apartment used for the purpose on special days in the lunar calendar.
12. In reality a committee of five mullahs supervises the fund: Hashemi-Rafsanjani (Speaker of the Islamic Majlis), Muhammad Khatami (Minister of Islamic Orientation), Mehdi Karrubi (President of the Martyrs' Foundation and Commander of the Mecca Pilgrims), Mahdi Hashemi (Coordinator of Islamic

Liberation Fronts) and Hadi Ghaffari (President of the Party of Allah).

13. Report presented by the War of Enlightenment to the Islamic Majlis in February 1986.
14. Ibid.
15. The newspaper has two editions, Persian and Arabic, and is based on the daily edition of *Kayhan* in Tehran. A third, Turkish, edition is printed in Tehran and distributed in Turkey and the Turkish-speaking sector of Cyprus. All copies are mailed free of charge to both individuals and associations. The total circulation of the three editions is estimated to be around 800,000 copies a month. All three editions are sixteen-page tabloids.
16. For more details on these 'fronts', see Chapter 10.
17. In a personal interview in New York in February 1986.
18. *Le Figaro*, 11 January 1986.
19. At the time of his murder he was the coordinator of a group of former army officers working for the National Resistance Movement led by Shapour Bakhtiar, the Shah's last Prime Minister.
20. A report by the Howzeh Elmieh (Scientific Centre) of Qom in March 1986 named the countries with theological students in the Islamic Republic as follows: Afghanistan (3500), Pakistan (3000) and Iraq (2800); also (all with between one and two hundred students) Turkey, Kuwait, Bahrain, the United Arab Emirates, Saudi Arabia, Oman, North Yemen, Qatar, Jordan, Lebanon, Syria, Palestine, Egypt, Sudan, Tunisia, Morocco, Algeria, Senegal, Guinea, Great Britain, France, Tanzania, South Africa, India, Madagascar, Bangladesh, Indonesia, Malaysia, the Philippines, the USSR, South Korea and Yugoslavia.
21. Most theological colleges are still dominated by traditional and conservative mullahs who teach a non-revolutionary version of Shi'ism. This 'deficiency' is corrected by the Party of Allah through the organization of non-academic sessions on the Islamic Revolution and Ayatollah Khomeini's vision of Holy War.
22. Some students are on scholarships from various liberation movements, and on graduation join their respective organizations as theological commissars.
23. *Iran va Jahan*, Paris, 12 December 1983; also *Maariv*, Israel, 15 November 1983.
24. Ibid.

25. Confidential Telex, 23 April 1986, Paris.
26. Both the Syrian and the Iraqi governments belong to rival factions of the Arab socialist Ba'ath (Renaissance) party.
27. In the summer of 1986 Massoud Barzani was in control of several villages in northern Iraq and was planning the establishment of a 'provisional government in liberated zones'.
28. *Al-Amal* (*Action*), organ of the Hezb al-Amal al-Islami (Islamic Action party), 9 February 1986.
29. *Jeune Afrique*, 24 January 1984.
30. *Pasdar Islam* (*Guardian of Islam*), monthly, vol. XII, Tehran, November 1985.
31. Ibrahim Hammud in *Tariqna* (*Our Path*), originally in Arabic, Tehran, 1984. It is also available in Persian, Turkish and Urdu.
32. Gary Sick, *Washington Post Weekly*, 2 June 1986.
33. *Mawaqifna* (*Our Positions*), Beirut, 1985.
34. Actually there is no such phrase in the Qur'an. The slogan 'War, war unto victory!' was coined by Khomeini in 1980 and was clearly inspired by the PLO's celebrated slogan '*Thawrah, thawrah hat al-Nasr!*', which means 'Revolution, revolution until victory!'
35. On 12 December 1984.
36. The speaker is Hojat al-Islam Shaikh Abbas Amjad, a leader of the Saudi branch of the Party of Allah, now in exile in Lebanon.

Chapter 9

1. *Al-Amal* (*Action*), organ of the Islamic Labour party, quoted by Muhammad Selhami in *Jeune Afrique*, vol. 1203, January 1984.
2. One of Imam Hussein's many titles.
3. Ayatollah Muhammad Aqda'i, in a taped sermon in Beirut on 25 March 1986.
4. *Harem* literally means 'off limits' in Arabic.
5. One of Khomeini's favourite slogans, scribbled on many walls in West Beirut and Baalbek.
6. The same word as 'mirage', originally used to describe the Prophet Muhammad's nocturnal voyages to the seventh heaven, where he met Allah and discussed with Him various matters of interest. In its more general application, the word describes the celestial journey of martyrs of the Faith to Paradise.
7. Israeli military authorities have consistently refused to publish details of the attack, beyond saying that 'fragments of a

woman's body were found'. See *The Times*, London, 11 April 1985.

8. *Jomhuri Islami*, Tehran, 13 April 1985.
9. *Jeune Afrique*, 24 April 1985.
10. Here is part of a poem written by a Party of Allah militant, Gholam-Ali Kuhi, in memory of San'ah:

    What a beautiful bride you became, San'ah!
    The envy of the full moon you became, San'ah!
    Wearing your bridal dress, your eternal shroud,
    You strolled amid the stars, San'ah!
    You scattered your body over the sacred land. . . .
    But angels came to collect the fragments, San'ah!
    Is there anything more beautiful than death?
    You say: 'Yes! To kill the enemy! You say San'ah!'

    In *Gozideh i az assar shoaray Hezb Allah* (*A Selection of Work by the Poets of the Party of Allah*), Tehran, 1986.
11. *Jeune Afrique*, vol. 1268, 1958.
12. According to the Hadiths the Prophet said: 'He who keeps a secret shall achieve his desired end.'
13. Commandant Kan'ani, commander of the Revolutionary Guard in Syria and Lebanon, in a speech quoted by *Pasdar Islam* (*Guardian of Islam*), vol. XXIV.
14. A declaration by Grand Ayatollah Milani in 1958.
15. Shi'ites claim to number over one million in Lebanon, ahead of Christians, who are estimated at around 780,000.
16. The majority of mercenaries serving in the Israeli-sponsored 'army' of Major Saad Haddad in southern Lebanon were Shi'ites. Haddad, who died in 1984, was succeeded by General Antoine Lahad.
17. Descent from the Prophet is an advantage but not an absolute requirement in seeking the position of Imam.
18. Shariatmadari died in Tehran in 1986 after four years under house arrest. Khomeini refused to issue him a passport to go abroad for medical treatment.
19. Ghotbzadeh, a close associate of Khomeini, served as his Foreign Minister in 1980. He was later charged with plotting to kill the Ayatollah and was executed. Bani-Sadr served as President of the Islamic Republic for a few months, but fled the country in 1981 and was granted political asylum in France.
20. See Ghassan Tueni, *Une Guerre pour les autres*, Paris, 1985.
21. According to private sources in Tehran.
22. Grand Ayatollah Abol-Qassem Mussavi-Kho'i and Ayatollah

Muhammad-Baqer al-Sadr were among Fadhl-Allah's teachers.

23. Quoted by Robin Wright in *Sacred Rage*, New York, 1985, p. 70.
24. Ibid.
25. In an interview with Tehran Radio (Arabic programme) on 20 December 1983.
26. In slogans chanted at Friday prayer sessions in mosques in the Islamic Republic as well as in Lebanon.
27. This did not include expenditure incurred by Revolutionary Guard units in Syria and Lebanon.
28. Israeli Intelligence presented a report to that effect to the United States in 1983, according to private sources.
29. One example was the murder of the French Ambassador, Louis Delamare, in 1982. PLO agents wanting to do France a good turn later identified his assassins and murdered them in Beirut, according to private sources. The assassins were Abdul-Wahab Husseini, Muhammad Yassine and Sadeq Mussawi.
30. See Chapter 10.
31. The Jund-Allah was created by Shaikh Sa'id Sha'aban in order to fight Alawite militiamen acting on behalf of Syria in the Tripoli region. But by 1986 the Jund-Allah had practically come under Iranian command. It was a Jund-Allah group that kidnapped four Soviet diplomats in Beirut in 1984, killing one of them. The rest of the Soviet hostages were released after Syrian militiamen began murdering known supporters of the Jund-Allah. In 1985 the leaders of the Jund-Allah, realizing they needed support from a foreign power, unsuccessfully tried to approach Libya's Colonel Gaddafi, who considers Shaikh Sha'aban a reactionary. Jund-Allah's turning to Tehran must be seen as an act of desperation.
32. According to US Intelligence sources, quoted by Robin Wright in *Sacred Rage*, p. 89.
33. The Syrian Vice-President Abdul-Halim Khaddam's phrase, in an interview with Tehran Radio, 11 June 1986.
34. In May 1986 Tehran dispatched Muhammad-Ali Besharati, a Deputy Foreign Minister, to Beirut to 'encourage' Party of Allah groups holding nine French citizens hostage to release two of them as a sign of goodwill from the Islamic Republic. In exchange France expelled Massoud Rajavi, leader of the Mujahedin Khalq, a guerrilla group opposed to Khomeini; Rajavi went to Baghdad.
35. Farsi is a member of the Islamic Majlis (Parliament), where he made these remarks on 19 May 1986. Quoted in *Mashruh*

Jalaseh Alani Majlis Showray Islami (*Minutes of the Open Session of the Islamic Consultative Assembly*), vol. 113.

Chapter 10

1. In *Resalat al-Anvar* (*Letter of the Rays of Light*), Shiraz, 1983, p. 174. Ayatollah Dast-Ghayb, who was assassinated in 1981 in Shiraz, was the author of more than fifty works on Shi'ite doctrine and was one of the leading theoreticians of the Islamic Revolution. Khomeini has given him the posthumous title of Shahid Mihrab (Martyr of the Altar).
2. A commando group threw two grenades into the garden of an Athens hotel on 3 September 1985, killing two hotel guests and wounding thirteen others. All the victims were members of a British tour group of handicapped people.
3. In *al-Fajr al-Jadid* (*The New Dawn*), 17 April 1986.
4. Khomeini, in *Kashf al-Asrar* (*Key to the Secrets*), Tehran, 1980, p. 67.
5. *Din al-Islam aqwi* (*Islam Is the Strongest Religion*), Beirut, 1983, p. 22.
6. Ibid., p. 97.
7. The theme is particularly developed in the works of the late Iraqi theologian, Ayatollah Muhammad-Baqer al-Sadr.
8. The phrase is Sadr's.
9. Including more than eighty thousand Americans and sixty-five thousand western Europeans. There were also thousands of Koreans, Filipinos, Japanese, Indians and citizens of the Eastern bloc states, among them over seven thousand Russians.
10. The phrase was first used by Muhammad Khoiniha, the leader of the 'students' who seized the US Embassy compound in Tehran on 4 November 1979.
11. Unofficial estimates. Government estimates put the number at under a million.
12. The number of political executions in the Islamic Republic between February 1979 and July 1986 is variously put at 9500 (government figure) and 55,000 (exile opposition figure).
13. *Nouvel Observateur*, Paris, 3 July 1986.
14. The expulsion of Palestinians remained incomplete in July 1986, despite a series of bloody battles in which hundreds of Palestinians were killed.
15. See Chapter 1.
16. From the French word *comité*.
17. Published by the Ministry of the Interior, Tehran.

18. Ibid.
19. Including political prisoners, whose number in 1986 was put at around 150,000 by opposition parties. Non-partisan estimates, however, put the number at 45,000.
20. See note 12 above.
21. There were at least twenty-five Western hostages in Beirut and Tehran in October 1986.
22. *Kayhan* weekly, vol. 104, London, July 1986.
23. According to private estimates, between 1980 and 1986 more than six hundred women were disfigured by acid in the Islamic Republic. In the same period throwing acid on unveiled women was also practised in Egypt, Morocco, Tunisia, Iraq, Pakistan and Indonesia. In July 1986, AFP (Agence France Presse) reported from Rabat, Morocco, the trial of two women charged with disfiguring a man by throwing acid on him.
24. In the spring of 1986 forty people were put on trial in Egypt for having burned and looted several shops selling videotapes. At the start of their trial, on 3 July 1986, the men, all members of a fundamentalist group, said they had acted in accordance with their 'sacred religious duties'. AFP report from Cairo, 3 July 1986.
25. The use of the machine has led to some controversy among Shi'ite theologians. Its supporters say it makes the task of cutting off the fingers and hands of the guilty more efficient. Its opponents argue that the machine also makes the punishment less painful, thus reducing its effect as a deterrent. Ayatollah Fadhl-Allah, the spiritual leader of the Lebanese fundamentalists, had still not approved its use in the autumn of 1986.
26. Private interview with Siavosh Bashiri in Paris, 1985.
27. Private interview in Paris, June 1986. The interviewee requested anonymity.
28. *Le Matin*, Paris, 20 October 1985.
29. Private interview in Paris, April 1986. The former hostage spoke on condition that he was not identified.
30. Ibid.
31. Kidnapping for money is, however, seldom aimed against foreign nationals. This is because freelance kidnappers dare not provoke retaliation from foreign powers; they limit their business to kidnapping local people or citizens of weak countries. In March 1986, two British citizens, Philip Padfield and Leigh Douglas, were kidnapped by 'freelance' gunmen. Both were sold to a pro-Libyan group after the US raid on Libya on 15 April 1986. Both were murdered as an act of revenge

against Britain's support for the US. In September 1986, British journalist David Hirst narrowly escaped becoming a hostage in the hands of another 'freelance' terror gang.

32. According to Pierre Blanchet in *Nouvel Observateur*, 27 June 1986, Paris. An American hostage, Stephen Donahue, was released on 2 July 1986 after his family had paid a ransom of 400,000 dollars.
33. He is in fact a Christian.
34. Two of them, Philippe Rochot and Georges Hansen, were freed in June 1986 as a result of negotiations between France and the Islamic Republic.
35. *The Guardian*, London, 19 January 1984.
36. He was freed after President Assad interceded personally with Khomeini. At the time Assad wanted to open up a dialogue with the United States.
37. In 1980 some of the fifty-two American diplomats seized in Tehran were also kept at that prison, probably selected because it is so near the border with the USSR. The idea was that if the USA attempted a rescue operation its aircraft might violate Soviet air space and provoke a superpower duel. The USA still denies that Buckley has been killed.
38. In 1983, under the pseudonym of Gérard Michaud, he wrote the Syrian section of the book *Les Frères Musulmanes*.
39. French authorities were unable to confirm or deny Seurat's death.
40. In 1986 the 'students' occupied seventy-six key posts in the top echelon of the Islamic Republic's government, including that of Deputy Prime Minister (Ali-Reza Moayeri). Two Deputy Foreign Ministers, Hussein Shaikh al-Islam and Ali-Muhammad Besharati, were also members of the group of 'students'.
41. In spite of the fact that the hijackers had murdered one of the passengers, Robert Stethem, a US Navy diver who was shot in cold blood and his body thrown out of the aircraft.
42. The French government expelled him, together with several other Islamic diplomats, a few weeks later.
43. Jamaran, in north Tehran, was where Khomeini lived after May 1980.
44. According to Edouard Sablier in *Le Fil rouge*, Paris, 1983.
45. Quoted in *Asnad Laneh Jassussi* (*Documents of the Nest of Spies*), vol. XXIV, Tehran, 1981.
46. Quoted in *Kayhan* weekly, vol. 33, 1984.
47. *Ettalaat* daily.

48. Alexandre Buccianti in *Le Monde*, Paris, 4 July 1986.
49. Ayatollah Abdul-Hussein Dast-Ghayb Shirazi, *Me'eraj* (*Celestial Voyage*), Tehran, 1985, p. 214. (Originally written in 1936, the book was refused a publication permit by the government until the victory of the Islamic Revolution in 1979.)
50. Ibid., p. 217.
51. Muhammad-Baqer Majlisi in *Bahar al-Anvar* (*Sea of Light*), vol. IV, Qom, 1960.
52. For more on this see my *The Spirit of Allah: Khomeini and the Islamic Revolution*, London, 1985.
53. The introduction of a solar calendar by Reza Shah in the 1920s was resented by the mullahs as an act of sacrilege. In 1978 Khomeini described the Shah's move as 'part of a vast scheme worked out by the Jews to destroy Islam by making its children forget that each day, indeed each hour of the day, has a meaning, and that every second of time belongs to Allah'. Quoted in *Sokhanane Imam* (*Sayings of the Imam*), vol. III, Tehran, 1980.
54. His birthday, the day he first ordered an insurrection against the government in 1962, the day of his exile to Turkey in 1965, the day he went from Najaf in Iraq to France in 1978, the day he returned to Tehran in 1979, and the day he won a 99.9 per cent victory in the referendum approving his Islamic Republic in 1979. Each of these days is preceded by a week of celebrations and demonstrations.
55. Boys cease to be children at the age of ten when they are said to achieve *tam'yeez* (the power to distinguish good from evil). They do not begin to exercise full political and social rights, including the right to take wives, until the age of sixteen. Girls can marry at the age of nine, though they are considered grown up from the age of five, when they must start wearing the Islamic *hijab* or veil. Some Shi'ite authorities, however, insist that women must cover their hair in front of 'unauthorized men' from the age of four.
56. Khomeini's expression.
57. Khomeini in *Kashf al-Asrar* (*Key to the Secrets*), Qom, 1979, p. 220.
58. Ibid., p. 117.
59. Quoted in Shojaeddin Shafa, *Towzih al-Masayel* (*Explanation of Problems*), Paris, 1983, p. 581.
60. Quoted in *Payam Islam* (*Message of Islam*), vol. 182, Qom, 1986.
61. Islamic Jihad statement on the first anniversary of Sadat's assassination.

62. Ibid. This is no doubt a much exaggerated figure, although until the early 1980s Cairo was indeed facing a serious prostitution problem.
63. A leaflet published in April 1986 by the Islamic Tendency, the main fundamentalist group in Tunisia, said: 'Why did they give women the vote? To deceive them and to bring them into public [places]. . . . The next step was persuading women to cast off their proper clothes, to walk around half naked. And then everyone could begin sleeping with everyone.'
64. Leaflet produced by Hezb al-Tahrir al-Islami (Islamic Liberation Party) of Egypt, March 1985.
65. Ibid.
66. See Khomeini's Kashf al-Asrar (Key to the Secrets).
67. Islamic Jihad leaflet against President Sadat, 1982.
68. Ibid.
69. Hamdi had paid a state visit to South Korea, where he had invited a folk dance company to perform in Yemen. The story started from there.
70. A former member of the Islamic Parliament, in an interview on 8 March 1986.
71. Interview in Paris, January 1986.
72. Private interview in Cairo. She did not wish to be named.
73. Meshkini is President of the Assembly of Experts. A junior mullah in the traditional hierarchy, he owed his influence to his political role.
74. This despite the fact that many people were executed after being found guilty of smuggling drugs into the country.
75. Emmanuel Jarry in *Le Monde*, 28 November 1983.
76. Vast smuggling networks also operate across the Islamic Republic's borders with Turkey, Afghanistan and Pakistan as well as through the Persian Gulf and the Gulf of Oman. Smuggling through the emirate of Dubai to Iran was estimated to have been worth more than 1000 million US dollars in 1984.
77. Making decisions with the help of worry beads (*mesbah*) is a well-established tradition in Shi'ism.
78. *Actuel*, no. 78, Paris, 1986.
79. The other was Ayatollah Hussein-Ali Montazeri, Khomeini's chosen heir as Wali Faqih (Jurisconsult).
80. The governments most often accused of plotting to assassinate the leaders of the Party of Allah include those of the United States, Israel, Iraq and Jordan. Syria and Libya are also suspected, but without being named. From 1979 the two countries formed a tactical alliance with the Party of Allah, but

were not prepared to let their allies monopolize the leadership of radical movements in the Middle East. Muhammad Sa'ad and Khalil Jiradi, two Party of Allah leaders in southern Lebanon, were killed by an Israeli commando in March 1985. But the murder of Abdul-Aziz Faqih, a moderate Shi'ite theologian, close to Nabih Berri in March 1986, was almost certainly the work of the Party of Allah.

81. The correspondent cannot be named. He still lives in Tehran and identification might endanger his life.
82. The expression was suggested by the correspondent cited above.

Chapter 11

1. The phrase is Fereidun Hoveyda's, who first used it in French: '*le Croissant gamme*'. (See Bibliography.)
2. Quoted in Shaikh Saduq Ibn Babuyeh, *Thawab al-Aamal* (*The Fairness of Acts*). The book was written in the sixteenth century; the latest edition is dated 1981 and printed in Qom.
3. Roland Jacquard, *Les Dossiers secrets du terrorisme*, Paris, 1985, p. 78.
4. The term is often used by French and German official sources in reference to the Party of Allah.
5. Ayatollah Mahalati, in a speech in Tehran, January 1982.
6. *Hezb-Allah* (*The Party of Allah*), Tehran, 1985, p. 63.
7. The Arabic for Mesopotamia. Khomeini does not like to use the name Iraq to describe that country, and often refers to it as 'Mesopotamia'.
8. Abd-Allah Nesh'at of the ad-Da'awah party, in a private interview in Paris, April 1986.
9. His real name is Mikha'il Yuhanna. A Nestorian Christian, Tareq Aziz was later promoted to the number two position in the Ba'athist regime. His name figures on the list of seven Iraqi leaders whose 'execution' is demanded by the Party of Allah. The others are Saddam Hussein (President of the Iraqi Republic), Taha Yassin-Ramadan (Deputy Premier), Izzat Ibrahim ad-Durri (number two in the ruling party), Adnan Khair-Allah Talfah (Defence Minister), Abdul-Jabbar al-Shenshal (Chief of Staff) and Sa'adun Hammadi (Speaker of the National Assembly). Between 1981 and 1986 at least five plots to murder the Iraqi leaders included in the black list were uncovered.
10. See my *The Spirit of Allah: Khomeini and the Islamic Revolution*, London, 1985.

11. According to Hussein Akhavan-Towhidi in *Dar Pass e Pardeh Tazvir* (*Behind the Mask of Hypocrisy*), Paris, 1986.
12. A copy of the report was made available by a former Party of Allah activist who broke with it and joined the opposition in 1985.
13. Ibid.
14. Mahri was eventually expelled from Kuwait in 1984, together with more than six thousand Shi'ites of Iranian and Iraqi origin. His functions were assumed by the Iranian Ambassador, Muhammad Shams-Ardakani. But he too had to leave after a scandal concerning the disappearance of funds collected among Kuwaiti Shi'ites, ostensibly for the construction of a new school.
15. Including Muhammad Jar-Allah, editor-in-chief and owner of the Arab nationalist daily *as-Sayassah* (*Politics*), who suffered serious injuries but survived.
16. No alcoholic drinks, however, were sold or consumed in either café. The Kuwaiti government already enforced very strict prohibition rules as a concession to the fundamentalists.
17. Issued in Tehran, July 1986.
18. Tehran Radio, Arabic programme, 12 March 1979.
19. Statement issued in Qom and subsequently distributed by the pan-Iranist party, which demanded the inclusion of Bahrain in Iran for nationalistic, and not Islamic, reasons.
20. Speech quoted by Tehran Radio, Arabic programme, 23 March 1979.
21. The Islamic Front for the Liberation of Bahrain (IFLB) was in existence in 1986, but mainly as a postal address in Tehran. Its most active members had become part of Mudarressi's new party. The 'front' retained some form of existence among Bahraini students in Britain, but seemed to be distancing itself from the Party of Allah and returning to its original roots within the Muslim Brotherhood.
22. No reliable statistics exist on Saudi Arabia's population. The government uses figures ranging from 7 to 10 million. Independent estimates vary between 4 and 6 million. The kingdom was host to nearly 2 million foreigners, including 1.1 million Yemenites, until 1986.
23. *Kashf al-Asrar* (*Key to the Secrets*), Tehran, 1980.
24. Speech in Qom, 13 January 1986.
25. The pamphlets were published under the collective title of *Al-Khotut al-Aridhah* (*Broad Outlines*). Their publication was stopped after Abbas-Ali Khalatbari, then Iran's Foreign

Minister, brought the matter up with King Faisal Ibn Abdul-Aziz during an official visit. The King ordered the campaign to be ended as a gesture of friendship towards the Shah.

26. Several schemes were discussed in the 1970s, with support from the United States. See also Chapter 12.
27. Khomeini's assertion has no basis in Islamic theology or history. Islam is neither pro- nor anti-monarchist in general.
28. Published in Tehran, 18 November 1979.
29. The movement, called al-Salafioun or Fundamentalists, was founded by the Syrian Rashid Radha and influenced the creation of the Muslim Brotherhood.
30. In Arabic: Thawrat al-Zanj. It broke out in southern Mesopotamia in the fourteenth century and quickly spread to southwest Iran and the Arabian shores of the Persian Gulf. An army of rebels also invaded Mecca and brought the black stone of the Ka'abah to Bahrain. Since black slaves from Africa formed the bulk of the rebel armies, the movement came to be known as 'The Revolution of the Negroes'.
31. Hojat al-Islam Karim Bojnurdi, an eye witness of the event, in his pamphlet *Qiyam dar Khaneh Khoda* (*Uprising in the House of God*), Qom, 1981.
32. Ibid.
33. Ibid.
34. Technically speaking there were no hostages, and at the start of their action the rebels had called on the pilgrims to leave if they so wished. In practice, however, at least six thousand were 'invited' to join the rebels in the vast basement halls of the shrine, according to eye witness accounts.
35. From *Qiyam*; see note 31 above.
36. The Saudis' appeal to King Hussein of Jordan to send in his army indicated their concern about possible indiscipline in their own armed forces.
37. Fahd was attending a conference in Rabat at the time the revolt started in Mecca. He returned home hurriedly and organized the counter-attack.
38. The commandos belonged to the Groupe d'Intervention de la Gendarmerie Nationale. During the Mecca operation they were commanded by Captain Paul Barril, the force's deputy chief.
39. Johaiman at no point claimed that he was the promised Mahdi (Guide) sent by Allah to bring Muslims back to the right path. Nor was such a claim made on his behalf by his companions. But the myth that he saw himself as Mahdi has persisted; it was

created by Saudi propaganda in order to discredit Johaiman and portray him as a megalomaniac, in addition to being 'inclined towards evil sexual practices'. Johaiman made a long speech in his own defence in front of the three Islamic judges who directed his so-called trial. A partial text, based on Johaiman's 'testament' which he had written, sealed and deposited with a close relative before leading the Ka'abah revolt, has been published and circulated in the Gulf States. In it Johaiman speaks of himself as 'a humble servant of the Only True Faith' and not as the 'Mahdi'.

40. Johaiman had met Mut'ee during successive Haj pilgrimages to Mecca in the 1970s.
41. Johaiman's text. See note 39 above.
42. It is a notorious fact that many Saudis cast off their traditional Arab dress and lifestyle as soon as they leave the kingdom, and become Western in every sense. Rich Saudis patronize the major casinos in Europe and the United States; one prince was reported to have lost millions of dollars in a single evening in 1977 in Monte Carlo. Gambling is of course strictly forbidden by Islam.
43. In 1985 more than seven hundred Islamic 'conversion missions' in forty-three countries received financial support from Saudi Arabia. The Saudis, according to unofficial estimates, spend as much as 1500 million dollars a year on these 'conversion missions'. In parts of black Africa Saudi-financed missions and those backed by Iran are engaged in ferocious competition, which at times confuses the local people and 'puts them off Islam altogether', according to one Senegalese observer.
44. This is an unofficial estimate. The Saudi government refuses to publish the results of a census it ordered in the 1970s.
45. These demonstrations were led by Hojat al-Islam Khoiniha, the leader of the 'student' group that seized the American Embassy in Tehran. Khoiniha was withdrawn in 1985 as a gesture of goodwill towards Riyadh, but agitations among pilgrims continued.
46. The Communist Party of the Arabian Peninsula, in a statement released in Rome in June 1985. The Popular Front for the Liberation of the Occupied Gulf (PFLOG) (see note 51 below) has also introduced an 'Islamic' flavour into its propaganda, which until 1980 was almost exclusively Leninist in tone if not in content.
47. Saudi militants are trained under the auspices of ad-Da'awah,

Hezb al-Amal al-Islami and Hezb al-Tahrir al-Islami, as well as the Party of Allah itself. They are reported by the Tehran media to be active in 'the struggle', not only in the kingdom itself but also in other Gulf States and Lebanon. Many of these militants are Shi'ites from al-Hasa.

48. According to Hilal ben Ahmad, Governor of Nizwah at the time of Sultan Sa'eed, in a private interview in Nizwah in 1973.
49. The custodianship of the Jurisconsult or the rule of the theologians.
50. The Ibadhis are a breakaway Islamic sect linked with the Kharejites, who were responsible for the murder of Ali, the first Imam of the Shi'ites and the fourth Caliph.
51. This was a communist-led uprising supported by South Yemen and, until 1972, both the USSR and China. In 1971 the rebels, grouped together as the Popular Front for the Liberation of the Occupied Gulf, itself an offshoot of the Dhofar Liberation Front, controlled the whole of the oil-rich province of Dhofar with the exception of its capital, Salalah. An Iranian task forced commanded by General Ali Khorsand was dispatched to the Omani province in 1972 and played a key role in crushing the rebellion. More than a thousand British, Canadian and Australian officers and NCOs, ostensibly 'working under contract and during sabbatical leave', also helped the British-commanded Omani army win the war in Dhofar.
52. The Iranian delegation was led by Ayatollah Muhammad Khonsari, who was to become Ambassador to Libya a few weeks later. According to Libyan sources, Khonsari was favourably impressed by the Omanis. But Tehran rejected his recommendations because the PFLOG remained suspect in the eyes of the mullahs, who considered it a communist 'front' organization. Cooperation with the PFLOG was nevertheless accepted by Tehran in the event of joint action against Arab emirates. But in every instance the mullahs have insisted that leadership must remain in the hands of the Party of Allah. The PFLOG's new charter, in which the 'front' announces its conversion to Islam, has not allayed the party's suspicion.
53. A US naval force was present off Ras al-Hadd in the Arabian Sea, while a multi-purpose base constructed on the Mussandam peninsula was ready for use by the US Rapid Deployment Force in 1986.
54. Pakistani estimates put the sums in question at over 50 million US dollars. Part of this was in the form of weapons smuggled

into Pakistan and distributed among Shi'ite militant groups.

55. Details of the allocations were published by the London *Kayhan* weekly on 10 July 1986. The sums approved for the United Kingdom came under the heading 'London Operations'.
56. Ministry of Islamic Orientation statistics, June 1986.
57. These inspectors acted as 'volunteers', according to the official media in Tehran, but they received 'donations' equivalent to 10–15 US dollars a day.
58. The fall in oil revenues has been a major factor in the decline of the Party of Allah's activities in India and elsewhere since 1985. In 1981 Mahalati had spoken of 'billions of dollars' that he planned to spend in the Indo-Pakistani subcontinent in order to promote Khomeini's version of Islam. But by 1986 the bulk of the Party of Allah's drastically reduced budget was taken up by Lebanese operations and the propaganda effort concentrated in London and Rome.
59. Published by the Ministry of Islamic Orientation, Tehran, November 1982.
60. The Sabilyoun are known in Filipino Spanish as the *jurimentado* or 'those who have taken the oath'.
61. Philippe Aziz, *Les Sectes secrètes de l'Islam*, p. 297.
62. Ibid.
63. Or 'the two testifications'. They are 'There is no God but Allah and Muhammad is His Prophet.'
64. The 'Great Satan' refers to the United States.
65. Indonesia, with a population of 130 million, of which 85 per cent are Muslims, is the largest Muslim nation in the world. Muslims are also in a majority in Malaysia. In the Philippines, Thailand and Burma Muslims account for around 12 per cent of the population, but are in a majority in most of the areas which they inhabit.
66. Also known as the Nusairis, they form a mere 11 per cent of the population of Syria, but they occupy more than 70 per cent of all the top positions in the armed forces, the civil service and the ruling party.
67. The ruling Ba'ath party describes itself as 'socialist', and Assad did all he could to prevent the mention of Islam as the state religion in the Syrian constitution; however he failed, under strong pressure from the Sunnis, in 1981.
68. According to Assad, the Brothers killed 'students, workers, peasants, teachers, soldiers, doctors, engineers, lawyers . . .' mostly while their victims were asleep. Quoted by Lucien

Bitterlin, *Hafez el-Assad*, Paris, 1986, p. 215.

69. Estimates of the number of dead on both sides vary between three and thirty thousand. The city of Hama was closed by the army for a whole week and was 'combed' house by house. Thousands of people were rounded up and sent to other cities for questioning. Many never returned, according to the Brothers.
70. A strong American lobby favours US support for Muslim fundamentalists opposing pro-Soviet regimes. See Paul Jabber's essay in *Foreign Affairs*, spring 1986.
71. The Syrian Brothers publish the periodical *an-Nazer* (*The Observer*), probably from Baghdad. In it they use against the USSR the same language that the Party of Allah uses against the USA.
72. The Islamic chargé d'affaires in Bonn had, however, arranged a secret meeting with Attar in 1981, apparently without knowing exactly what group he represented. The Syrians protested strongly against the meeting and Tehran promptly apologized, according to private sources in Lebanon.
73. Sadr-Eddin, in an interview published by the pro-Iraqi weekly *al-Watan al-Arabi* (*The Arab Fatherland*) in Paris, 22 April 1982, claimed that he had contacted Khomeini on a number of occasions but had been told first to mend his relations with the Assad government.
74. According to private sources. The Brothers were led by a man named Omran Yunus.
75. The Ba'ath party was founded by a Syrian Christian, Michel Aflaq, and in its constitution describes itself as secular. This is perhaps why President Assad set up the Ali al-Murtadha Society – to mobilize religious support for his regime. The society, which has branches throughout Syria and in parts of Lebanon, is said to be run by Alawite 'shaikhs' in close consultation with the Assad clan.
76. The process is known as *al-Itizal al-Shu'uriyah* or the isolation of consciousness, a theme developed in Shukri Mustafa's writings. The true Muslim, according to Mustafa, must forget all that he has learned from 'un-Islamic sources' before he can liberate his consciousness and 'sharpen' it as a 'sword with which the infidels are cut down'.
77. Unpublished research paper by Imadeddin Adham.
78. The Party of Allah's operational handbooks have been translated into Arabic and printed in Lebanon. Some copies were smuggled into Egypt between 1983 and 1986 and figured

among 'dangerous material' seized by the police in raids against Qutbist hideouts in Cairo and Asyut.

79. The particular country varies according to the circumstances of the day, but the two most often named were Libya and the Islamic Republic.
80. Islambouli's cry of 'I killed the Pharaoh' is the source of the title given him by fundamentalist propagandists.
81. Estimate by Imadeddin Adham. See note 77 above.
82. One of the most popular of Egyptian singers, whose career spanned nearly four decades until her death in 1980.
83. *Crowds and Power*, London, 1983.
84. An Egyptian variety of broad bean, the country's staple food.
85. Traditionalist fundamentalist groups such as those formed around Shaikh Ahmad al-Mahlawi, Shaikh Hafez Salamah and Shaikh Salah Abu-Isma'il have adopted what could be described as a non-violent posture since 1985. They seemed more interested in forcing some concessions out of the government than in planning to overthrow it. Some of these groups, notably the one led by Salamah, had nevertheless been involved in violent activities in the 1970s. Salah Serrieh, a doctor of philosophy who led an armed attack on the Military Technical College in Cairo in 1974, apparently in a bid to assassinate President Sadat and other government officials, was a member of the Tahrir (Liberation) group which now forms the basis of Salamah's support. Serrieh and one of his accomplices, Karem al-Anaduly, were sentenced to death and executed.
86. The existence of a strong Christian minority in the south and the presence of well-organized communist and nationalist parties in the major towns and cities of the north, notably Khartoum itself, further limited the appeal of Khomeinist groups.
87. Several parties of the same name exist in Muslim countries, but the original Tahrir party was founded in Jordan by Taqi-Eddin al-Nabhani in 1954. During the 1980s Tahrir parties were active in Iraq, Syria and the Gulf States.
88. Numeiri's experiment showed that rulers who claim to have become guardians of Islam overnight have no credibility. Numeiri had come to power as an 'Arab socialist' and, taking his cue from Nasser, had at first fought the Muslim Brotherhood, the Ansars and other Sudanese fundamentalist parties.
89. In 1986 Islam was the majority religion in the African continent. Statistics published by *Dar al-Tabligh* (*House of*

Propagation) in Saudi Arabia in 1980 showed that Islam was making rapid progress even in countries such as Mozambique and Madagascar, where various Christian churches on the one hand, and Marxist parties on the other were traditionally strong and actively opposed to Muslim 'expansionism'.

90. *Jama'ah* means 'group' as well as 'association'. The term is used by numerous Islamic study and action groups throughout the Muslim world.
91. Yoweri Musseveni, who became Uganda's ruler after winning the civil war in 1986, tried to stem the tide of Islam by equating it with Arabism – which, in turn, he equated with the slave trade.
92. According to an article in *Pasdar Islam* (*Guardian of Islam*), vol. XXV, Tehran, recounting a tour of West Africa by a Party of Allah delegation in 1985.
93. Ibid.
94. For more background see Moriba Magassouba, *L'Islam au Sénégal*, Paris, 1985.
95. *L'Evénement de jeudi*, Paris, 1 January 1986.
96. *Hegira* communes were first set up in Egypt in the 1970s, but were opened in many other countries as well. In the United States the first 'completely Islamic' city, called Dar es-Salaam (The House of Peace), was inaugurated near Santa Fé in New Mexico in 1985. Its population of less than a thousand lived in accordance with the *shari'ah* and for women the Islamic veil was obligatory.
97. The school, housed in the former Sepahsalar mosque, is financed by the Society of the Combatant Clergy in Tehran, led by Ayatollah Muhammad-Reza Mahdavi Kani.
98. See note 95 above.
99. Plural of *al'em* or 'scientist', which is used to refer to theologians. In Islam theology is considered as the ultimate 'science'.
100. Including laws concerning gambling, the sale of alcoholic liquor and the publication of literature about religions other than Islam.
101. Hamza Kaidi gives a detailed account of the attack in *Jeune Afrique*, vol. 1301, Paris, 1985.
102. In a statement issued on his behalf by the Jund Allah, dated 30 December 1985.
103. The statement, dated 16 April 1986, announced the new movement's slogan as 'Allah is our aim, the Prophet is our leader, the Qur'an is our constitution, death in the service of

Allah is our supreme desire.' It also named the movement's leaders as Bou-Ali, Muhammad-Tayyeb Amarra, Muhammad Ben-Omar, Jaafar Berkani, Khaled Touati, Abdul-Aziz Lehoudi and Abdul-Qader Shebouti. All of them, with the exception of Berkani, had spent some time in the Party of Allah's training camps in the Islamic Republic and Lebanon.

104. Ben Bella was strongly influenced by his wife's fundamentalist opinions, according to sources close to the couple.
105. The USSR honoured him by granting him in 1963 the Order of Lenin, the country's highest distinction.
106. Statement by the Algerian section of the Islamic Jihad, dated 7 June 1986, released in Paris.
107. AFP report from Algiers, 10 March 1986.
108. A leaflet issued in February 1986 by the students' section of the Party of Allah at the University of Constantine said: 'The atheist socialist Marxists who are inspired by Marxism, itself a sinister invention of the God-hating Jews, are now piercing the ears of the people with their talk of Islam. . . . But no one will be fooled as they cannot hide behind the thin veil of the National Charter.' The 'National Charter' was approved in January 1986 as the country's new constitution. The leaflet was published to mark the 'martyrdom' of Abdul-Latif Soltani and Abdul-Aziz Mansouri, who died, it said, 'gun in hand, fighting'.
109. From the memorandum of association published by the Moroccan branch of the Islamic Jihad in 1980.
110. Ibid.
111. See Appendix C for a translation of one of Yassine's texts.
112. This group has its 'hegira' headquarters in Brussels.
113. Private interview in Brussels, February 1986.
114. Ibid.
115. *Middle East Journal*, vol. 40, no. 2, Washington DC, 1986.
116. Private interview with Moroccan Muslim militants in Paris, May 1986.
117. One such was Habib Moammar, arrested in Nancy, north-eastern France, in 1985, who confessed to having placed bombs in several department stores, including a branch of Marks and Spencer in London. He was denounced to the police by his girlfriend and 'companion of struggle' Souad Issaoui, who was later released in recognition of her cooperation. Moammar claimed that he had joined the terrorist group in question for money, but had later come to share its ideals.
118. Islamic Orientation Movement statement, 30 August 1982.

119. Islamic Jihad statement, Marseilles, February 1985.
120. Ibid.
121. *Le Monde*, Paris, 12 July 1986.
122. The only major exception occurred when an effigy of Atatürk was burned by fundamentalists in Kayseri in 1978. In the same year Sunni Muslims massacred Shi'ites in Karaman-Marash. Ironically, the Shi'ites were defending Kemalist values against the Sunnis' programme for a return to the Caliphate.
123. According to Muslim fundamentalists Atatürk was a Jew. Mustafa Kemal was in fact born into a Muslim family.
124. Atatürk was born in Salonika, now part of Greece, where the Dönme sect of Jews formed an important minority. A legend invented by the Party of Allah traces Atatürk's origins to a Dönme Jewish family.
125. The statement was published in a leaflet dated 12 December 1982.
126. The first Islamic summit, jointly sponsored by the Shah of Iran and King Faisal of Saudi Arabia, was held in Rabat, Morocco, in 1968. Turkey was represented by Orhan Aralp, a Deputy Foreign Minister. The Turks sent their Foreign Minister to later summits.
127. In 1984 Turkey issued a strong warning to the Islamic Republic against attempts at interfering in its domestic affairs. The Party of Allah took the message and armed bands of Muslim fundamentalists, Armenian guerrillas and Kurdish secessionists which had taken up position along the Iran–Turkey border were removed.
128. One popular Turkish preacher operating from Qom was Hojat al-Islam Mehmet Samad Karsi, who frequently visited Western Europe to address meetings of Turkish workers and students. In June 1985 he was in Switzerland and spoke at meetings in Geneva, Zurich and Lausanne. He talked of Turkey 'emerging out of the black night of Kemalism to hail the sun of Islam that has risen from the heart of the East'.

Chapter 12

1. Faraj, the mastermind behind President Sadat's assassination, was also the author of a pamphlet called *Al-Faridhaat al-Ghayabah* (*The Occulted Duty*), one of the most popular texts of Holy Terror. He was hanged in the Bab al-Khalq Prison in central Cairo on 15 April 1982 together with two companions. The concept of 'occultation of one's supreme duty', or the

assassination of 'impious rulers', was borrowed by Faraj from Shi'ism, which advocates *taqiyeh* or the dissimulation of one's purpose and beliefs until 'the right moment'.

2. The theme is developed by Qutb, Khomeini and Faraj.
3. Dr Aziz Pasha, in an interview with BBC Radio 4, 20 July 1986.
4. The term belongs to Ayatollah Mahalati and was used in his pamphlet *Tariqat va Shariat* (*The Path and the Law*), Tehran, 1983.
5. Ibid.
6. This is how Shaikh Omar al-Talmassani, Supreme Guide of the Egyptian Muslim Brotherhood until his death in 1986, put the point in *Memories, not Memoirs*, Cairo, 1985, p. 52:

> Is there anyone who believes it is possible to have [normal] relations with the Jews? . . . Any attempt in that direction cannot but lead to the destruction of all Muslims. . . . We are Muslims, and Allah, in Whom we all believe, told us in the Holy Qur'an: 'Thou shalt note that Jews and pantheists are the ones that are most hostile to Muslims.' This is a divine decree which permits of no confusion, no interpretation. . . . Can we claim to know the Jews better than Allah himself?

7. Mawlana Mufti Muhammad, leader of the Pakistani Jama'at Islami movement, quoted by Mahalati in his pamphlet. See note 4 above.
8. Ibid.
9. Talmassani, in a private interview in Geneva, June 1985.
10. Khomeini invented the rumour according to which Reza Shah had converted first to Zoroastrianism and then to Judaism. In 1963 the Ayatollah told a meeting in Qom that Muhammad Reza Shah, too, had 'probably gone over to the Jews'.
11. Broadcast by Radio Tripoli, 7 October 1982.
12. A pamphlet, produced probably by the Syrian secret service in 1984, related what it called the 'true history of Arafat's Jewish origins'. Rumours concerning Arafat's supposed 'Jewish blood' were heard in Cairo, Baghdad, Tehran, Beirut and Amman in 1985 and 1986.
13. Mir-Javad Alim-Na'ini in *Hezb-Allah* (*The Party of Allah*), Tehran, 1985, p. 116.
14. Ibid., p. 43.
15. The author is probably a Pakistani. The Arabic edition, probably translated from Urdu, is entitled *Al-Islam al-Asri* (*Contemporary Islam*), Beirut, n.d.

16. Cousteau has categorically denied his conversion but continues to be listed among those 'who have seen the light'. Béjart's profession as a dancer and choreographer is carefully dissimulated in articles written in his praise – dance is forbidden in Islam – and he is described as a 'master of Western creative arts'. Roger Garaudy, a former member of the French communist party and a pamphleteer in his spare time, is called 'the greatest Western philosopher of our time' in articles and speeches reporting his conversion to Islam. The fact that most of the Western converts to Islam, such as the French publisher Michel Chodkiewicz, advocate the humanist version as presented by the Sufis, is conveniently ignored by the propagandists of Holy Terror.
17. By the Turkish writer Attila Ilhan.
18. *Kashf al-Asrar* (*Key to the Secrets*), Tehran, 1980, p. 274.
19. Yahya Danesh, *Naqshe Imam dar Enqelab* (*The Role of the Imam in Revolution*), Tehran, 1982, p. 97.
20. Attila Ilhan, quoted in *Le Monde*, Paris, 27 May 1986.
21. Danesh. See note 19 above, p. 103.
22. Khomeini, quoted in Muhammad Khalil Zayyen, *Fi Sabil Allah* (*In the Way of Allah*), Rome, 1985, p. 44.
23. The Iranian philosopher Ehsan Naraqi, in a private conversation in Paris, June 1986.
24. *Montakhab Asar Nevisandegan Hezb Allah* (*A Selection of Works by Party of Allah writers*), Rasht, 1985.
25. Ibid.
26. Andrew Young, Carter's Ambassador to the United Nations, for example, described Khomeini as a 'twentieth-century saint'. Most of Carter's advisers on Iran viewed the Ayatollah as a pious man who was leading a revolution against corruption and tyranny, and whose anger against the USA was legitimate. They believed that Khomeini was acting in a hostile way because he misunderstood the true intentions of the Carter administration. These advisers also deluded themselves into thinking that once Khomeini was properly informed of the fact that the Carter administration was not like its predecessors and had no intention of moving against the Islamic Revolution, Tehran and Washington would become friends again. They did not realize that the Party of Allah saw the United States as an empire of evil that in time must be destroyed.
27. Unpublished monograph, Paris, 1984.
28. Ibid.
29. *Sobh Azadegan*, Tehran, 19 November 1982.

30. Britain was the prime mover in the creation of the Baghdad Pact, which later became known as the Central Treaty Organization (CENTO), with Turkey, Iran, Pakistan and the UK as full members and the United States as associate member. The treaty died in the confusion of the Islamic Revolution.
31. *Le Figaro*, Paris, 6 March 1986.
32. Moayeri came to Paris in his official capacity as assistant to the Prime Minister of the Islamic Republic.
33. Unofficial estimates. No official statistics were available, since most of the trade between the two countries passed through third countries, notably Turkey.
34. Minutes of the Islamic Majlis in *Ruznameh Rasmi Keshvar* (*The Official Journal*), 2 February 1985.
35. In a private conversation in Paris, August 1980.
36. British journalist David Hirst, quoted in *The Sacred Rage*, p. 262.
37. Quoted in *The Sacred Rage*, p. 31.
38. Quoted in Muhammad Khahl Zayyen, *Fi Sabil al Allah* (*In the Way of Allah*), Rome, 1985, p. 22.
39. Quoted in *Ebadat va Khodsazi* (*Prayer and Self-improvement*), Mashhad, 1986, p. 45.
40. The terms *adalat* (justice) and *mussavat* (equality) are extremely popular in the revolutionary movements of all Muslim countries. Most militant groups in the Muslim territories of the USSR choose one or other as their codename.
41. The term extends beyond its Islamic undertones and also implies pan-Turkism. Among other crimes, Galiev was accused of wanting to create a new Turkish empire uniting all Turkic people from the Chinese province of Sinkiang to the Mediterranean. A biography of Sultan Galiev published in Paris by Alexandre Benningsen and Chantal Lemercier-Quelqejay in 1986 had the sub-title *Le Père de la révolution tiers-mondiste* (*Father of Third-world Revolution*).
42. In a private conversation with an Iranian diplomat in Moscow, January 1979
43. Some resistance groups try to conceal their Islamic sentiments and projects when addressing Western audiences. However every one of them advocates a fully Islamic agenda and the application of the *shari'ah*.
44. Some 30 per cent of Afghans are Shi'ites, dominated by the mullahs. The Sunni majority, with the exception of the Tatars in the north, are under the influence of mawlavis who, although not as powerful as the Shi'ite mullahs, enjoy virtually unlimited

influence in deciding what is right or wrong in society. None of the resistance groups advocates the creation of a secular, pluralist-democratic nation state based on the Universal Declaration of Human Rights. In some cases, the hatred felt and expressed for the West, albeit in private, is as strong among the resistance groups as their hatred of the USSR and communism.

45. Statement by Lajnat Movahedeen (Alliance of Monotheists), published in Sofia in October 1985 as an open letter addressed to delegates attending the UNESCO General Assembly there.
46. Ibid.
47. Ibid.
48. Ibid.
49. In 1986 the Alliance had a postal address in Tehran.
50. Statement by the Alliance of Monotheists, published in Paris, June 1986.
51. Ibid.
52. Ibid.
53. For an insight into Bulgarian thinking about Muslim fundamentalism I am indebted to Celal Metin's monograph, *Les Mussulmans en Bulgarie*, prepared in 1986.

Chapter 13

1. Shayegan is an Iranian philosopher who originally supported the Islamic Revolution and described Khomeini as 'the Gandhi of Islam'. Forced into exile in 1981, he moved to Paris where he published two books on Islam and revolution.
2. In addition to publishing articles in non-government newspapers Farwaj devotes considerable time to lecturing on Islam and modernization.
3. Introduction to his pamphlet of the same title, Cairo, January 1986.
4. Dashti, a veteran of Persian letters and politics, died in 1984 after spending three years in Khomeini's prisons. He was already eighty-three when he was tortured and imprisoned. His book, an account of the Prophet Muhammad's career from his escape to Medina until his death, depicts Islam as a tribal code for largely nomadic Arabs in the seventh century. Written in 1937, the book was first banned under the Shah; it was put aside by the author until 1980, when Dashti authorized its publication by underground opposition groups. He told a friend before he died: 'Had the Shah allowed books like this to be published and read by the people, we would never have had an Islamic revolution.'

According to unofficial estimates Dashti's book, published in countless pirated editions by opposition parties of Left and Right, may have sold more than half a million copies between 1980 and 1986.

5. Such as the Muslim Brotherhood, the Ansar in the Sudan and the Society of Muslim Ulama in Pakistan.
6. In a private conversation in Cairo, 1985.
7. Quoted in Claire Brière and Olivier Carre, *Islam, guerre à l'occident*, Paris, 1983, p. 207.
8. See, for example, Wafik Raouf, *Irak-Iran: des vérités inavouées*, Paris, 1985.
9. Quoted in *al-Akhbar*, 16 January 1985.
10. The speaker was Ayatollah Muhammad Hassan Khameneh'i, a brother of the Islamic Republic's President, Ali Khameneh'i. Muhammad Hassan Khameneh'i, who resigned as Chairman of the Islamic Majlis's justice sub-committee, made his observations in his 'open letter of resignation' published in Tehran in July 1986. The letter was extensively quoted in the government-owned media in Tehran as well.
11. Some unions came under the control of Islamic Marxist groups or students linked to the Muslim Brotherhood's moderate faction in Egypt. In Beir Zeit University, on the occupied West Bank, a coalition of PLO supporters, Nasserites and pro-Jordanian students won control of the unions in 1986. The Khomeinists were almost totally excluded for the first time in six years.
12. The expression is Shayegan's.
13. The Islamic term is *hareem* – which comes from the same root as 'harem' – the preserve of every individual in which the state has no right to interfere.
14. This argument was developed by Bechir Ben Yahmed in a private conversation in Paris, April 1986.
15. The view of Grand Ayatollah Qomi, number six in the Shi'ite religious hierarchy, expressed in a private interview in Paris, May 1986.
16. An exception was provided by Syria, when its leaders ordered the massacre of fundamentalists in Homs and Hama in 1981.
17. The most populous Muslim countries are Indonesia, Nigeria and Bangladesh, whose conversion to Islam was accomplished by traders and missionaries rather than by invading armies.
18. The expression was coined by Habib Boulares. (See bibliography.)
19. Shayegan, in an interview with *Nouvel Observateur*, 23 September 1982.

Select Bibliography

Mir-Fathollah Aban, *Jahad dar Islam* (*Holy War in Islam*), Qom, 1983.

Abbas Ali Abhari, *Maqam Shaheed dar Islam* (*The Place of the Martyr in Islam*), Qom, 1980.

Ali Abiri, *Yeksad Mosahebeh Imam Khomeini* (*One Hundred Interviews with Imam Khomeini*), Tehran, 1979.

Nematallah Abiri-Golpayegani, *Rah e Haq* (*Path of Justice*), Tehran, 1980.

Karim Abolhoda, *Ahl e Bayt* (*Members of the Household*), Qom, 1974.

Gholam R. Afkhami, *The Iranian Revolution: Thanatos on a National Scale*, Washington DC, 1985.

Fouad Ajami, *The Vanished Imam*, New York, 1986.

Fouad Ajami, *The Arab Predicament: Arab Political Thought and Practice since 1967*, New York, 1982.

Firuz Akbari, *Tariq e Shohada* (*The Way of the Martyrs*), Tehran, 1979.

Shahrough Akhavai, *Religion and Politics in Contemporary Iran: The Clergy–State Relationship in the Pahlavi Era*, Albany, New York, 1980.

Hussein Akhavan-Towhidi, *Dar Pas e Pardeh Tazvir* (*Behind the Mask of Hypocrisy*), Paris, 1986.

Mir-Javad Alim-Na'ini, *Hezb-Allah* (*The Party of Allah*), Tehran, 1985.

T. D. Allman, *Unmanifest Destiny*, New York, 1984.

Said Amir-Arjomand, *The Shadow of God and the Hidden Imam: Religion, Political Order and Societal Change in Shi'ite Iran from the Beginning to 1890*, Chicago and London, 1984.

Hojat al-Islam Ansari-Kermani, *Vizhehgihay i az Zendegi Imam* (*Anecdotes from the Life of the Imam*), Tehran, 1983.

Taqi Azimi-Far, *Ijtihad dar Islam* (*Religious Ruling in Islam*), Qom, 1972.

Philippe Aziz, *Les Sectes secrètes de l'Islam*, Paris, 1983.

Imadeddin Badr, *Nahdhat al-Islamiah fel Iran* (*Islamic Movement in Iran*), Qom, 1984.

Yazdanbkhsh Bahrami, *Qahramanan e Jahan Islam* (*Heroes of the World of Islam*), Tehran, 1980.

Sadreddin Bakhtar, *Hezb-Allah dar Lobnan* (*The Party of Allah in Lebanon*), Tehran, 1986.

George W. Ball, *Error and Betrayal in Lebanon*, Washington DC, 1984.

Paul Balta, *L'Islam dans le monde*, Paris, 1986.

Muhammad-Hussein Bani-Yaqub, *Khomeini cheh Amukht?* (*What Did Khomeini Teach?*), Tehran, 1984.

Claude Barril, *Missions très spéciales*, Paris, 1984.

Muhammad-Hussein Beheshti (Ayatollah), *Majmueh Sokhanraniha* (*Collected Speeches*), Tehran, 1986.

Monroe Berger, *Islam in Egypt Today*, Cambridge, 1970.

Cheryl Bernard and Zalmy Khalilzad, *The Government of God*, New York, 1984.

Abdul-Karim Biazar-Shirazi, *Ebadat va Khodsazi* (*Prayer and Self-improvement*), Mashhad, 1986.

Fath-Allah Bidar, *Nahayat e Amr* (*The Finite of the Infinite*), Tehran, 1986.

Habib Boulares, *L'Islam: la peur et l'espoir*, Paris, 1982.

Claire Brière and Olivier Carre, *Islam: guerre à l'occident?*, Paris, 1983.

John Bulloch, *The Final Conflict: the War in Lebanon*, London, 1977.

Olivier Carre and Gérard Michaud, *Les Frères Musulmans (1928–1982)*, Paris, 1983.

Gérard Chaliand, *Terrorismes et guerrillas*, Paris, 1985.

Jean-Paul Charnay, *L'Islam et la guerre*, Paris, 1986.

Bahram Chubineh, *Tashayu va siyassat* (*Shi'ism and Politics*), 2 vols, Düsseldorf, 1983.

Arthur Conte, *Les Dictateurs du XX siècle*, Paris, 1984.

Yahya Danesh, *Naqsh e Imam dar Enqqelab* (*The Role of the Imam in Revolution*), Tehran, 1982.

Ali Davani, *Nehzat e Ruhaniyat dar Iran* (*The Clerical Movement in Iran*), 11 vols, Tehran, 1980–83.

Marius Deeb, *The Lebanese Civil War*, New York, 1980.

Fath-Allah Derakhshan, *Rah e Imam* (*The Path of the Imam*), Qom, 1984.

Wilhelm Dietl, *Holy War*, New York, 1984.

Ali El-Ganari, *Bourguiba, le combattant suprême*, Paris, 1985.

John L. Esposito (ed.), *Voices of Resurgent Islam*, Oxford, 1983.

Abdul-Aziz Essaid, *Le Réveil de l'Islam*, Marseilles, 1985.

Gholam-Reza Ethna-Ashari, *Gozidehi az vassiyatnameh hay Shohada (A Selection of Testaments by the Martyrs)*, Tehran, 1984.

Gholam-Reza Fada'i-Araqi, *Hezb-Allah va Hezb-Shaytan (The Party of Allah and the Party of Satan)*, Qom, 1986.

Muhammad-Hussein Fadhl-Allah (Shaikh), *Islam and the Logic of Force*, Beirut, 1981.

Muhammad-Javad Fazel-Harandi, *Shahadat dar Islam (Martyrdom in Islam)*, Tehran, 1984.

Claude Feuillet, *Le Système Saoud*, Paris, 1983.

Michael M. Fischer, *Iran: From Religious Dispute to Revolution*, Cambridge, Mass., 1982.

Franklin L. Ford, *Political Murder*, Cambridge, Mass. and London, 1985.

Moammar Gaddafi, *Je suis un opposant à l'échelon mondial*, Lausanne, 1984.

Yahya Ganjavi, *Jonbesh Towhidi Saff (The Unitarian Movement of the Line)*, Qom, 1979.

Ben-Yussef Gharbi, *L'Islam et l'avenir du Maghreb*, Marseilles, 1985.

David Gilmour, *Lebanon: The Fractured Country*, New York, 1984.

M. Hamidullah, *Le Prophète de l'Islam*, Paris, 1959.

Ragheb Harb, *Din al-Islam Aqwa (Islam Is the Strongest)*, Beirut, 1983.

Muhammad Heikal, *Autumn of Fury*, London, 1983.

Ubaid Hilwan, *Thawrat al-Islamiyah fel Eraq (Islamic Revolution in Iraq)*, Rome, 1983.

David Hirst, *The Gun and the Olive Branch*, London, 1983.

David Holden and Richard Johns, *The House of Saud: The Rise and Rule of the Most Powerful Dynasty in the Arab World*, New York, 1982.

I. M. Hosaini, *The Moslem Brothers*, Beirut, 1969.

Fereydoun Hoveyda, *Les Nuits féodales*, Paris, 1983.

Fereydoun Hoveyda, *Les Miroirs du mollah*, Paris, 1985.

Assaf Hussein, *Political Perspectives of the Muslim World*, New York, 1985.

Assaf Hussein, *Iran, Revolution and Counter-Revolution*, New York, 1985.

Muhammad Iqbal, *Knowledge and Religious Experience*, Lahore, 1968.

Sorush Irfani, *Revolutionary Islam in Iran*, London, 1982.

Muhammad Itani, *Al Niza al Mussalahah fi Islam (Armed Struggle in Islam)*, Beirut, 1981.

Roland Jacquard, *Les Dossiers secrets du terrorisme*, Paris, 1985.
Godfrey H. Jansen, *Militant Islam*, London, 1979.
Michael Jansen, *The Battle of Beirut*, London, 1982.
Bizhan Jazani, *Capitalism and Revolution in Iran*, London, 1980.
Brian Jenkins, *International Terrorism: A New Mode of Conflict*, Los Angeles, 1979.
Benjamin Z. Kadar, *Crusade and Mission: European Approaches Towards the Muslims*, Princeton, New Jersey, 1984.
Adnan Kamal, *As-Sarat al-Mustaqeem* (*The Right Path*), Rome, 1985.
Ahmad Kasravi, *Shiagari* (*Shi'ism*), West Germany, 1984 (originally published in Tehran in 1943).
Nikki R. Keddie, *Religion and Politics in Iran*, London, 1983.
Nikki R. Keddie, *Roots of Revolution*, London, 1981.
Gilles Kepel, *Le Prophète et Pharaon*, Paris, 1984.
Rashid Khalidi, *Under Siege: PLO Decision-making during the 1982 War*, New York, 1986.
Mehdi Khaza'i, *Shahid Mehrab* (*Martyr of the Altar*), Shiraz, 1984.
Ruhollah Khomeini, *Hokumat Islami* (*Islamic Government*), Tehran, 1979.
Ruhollah Khomeini, *Tahrir al-Wassillah* (*Liberation of Means*), Tehran, 1985.
Ruhollah Khomeini, *Kashf al-Asrar* (*Key to the Secrets*), Tehran, 1980.
Thomas Kiernan, *The Arabs*, London, 1978.
Robert Lacey, *The Kingdom*, London, 1983.
John Laffin, *The Dagger of Islam*, London, 1981.
John Laffin, *Fedayeen*, London, 1973.
Henri Laoust, *Les Schismes dans l'Islam*, Paris, 1965.
Walter Laqueur, *Terrorism*, Boston, Mass., 1977.
Abdallah Larout, *L'Idéologie arabe contemporaine*, Paris, 1967.
Bernard Lewis, *The Assassins*, London, 1982.
Abtin Livani, *Nehzat Islami dar Qafqaz* (*Islamic Movement in the Caucasus*), Tehran, 1981.
Neil C. Livingstone, *The War Against Terrorism*, Toronto, 1982.
David E. Long, *The United States and Saudi Arabia: Ambivalent Allies*, Boulder, Colorado, 1985.
Moriba Magassouba, *L'Islam au Sénégal: demain les mollahs?*, Paris, 1985.
Marie-Agnès Malfray, *L'Islam*, Paris, 1980.
G. S. Hodgson Marshall, *The Venture of Islam*, 3 vols, Chicago, 1974.
Abul-Ala Mawdoodi, *Islamic Law and Constitution*, Rome, 1984.
Richard Mitchell, *The Society of Muslim Brothers*, London, 1969.

Hussein-Ali Montazeri, *Towzih al-Masayel* (*Explanation of Problems*), Tehran, 1985.

Vincent Monteil, *L'Islam noir*, Paris, 1980.

James W. Morris, *The Wisdom of the Throne: An Introduction to the Philosophy of Mulla Sadra*, Princeton, 1981.

Morteza Motahari, *Nehzat Islami dar Sadsal Akhir* (*The Islamic Movement in the Last One Hundred Years*), Tehran, 1985.

Saeed Mutallebi, *Shahid dar Mehrab* (*Martyr at the Altar*), Tehran, 1985.

V. S. Naipaul, *Among the Believers, an Islamic Journey*, London, 1981.

Emile Nakhleh, *The Persian Gulf and American Policy*, New York, 1982.

Ihsan Naraqi, *Ancheh Khod Dasht* (*What We Already Had*), Tehran, 1977.

Sayyed Hussein Nasr, *Islam, perspectives et réalités*, Paris, 1978.

Muhammad Navab-Safavi, *Ayandeh Islam*, 2 vols, Tehran, 1980.

Muhammad Navab-Safavi, *Jame'eh va Hokumat Islami* (*Islamic Government and Society*), Qom, 1985.

Abdul-Ghaffar Nava'i, *Nehzat Islami dar Afghanistan* (*Islamic Awakening in Afghanistan*), Peshawar, 1985.

Amir Nejat, *Islam Re-evaluated*, California, 1986.

Benjamin Netanyahu (ed.), *Terrorism: How the West Can Win*, New York and London, 1986.

Gholam-Hussein Omrani, *Tarikhcheh Mobarezat Ruhaniyat dar Iran* (*Brief History of the Struggle of the Clergy in Iran*), Mashhad, 1979.

J. P. Peroncel-Hugoz, *Une Croix sur le Liban*, Paris, 1984.

J. P. Peroncel-Hugoz, *Le Radeau de Mahomet*, Paris, 1983.

J. Piscatori (ed.), *Islam in the Political Process*, Cambridge, 1983.

Léon Poliakov, *De Moscou à Beyrouth*, Paris, 1983.

M. D. Qajar, *Payam Enqelab* (*Message of the Revolution*), Tehran, 1983.

Sayyed Qutb, *Islam, the Misunderstood Religion*, Rome, 1984.

Sayyed Qutb, *Islam, the Religion of the Future*, Lahore, 1976.

Sayyed Qutb, *Mashahid al-Qiyamah fi Qur'an* (*Signs of Resurrection in the Qur'an*), Cairo, 1947.

Jonathan Raban, *Arabia Through the Looking-glass*, London, 1979.

Fazlur Rahman, *Islam*, Chicago, 1979.

Fat'hz Radhwan, *Al Jihad, Qanun al Hayat* (*Holy War: The Law of Life*), Cairo, 1973.

Xavier Raufer, *Terrorisme, violence*, Paris, 1984.

Maxime Rodinson, *Islam and Capitalism*, London, 1977.

Maxime Rodinson, *Mohammad*, London, 1973.

Barry M. Rosen (ed.), *Iran Since the Revolution*, Boulder, Colorado, 1985.
Olivier Roy, *L'Afghanistan, Islam et modernité politique*, Paris, 1985.
Muhammad-Baqer Rusta, *Rah e Ali* (*The Path of Ali*), Mashhad, 1983.
Malise Ruthven, *Islam in the World*, London, 1984.
Edouard Sablier, *Le Fil rouge*, Paris, 1983.
Muhammad-Baqer al-Sadr, *Eqtesadna* (*Our Economics*), Tehran, 1982.
Muhammad-Baqer al-Sadr, *Ossul Hokumat Islami* (*Principles of Islamic Government*), Tehran, 1983.
Morteza Sadeqi-Nezhad, *Nehzat Islami dar Hend* (*Islamic Awakening in India*), Qom, 1985.
Nadav Safran, *Saudi Arabia, the Ceaseless Quest for Security*, Cambridge, Mass., 1985.
Kamal S. Salibi, *Crossroads to Civil War: Lebanon, 1958–1976*, New York, 1976.
Peter Scholl-Latour, *Les Guerriers d'Allah*, Paris, 1986.
Jean Servier, *Le Terrorisme*, Paris, 1984.
Ali Shariati, *Insan va Islam* (*Man and Islam*), Tehran, 1976.
Ali Shariati, *Tashayu Alavi va Tashayu Safavi* (*Alawite and Safavid Shi'ism*), Tehran, 1971.
Faruq Sharif, *A Guide to the Contents of the Qur'an*, London, 1986.
Daryoush Shayegan, *Qu'est-ce qu'une révolution religieuse?*, Paris, 1983.
Kalim Siddiqi, *Al-Harakat al-Islamiah: Qadaya wa Ahdaf* (*The Islamic Movement: Issues and Goals*), London, 1985.
Jaafar Sobhani, *Hokumat Islami dar Cheshmandaz Ma* (*Our Vision of the Islamic State*), Tehran, 1986.
Robert Sole, *Le Défi terroriste*, Paris, 1980.
Amir Taheri, *The Spirit of Allah: Khomeini and the Islamic Revolution*, London, 1985 and Washington DC, 1986.
Abdel-Majid Tarab-Zamzami, *La Guerre Irak–Iran*, Paris, 1985.
E. H. C. Touré, *L'Etat Islamique, ses spécifités et ses caractéristiques*, Dakar, Senegal, 1985.
Ghassan Tueni, *La Guerre pour les autres*, Paris, 1985.
Sayyed Ibrahim Ulumi, *Ayandeh Islam dar Lobnan* (*The Future of Islam in Lebanon*), Tehran, 1986.
Manuchehr Vakilian, *Imam, Jang va Shahadat* (*Imam, War and Martyrdom*), Tehran, 1983.
Harald Vocke, *The Lebanese War*, London, 1978.
Grant Wardlaw, *Political Terrorism*, Cambridge, 1982.
Montgomery Watt, *Islam and the Integration of Society*, London, 1970.

Robin Wright, *Sacred Rage*, New York, 1985.

Abdul-Ghani Yadegar, *Zendehgi Shahid Ghaffar* (*Life of the Martyr Ghaffari*), Tehran, 1986.

Abd Assalam Yassine, *La Révolution à l'heure de l'Islam*, Tunis, 1981.

Ayman A. Yassini, *Religion and State in the Kingdom of Saudi Arabia*, Boulder, Colorado, 1985.

Abdul-Aziz Yazid, *Ahdaf al-Thawrat al-Islamiah* (*The Goals of Islamic Revolution*), Beirut, 1983.

Bashir Yunus, *Hawar ma al-Athwar* (*Conversations with Revolutionaries*), Beirut, 1986.

Muhammad Khalil Zayyen, *fi Sabil Allah* (*In The Way of Allah*), Rome, 1985.

Abdul-Karim Zubin, *Labayk ya Khomeini* (*Hail to Khomeini*), Tehran, 1984.

Index